Human Resource Management

HUMAN RESOURCE MANAGEMENT

(In Two Volumes)

(Volume–2)

H.L. Kaila

Publications

KALPAZ PUBLICATIONS

DELHI-110 052

Human Resource Management
(In Two Volumes)

Rs. 1800 (Set)

ISBN : 81-7835-438-1 (Set)
ISBN: 81-7835-440-3 (Vol. 2)

Published in 2005 in India by
Kalpaz Publications,
C-30, Satyawati Nagar,
Delhi-110 052
Email : kalpaz@hotmail.com

Lasertype Setting by: Tact Computer Graphics, Delhi
Printed at: Salasar Imaging System, Delhi

Contents

17

Dimensions of Data Collection and Management by Objectives

The planning and implementation of organizational change in OD is based upon a systematic diagnosis of the organization and the work-related problems that it's members are experiencing. In addition, since OD is also a collaborative process, the diagnosis phase of OD actively involves the members of the organization in the process of generating data and information about the organization and it's problems. In the diagnosis phase, we determine the types of information that would be most helpful in assessing the current state of the organization and the existing barriers to it's effective functioning. A variety of data collection techniques are available:

Data Collection Techniques

Interviews : Interviews are probably the most widely used method of collecting data on OD, partly because they are an extremely flexible tool for gathering information about an organisation and it's problems. During interviews, organisation members are free to mention any sources of problems or difficulties that they might be experiencing. In addition, when particular issues are mentioned, additional probing questions can be asked in order to understand more clearly the nature of a particular problem and what may be causing it.

Interviews are not without their drawbacks however. Collecting diagnostic information by interviews is time-consuming and expensive and so it is also generally necessary to select a small sample of members of the organisation to be interviewed. This introduces the risk that a valid picture of the organisation may not be obtained. The information collected in interviews is also subject to potential bias by the interviewer, who may unconsciously ask certain types of questions and not others. The final problem with interviews is the difficulty of generating clear and accurate summaries from a large number of interviews.

Questionnaires : The diagnostic phase of OD frequently involves the administration of a questionnaire especially designed to focus on major problem areas being experienced in the organisation. Questionnaires have the advantage of providing a large amount of standardized information in a short period of time. The perceptions and opinions of everyone in the organisation can be obtained in response to a standard set of questions that people answer in terms of numerical response scales. The fact that the data generated from questionnaires is standardized and numerical greatly facilitates it's analysis and the determination of the general trends in results.

While the ease and efficiency of questionnaires are strong positive points, there are also some problems associated with it's use. Questionnaires lack the flexibility of interviews. With the questionnaire, you have no way of determining whether you have asked the right questions. The questionnaire may ignore some important problems in the organisation that might have come to light during an interview. In addition, administering a questionnaire does little or nothing to develop rapport and understanding between the members of the organisation. Questionnaire administration does not usually involve face-to-face, one-to-one meeting and can be experienced as relatively cold and impersonal.

Direct Observation: One can often learn a great deal about the organisation simply by being sensitive to his or her observations of the organisation and it's members. By witnessing relationships, the tone of interaction among members, and the general climate of the organisation, and gain considerable insight into the nature of the organisation and it's problems. One can focus attention on any or all parts of the organisation and in the process obtain a great deal of useful information.

Observation is also unfortunately very time-consuming and difficult to do in a systematic fashion. It is difficult to ensure that these observations are representative of what occurs in the organisation in general. Further it is extremely difficult to adequately record and summarize the results of observations for systematic feedback to members of the organisation. Finally it is difficult to know to what extent the behavior was influenced by the very fact that the observer was present observing the members of the organisation. Would the organisation members have acted differently if the observer had not been present? These problems are formidable, and as a result, observation tends to serve as a supplementary, rather than a primary, source of diagnostic information for OD.

Organisational Development

Organizational Development (OD) has emerged as one of today's major areas of research of organisation theorists and practitioners which aims at improving organisation effectiveness and achieve organizational excellence. It provides a viable and robust strategy for improving organisation effectiveness and enhancing the quality of work-life for organisation members. The field of OD has grown in popularity and usage.

OD, as the term implies, seeks improvement in the total organisation. OD is an effort planned, organizational wide and managed from the top, to increase organisation effectiveness and health through planned intervention in the organization's processes using behavioral science knowledge. It is a long term, intervening strategy meant to move the entire organisation to a higher level of functioning while improving greatly the performance and satisfaction of organisation members. It applies the principles of behavioral science to improve the effectiveness of individuals, groups and the entire organisation. Although it's primary focus is on changing people and the nature and quality of their working relationships, it frequently includes structural and behavioral changes also. It is basically a long-range programme, not a short-term deal designed to solve isolated or temporary problems, which attempts to change the behavioral attitudes and performance of the whole organisation. Further, it is not one-time training and development programme but it is an ongoing an cyclical process. It is an orþganisation-wide or large-scale effort because it brings about an all round improvement in the organisation and it's processes rather than confined to one small segment of the organisation.

Organisational Development Versus Management Development

Organizational development is different from management development. Management development is a personal development strategy that focuses on training of managers and supervisors to improve their knowledge, skills and job performance. OD goes beyond, it aims at changing organizational climate where people work. In other words, OD tries to fit the entire organisation to the men while MD tries to fit the men to the organisation, with their existing objectives and structures. Thus, OD is a broader concept and includes in itself management development.

Why Organisational Development?

The use of OD as a strategy for planned change is necessary in an organisation due to the following reasons.

First, training for change does not work properly through reward structure only. There has to be better job environment. Thus, there is a need to change the entire organisation so that it will support the training. This is exactly what OD tries to do.

The second reason is the change itself. Modern organizations are surrounded by dynamic, often turbulent environment. Organisation must adopt and adjust itself to these changes in order to survive and prosper. OD attempts to develop the whole organisation so that it can respond to change more uniformly and capably.

OD efforts usually have some of the following operational goals:

1. To develop a self-renewing, viable system that can organize in a variety of ways depending upon tasks.
2. To increase the level of trust and mutual emotional support among all organisation members and thus move towards high collaborative and low competition between independent units.
3. To create such conditions where conflict is brought out and managed.
4. To increase the openness of communication laterally, vertically and diagonally.
5. To increase the level of enthusiasm and personal satisfaction in the organisation.
6. To increase the effectiveness of the organisation in terms of all of it's goals.

OD Process

OD is a complicated process that tends to take a year or more in an organisation and may continue indefinitely. The programme is generally designed, implemented and monitored by a behavioral science consultant who is not a regular member of the organisation. There are many different approaches to OD but a typical complete program includes the following steps.

1. **Problem Identification:** OD programme leads to meet a certain objective in the organisation because OD is a means and not the end itself. Thus, it attempts to solve some organisation problems. For instance, it may deal with problems related to growth, use of human resources or organizational effectiveness.

2. **Data Collection:** Collection of data is undertaken through various methods like personal interviews, observation, questionnaire etc. The use of a particular type of method depends upon the nature of the problem.

3. **Diagnosis:** The collected information gathered must be subject to examination so as to grasp the problem well. The important factors like attitudes, assumptions, available resources etc. must be taken into consideration in diagnostic phase. Diagnosis reveals the sources of problem and helps in identifying the areas where changes are necessary and what changes are required in the system, the structure or group.

4. **Planning Strategy for Change**: After diagnosing the problem, the consultant prepares a proper action plan which outlines the goals for change, determination of basic approach to attain these goals and detailed scheme for implementing the approach.

5. **Intervening in the System :** Intervening in the system means a planned programme of activities which bring certain changes in the organizational system. These activities are designed to improve the organization's functioning through enabling the organisation members better to manage their team and organizational culture. There are various ways through which the external consultant intervenes in the system, such as laboratory training, process consultation, team development etc.

6. **Evaluation and Feedback :** Evaluation helps to know whether the programme has been launched correctly. A feedback of the effect of OD strategy on different parts of organisation is required. For this, certain techniques like pre and post-training behavioral pattern, the use of critique sessions, systematic appraisal of change efforts are quite useful.

Limitations

OD has been criticized on the following grounds:

1. OD emphasizes too much on human and social dynamics of organisation and gives too little attention towards task, technical and structural aspects and their inter-dependencies.
2. OD uses behavioral science concepts for bringing a planned change in the whole organisation but behavioral science itself has various limitations and they are applicable to OD too.
3. The results of OD are difficult to measure. For example, how one is going to measure 'openness and trust' and 'organizational climate'.
4. OD programme aims at bringing planned changes in the organisation, at large faces the tough problem of resistance to change by the people and this impedes desired progress.

Management by Objectives Evaluation–Making MBO Effective

Management By Objectives (MBO) was first introduced by Peter Drucker in 1954. It is a popular intervention for bringing about clarity in job and unit-performance outcomes by involving employees in the establishment of individual and group goals. It encourages individuals to participate in the establishment of job-related objectives for themselves and their units. In MBO, the superior and subordinate managers collectively (jointly) fix the objectives of the organisation and monitor, evaluate and measure the performance of the subordinate managers. Successful use of MBO depends on the ability of participants to define their objectives in terms of their contribution to the total organisation and to accomplish those objectives. (Gibson et.al, 1993).

Application of MBO

The application of MBO involves the following three steps:

1. Superiors and subordinates meet and discuss objectives that, if met, would contribute to overall goals.
2. Superiors and subordinates jointly establish attainable objectives for the subordinates.
3. Superiors and subordinates meet at a predetermined later date to evaluate the subordinate's progress towards the objectives. (Kondrasuk, Flagler et.al., 1984).

Process of MBO

Organizations require consistent levels of high performance from their employees in order to survive in a highly competitive environment. Many firms use some form of results-oriented planning and control systems. MBO is a cyclical process that consists of four steps to attain the desired performance (Newstrom, Davis, 1998).

1. **Collectively Fixing Objectives:** The superior and subordinate managers collectively fix the objectives. The objectives are fixed for the Key Result Areas (KRA's). KRA's are those areas which are very important for the long-term success of the organisation. For eg. Production, finance, marketing etc. Definite and measurable objectives should be fixed for each KRA. The time limit for achieving the objectives should also be fixed. The subordinate manager should achieve the objectives.
2. **Collectively Making a Plan:** After fixing the objective, the superior and subordinate managers make an action plan. This plan will be used by the subordinate manager to achieve the objectives.
3. **Collectively Making a Plan :** The subordinate manager implements the plan. That is, he puts the plan into action. He makes optimum use of the resources. If required he takes guidance from the superior managers.
4. **Collectively Monitoring Performance:** This is the final stage in the MBO process. Here, the subordinate monitors (evaluate or measure) his own performance. He compares his performance with the planned targets (objectives). If there are any deviations (differences) then the superior and subordinate managers fix new objectives. In this stage, the superior acts like a coach and guide. He does not act like a judge.

Advantages

1. **Better Utilisation of Resources :** In MBO, there is optimum utilization of physical, financial and human resources for achieving the objectives.
2. **Development of Personnel :** MBO helps to train and develop the subordinate managers. It improves their skills in planning, decision-making, controlling, directing, leadership, etc. So these managers are ready for promotion to higher posts.

3. **Making Planning Effective :** In MBO, the objectives are very clear. So, feasible plans can be made for achieving these objectives. Therefore, MBO makes planning effective.

4. **Better Team Work :** The superior and subordinate managers work together for fixing objectives and monitoring the performance. This develops good relations and they work as a team.

5. **Concentration on KRA's :** In MBO, objectives are fixed for the Key Result Areas. All the plans are made for the KRA's. Therefore wasteful activities are avoided.

6. **Objective Evaluation :** In MBO, the objectives are tangible and measurable. The actual performance of the subordinate can be accurately compared with the objectives. So, an objective evaluation is possible without any favor to anyone.

7. **Results Oriented :** MBO is result oriented. It gives more importance to results i.e. achieving the objectives. It gives less importance to activities, methods, etc. In fact, MBO is also called "MANAGEMENT BY OBJECTIVES."

8. **Sound organisational stucture :** In MBO system, the organizational structure is very sound. This is periodically reviewed and necessary changes are made to suit the needs of the company.

Disadvantages

1. **Time Consuming:** The MBO system is very time-consuming. It takes a lot of time for fixing objectives, evaluating the performance and refixing the objectives.

2. **Paper Work:** MBO involves a lot of paper work. It requires a lot of forms, reports, instruction books,etc.

3. **Clash in Objectives :** sometimes, the objectives of a subordinate may clash with the objectives of another person/individuals or departments.

4. **Problem in Fixing Objectives :** the superior and subordinates may not agree with each other while fixing objectives. This results in many problems. These problems have to be solved before fixing the objectives.

5. **Rewards May not Match with the Objectives:** the subordinates are given very small rewards for very good performances.

Therefore they get frustrated.

6. **Dominance by Superiors:** the superiors may dominate while fixing the objectives. He may not allow the subordinates to participate in fixing the objectives. This will make MBO meaningless.

Conclusion

Organisational development induces the employers to put greater efforts and ensure a high degree of commitment to work therby contributing significantly to create excellence in management. Every organistion strives to create excellence and a number of mechanisms and techniques are available and one of them is organisational development. It is the most important and a potent tool to create and achieve organisational excellence. Although organisational development has it's limitations, it is an excellent practice for introducing change and self-renewal in the organisation. Organisational development holds bright and promising future and it will become more widely used by different kinds of organisations.

Management by objectives refers to a process in which managers set specific and measurable goals with each individual employee on a regular basis. The employee is then responsible for achieving his or her own goals within a certain time. Under MBO, individuals are evaluated on the basis of what they accomplish now and how they get the job done. it encourages the individuals to set specific, challenging goals. It has the potential of increasing employee motivation and performance. Since organisations are ultimately concerned with concrete results, evaluating employees on the basis of the results they have personally accomplished is consistent with the overall needs and objectives of the organisation. Employees know exactly what is expected of them and what they must achieve if they are to be evaluated positively. Systematic goal setting throughout the organisation facilitates planning and coordination by clarifying exactly what is expected of each person on an ongoing basis.

Though a heavy emphasis on MBO may lead to a lack of attention to how results are being accomplished. There is a risk that managers might not give enough attention to providing their subordinates with advice and assistance regarding how to achieve their goals effectively. It also makes difficult to compare the level of performance of different individuals. They are difficult to implement effectively. The primary factor distinguishing effective and ineffective MBO programs seems to be the extent to which the implementation of MBO recognizes the need for social skills on the part of managers conducting MBO goal-setting and performance appraisal meetings. Since managers rarely possess all the skills required for conducting and implementing MBO programs, MBO must be accompanied by training and development designed to assist managers in the acquisition of the necessary skills.

References and Further Reading

1. Hugh J. Arnold, Daniel C. Feldman, "Organisational Behaviour", Tata Mcgraw Hill, pp. 322-325.
2. Jack N.Kondrasuk, Keith Flagler, Dennis Murrow, and Paul Thompson, "The Effects of MBO on Organisational Results", Group and Organisational Studies, 1984, pp. 531-539.
3. James L. Gibson, John M. Ivanovich, James H. Donnelly, "Organisations", 7 Edition, 1993, pp. 672-674.
4. John W. Newstrom and Keith Davis, "Organisational Behaviour-Human Behaviour at Work", 10 Edition, Tata Mcgraw Hill, pp. 173.
5. Michael Vaz, Vinayak Paralikar, "Management and HRD", 9 Edition, 1997, pp. 55-58.

18

Employee Satisfaction Survey

Introduction

Job satisfaction is, "a variable — a point on a pleasant-unpleasant continuum that has implications for action."

The term job satisfaction came into vogue in 1935 when Hoppock published his classic work "job satisfaction".

He defined job satisfaction as "any combination of psychological, physiological and environmental circumstances that causes a person truthfully to say, I am satisfied with my job." Hence it is the verbal expression of employee's evaluation of his work. It is in regard to one's feelings or state-of-mind regarding the nature of their work. Job satisfaction can be influenced by a variety of factors, e.g., the quality of one's relationship with their supervisor, the quality of the physical environment in which they work, degree of fulfillment in their work, etc.

Job satisfaction is an attitude, which results from a balancing, and summation of many specific likes and dislikes experienced in connection with the job. It is the employee's judgment of how well the job on the whole is satisfying his various needs. However, a global concept of job satisfaction is not warranted by findings from job satisfaction studies. Job satisfaction is not a single unified entity but a multi-dimensional concept. It can be broken down into such dimensions as- intrinsic task satisfaction, attachment to the work group, and satisfaction with superiors, identification with the company, satisfaction with job security and income, chances of promotion, etc.

Theories of Job Satisfaction

There are five approaches to understanding job satisfaction. These approaches purport to describe the process by which job satisfaction is determined for individuals. These approaches are—

- **The Comparison Theory:** according to this theory the magnitude of job satisfaction is a function of the size of the discrepancy between the individuals standards and what he believes he/she is receiving. The standard is considered by some as the individuals needs (Porter, 1962; Morse, 1953), and by others as his values (Locke, 1976).
- **Aspiration-Achievement or Expectation-Achievement Discrepancy Theory :** Aspiration or expectations can be set by the minimum needs of the individuals and/or by his current level of achievement of needs. It is undoubtedly true that job satisfaction is determined by a comparison of the desired standards and perception of the achieved level, the standard itself is not fixed but a 'moving' one, linked in a significant way to the achievement level.
- **Instrumentality Theory:** It postulates that individuals assess their satisfaction with jobs by considering the extent to which the job leads to valued outcomes. It is assumed here that each individual has a set of judgments about how much he values certain outcomes such as pay, promotion, good working conditions, etc. the person then estimates the extent to which holding the job will lead to these valued outcomes. His job satisfaction then results from the summation of the outcomes or instrumentalities obtained multiplied by the valences of these outcomes.
- **Equity-Based Models:** Lawler's Facet satisfaction model: satisfaction is a function of the extent to which the ÿperceived amount of job rewards one receives matches the perceived deserved rewards.
- **Locke's Value theory:** Satisfaction is a function of the extent to which one's job is perceived as fulfilling important values. Thus the discrepancy between preferred levels of job factors (pay, autonomy, etc.) and the actual level determines the level of satisfaction.
- **Social Influence Theory of Job Satisfaction:** This theory states that an individual may come into a new job not knowing how satisfied they will be with these. They look around, see others like themselves who are satisfied or dissatisfied with these, and then influenced by these observations. Thus they decide their level of satisfaction not by processing all types of information

about themselves but by observing others on similar jobs and making inferences about their satisfactions (Salsncik and Pfeffer, 1977). Finally satisfaction is more a product of self-perception and social perceptions, rather than determined by intrinsic characteristic of the job. An individual simply infers a level of his personal satisfaction by their perception of others satisfactions.

- **Herzberg's Two-Factor Theory :** Herzberg's theory proposes that job satisfaction is derived from two sets of factors. The first set associated with positive feelings about the job and to the Content of the work it-self and called them "motivators"(intrinsic factors), such as responsibility, recognition, the nature of work itself, achievement and advancement, are responsible for presence or absence of job satisfaction. The second set of factors are external to the job i.e. Context factors and have been labeled "hygiene factors". These factors include, pay, policies and practices, supervision, interpersonal relationship with coworker and working conditions. These factors do not promote satisfaction but reduce dissatisfaction.

Critical Analysis of the Theories

The above theories deal with causes of satisfaction and dissatisfaction and not with the nature of job satisfaction per se.

1. In these theories four parameters are involved—(a) the person's own needs and values; (b) the person's education, ability, experience, skill, etc that determine his contribution to the job;(c) reward the employer provides him with; and reward given to other employees in the organizations. These theories then take up different combination of the above factors and base their theories only on the parameters they choose.
2. The theories are not exclusive of each other but overlapping.
3. Operationally, applicability and validity of these theories depend upon the career stage of employee and other factor inside and outside the job.
4. Thus no one theory can completely or fully explain the concept of job satisfaction; but a combination of two or more theory is needed.

To conclude each theory embodies a partial truth, but none covers the entire spectrum of job satisfaction-dissatisfaction. A perspective and discerning manager or researcher should opt for that particular theory which enables him to understand his empirical data adequately.

Factors Contributing to Job Satisfaction

The following factors increase job satisfaction and staff motivation to perform:

- Achievement,
- Recognition for accomplishment,
- Challenging work,
- Increased responsibility,
- Growth and development,
- Pay,
- Autonomy,
- Hours of work,
- Inter-personal relationship, and
- Co-worker satisfaction.

Each of these factors is described below along with ways in which supervisors can enhance these factors in their units.

Achievement

Achievement is a sense of accomplishment or successful closure of a task or activity. Supervisors can enhance workers' sense of achievement on the job by:

- Encouraging employees to set professional goals,
- Setting goals with individual employees regarding specific work activities,
- Establishing unit goals, and
- Gradually increasing the complexity of assignments so that employees are challenged and experience success in more difficult situations.

Recognition

Recognition is the acknowledgment of an individual's or group's efforts, accomplishments, or contributions. There are many ways supervisors can recognize staff efforts and accomplishments, including the following:

- Highlight staff efforts and contributions in unit meetings.
- Celebrate client success and the worker's contributing efforts.
- Let a worker know verbally and/or in writing that his/her work is appreciated; (e.g., memos, with a pat on the back, or by notes placed on completed paperwork).
- Give awards, certificates, or other commendations for specific accomplishments and contributions.
- Encourage community service providers who compliment staff to put the praise in writing for placement in the worker's personnel file, with a copy forwarded to upper-level administrators.
- Give a genuinely positive performance evaluation.
- Promote staff or encourage them to apply for promotions.
- Allow and encourage staff to attend specialized training programs and conferences.
- Hold award dinners or lunches.
- Hold staff retreats.

When workers are reçognized for their efforts and accomplishments, they experience positive feelings about themselves and their professional competence, which create an increased sense of self-worth.

Challenging Work

For work to be satisfying, there must be tasks that are challenging or motivating. Just as each individual prefers some tasks to others, each finds some tasks more challenging than others. It is important for supervisors to identify with their staff the tasks or activities they find challenging. The following are activities that employees may find challenging:

- Specialized work requiring some complex skills.
- Public speaking – that is through presentations.
- Participating on a multidisciplinary team;
- Coordinating a new service program; and
- Serving as a liaison to a community service provider.

Responsibility

When employees feel responsible and accountable for their own work, their job satisfaction increases. Strategies for enhancing responsibility and accountability include the following:

- Gradually increasing staff autonomy in employee activities and decision making to gain expertise;
- Giving employees the freedom to be creative;
- Identifying the decisions that the individual employee and the unit can make alone and the decisions that they can be involved in making;
- Requesting that a particular employee to be in charge when the supervisor is away from the office;
- Asking an experienced employee to model specific aspects of the work for a new employee.
- Encouraging employees to contribute to the agenda for unit meetings.

Growth and Development

Everyone needs to continue to grow and develop personally and professionally on the job. When there are limited opportunities for growth and development, motivation wanes. Employees may commit energy to other aspects of their personal lives, seek other employment, or burn out. Some strategies for encouraging worker's growth and development include the following:

- Encouraging employees to attend training programs and conferences, followed by presentations at unit meetings about what they learned;
- Encouraging or advocating educational or special training leave for staff;
- Maintaining and updating a unit library and encouraging staff to read books and articles relevant to the job;
- Keeping staff informed about current research and issues as well as new intervention techniques and advances in the field of their respective jobs.
- Assigning tasks that challenge employees' growth and promote their professional development; and
- Encouraging creativity and innovation among staff.

How Employees Express Dissatisfaction?

Employee dissatisfaction can be expressed in a number of ways. For example they can complain, quit the job, be in-subordinate, steal organizational property, or shrink a part of their responsibility. The reaction to dissatisfaction can be classified along two dimensions: constructive/destructive and active/passive. They are defined as follows-

- **Exit:** Dissatisfaction expressed through behavior directed towards leaving the organization.
- **Voice:** Dissatisfaction expressed through active and constructive attempts to improve conditions. It includes suggesting improvements, discussing problems with superiors and some form of union activity.
- **Loyalty:** Dissatisfaction expressed by passively waiting for conditions to improve.
- **Neglect:** Dissatisfaction expressed through allowing conditions to worsen. It includes chronic absenteeism or lateness, and increased error rate.

Employee Satisfaction Survey

Methodology

The survey began with administration of Udai Pareek's questionnaire on intrinsic and extrinsic motivation. Here the participants were asked to rank the 14 factors in terms of their importance to them. Following which an interview was taken, certain fixed questions were asked, but their order depended on the flow of the interview.

The second phase was development of the questionnaire. The employee satisfaction survey questionnaire was developed by HCC. Here there were 65 questions asked with five options. The participant had to tick one of the 4 options which best described his situation.

The data of this survey was used for further analysis and discussion.

Scoring

The raw data was first converted into percentage. Then the options measuring satisfaction for positive statement and the options measuring satisfaction for negative statement were added and the option measuring dissatisfaction for both the statement was added together. The two totals would then give the overall satisfaction and dissatisfaction level of the employees. The option of can't say was used as it was. It gave the percentage of employees who have reserved their opinion.

Sample Description

The sample size of the survey conducted was 654 covering all the major sites of HCC and representing the heterogeneous group in terms of age, experience, qualification etc. These employees belonged to different construction sites. The sample included engineers and managers. While skilled, unskilled and semi- skilled employees were not included in the survey. The age of the participants ranged from 21years to over 55 years with participants experience ranging from one year or less to more than 20 years.

The project sites covered under the survey were- Rajasthan Atomic Power Project, Kudankulam Nuclear Power Project, Jharkhand Road Project, Gujarat State Highway Road Project, West Bengal Road Project Package 2, TALA C-4, Purulia Pumped Storage Project, BMC W3 A, Tirupur Bulk Water Supply Project, Dhauliganga Hydro Electric Project, Bandra Worli Sea Link, Naini Bridge Project.

Tool Used

There were two questionnaires used. The first questionnaire used was Intrinsic and Extrinsic Motivation: what people look for in a job? This questionnaire was taken from Udai Pareek's book titled "training Instruments For Human Resource Development". It's self administered, and respondent's are asked to rank order the 14 1tems depending on their importance to them from 1(highest) to 14 (lowest).

The second questionnaire was constructed by HCC. This question had 65 statements with 5 options to tick from; they were- strongly Agree, Agree, Can't Say, Disagree, Strongly Disagree. Out of the 65 statements,15 statements were negatively framed so that a tick on disagree will lead to inferring satisfaction and a tick on agree will mean dissatisfaction. Similarly in the remaining 55 statements a tick on agree would mean satisfaction and a tick on disagree would mean dissatisfaction.

These 65 statements were scattered around 13 factors or parameters of satisfaction. These parameters were- quality, customer orientation, others (perception), co-operative working, immediate boss support, work, working environment, own preferences, awareness of policies and practices, performance management, safety reward and recognition and growth and development.

Analysis of Data

HCC conducted an employee survey to asses the satisfaction level of it's employees.

The project sites covered are located at different locations all over India and sometimes outside India. Some of them are situated in the cities at remote locations. At the sites the climatic conditions are very extreme and poses a challenge to the employees. Also for certain projects, the employees have to work under ground for all most 10 to 12 hours.

Only a small percentage of employees are dissatisfied with quality that is 6% of the total population in the study. About 7% of the employees are in a state of confusion with respect to quality.

Table 1.1

Represents the Overall Result of the Survey Conducted by HCC (in percentage)

Factors	*Dissatisfaction*	*Can't Say*	*Satisfaction*
Quality	6	7	87
Customer Orientation	7	13	80
Others (perception)	15	11	74
Co-operative Working	18	10	72
Immediate Boss Support	19	9	72
Work	27	9	64
Working Environment	28	10	62
Own Preference	28	12	60
Awareness of Policies and Practices	22	21	57
Performance Management	28	18	54
Safety	38	8	54
Reward and Recognition	29	18	53
Growth and Development	45	11	44

Around 80% of the employees feel that HCC is regarded highly by its client, about 7% of them disagree and 13% are confused. Customer Orientation, under this factor there were two statements asked, these were-"HCC is regarded highly by its client". And "I think that our client at my location is happy with the performance of our project/department".

The client of HCC is usually the state or central government of India. In case of foreign project it is the government of that country. Depending upon the nature of the project, the requirements of the clients differ.

What does a client want from its supplier? Good quality of the delivered product. Delivery of the product on time. HCC has satisfied the above two criteria time and again. The best example of the efficiency in functioning comes from The Mumbai-Pune Express way. It is the first concrete six payment lane in India. It is not only good in terms of quality but was also completed before the scheduled date.

"Team work is always encouraged at my location"; "It is easy to get required information & support from other departments at my location"; and "The department receives adequate information & support from projects or head office". The above mentioned were the three statements asked under Co-operative Working. All of them were positive statements.

72% of the employees of HCC agree to the above dimension, promoting the notion that team efforts are encouraged and that the departmental work is well coordinated. Also there exists a good communication network between various departments and the site plus the HO. 10% of the employees are confused and 18% of them disagree with it.

Immediate Boss Support as a factor deals with the relationship between an employee and his immediate superior. There were a total of seven statements asked and only one was negative.

72% of the employees believe that there exists a healthy relationship between superior and subordinate, that the superiors are interested in the growth and development of the employees; also they are keen and ready to spend time to promote professional growth of the subordinate. Finally they feel they can look up to their superiors when faced with a problem. 19% of them disagree and 9% of them are confused.

The two positive statements under Work were on providing necessary tools and resources to deliver results and that the skills and the job performed are in line or well matched. The negative statements were on lack of authority to perform effectively and on people being stressed because of work overload.

The result of the survey show a positive trend as 64% of the employees are satisfied with their work, 27% are dissatisfied and a small percent i.e. 9% is confused.

Work environment as a parameter to study employee satisfaction is looked upon in two ways- physical and emotional aspect of work. Physical aspect includes good facilities at site in terms of food, accommodation, etc., resources to carry out the job effectively, and rules and regulation. With respect to emotional aspect, relationship and communication between employees as well as with the superiors, and mutual respect for each other was assessed.

The result of the survey is in favor of HCC. 62% of the participants are satisfied with current work situation, 28% of them are dissatisfied and 10% of them are confused.

Own Preferences discuss about the current pay offered and whether the participants are happy with it. It also discusses about job security, over-load of work and experience plus immediate feedback. Out of the five statements asked two were negative.

Keeping all the five statements in mind, the survey shows positive result. 60% of the participants are satisfied with the pay package, security, feedback and experience. 28% of the participants are dissatisfied and 12% of them are confused.

Awareness of Policies and Practices as a parameter deals with transparency in policies and their implementation. 57% of the employees are satisfied with the policies regarding fixing up of grades, salary, and, promotion; 22% are dissatisfied and 21% are confused.

The employees and their immediate superiors together decide the KRA/KPI of each employee. This is done at the beginning of each appraisal year. This is the base of appraisal at HCC. Also not only the immediate superior and the subordinate do the evaluation after proper analysis but also by other senior heads of the company.

There were seven statements under Performance Management. Out of them four were positive. They were concerned with matching skills and ability to the actual job, on deciding KRA/KPI and how does management handle poor performance? Negative statements were pertaining to poor performance, ignorance on part of the employees with regard to appraisal.54% of the participants are satisfied with performance management system of the company, 28% are dissatisfied and 18% are confused.

SAFETY is one of the values held very strongly at HCC. There are regular safety checks at all the construction sites. Secondly, employees cannot enter the construction area without proper gloves, helmets and boots. The safety of its employees is the first priority. HCC has also received safety certification by OHSAS 18001 (Occupational Health and Safety Assessment Series). Out of the two statement, one was positive and stated "Management at my location gives adequate attention to safety matters". The negative statement was "Creating safe working conditions at our location is a very difficult task".

53% of the participants are satisfied with Reward and Recognition offered by HCC. They feel they have better jobs as compared to most of their batch mates, also their efforts are well rewarded and lastly the company pays them adequately. 29% disagree with the above and are hence dissatisfied. 18% are confused.

Growth and Development, this is the only factor out of the 13 factors that shows dissatisfaction. About 45% of employees are dissatisfied, 44% are satisfied and 11% are confused. Out of the six statements, only one negative statement and five positive. The statements were pertaining to personal growth in terms of skills acquired, coaching and training, and about advancement in terms of promotion. The negative one was on lack of skills to perform effectively.

Conclusion

The data obtained from the survey was in the positive direction. That is most of the employees seemed satisfied with the factors under the survey. However certain factors were more satisfying than the others. Growth and development was the only factor that showed dissatisfaction. The discrepancy between the participants with regards to the factor can be attributed to such factor as the age of the participants, and years of experience. The overall result otherwise was quite satisfying.

This survey suggests that there are more aspects of a good or satisfying job than just pay and hours. Concentration on only one or two of these aspects is likely to give a misleading picture both of where the good jobs are and of workers' behaviour.

References and Further Reading

1. Ganguli H.C. (1996). Job Satisfactiuon Scales For Effective Management. Manual For Managers and Social Scientists. Concept Publishing Company, New Delhi.
2. Harward Business review, Jan.2003
3. Harward Business Review, Nov. 2003.
4. Managing job satisfaction/Bavandam research. Inc
5. Paul M. Muchinsky (1999). Psychology applied to work. 6th edition.. Wadsworth Thomson Learning.
6. Stephen P. Robbins (1998). Organizational behaviour. 10th edition.. Prentice Hall India.
7. Udai Pareek (1997). Training Instruements For Human Resource Development. Tata McGraw-Hill Publishing Company, New Delhi.
8. www.hbr.com
9. www.HR.com
10. www.workfamily.com

19
Emotional Intelligence

Emotional Intelligence

Emotional intelligence (EI) is one of the recent developments in the area of intelligence. The merging of emotion and intelligence as a cognitive ability under the caption of EI was proposed by Peter Salovey and John Mayer (1990). They defined it as "ability to monitor one's own and others felings and emotions, to discriminate among them and to use them to guide one's thinking and actions".

The concept of EI however, received popularity by the best selling book, Emotional intelligence by Daniel Goleman. (1995), the cover articl in 'Time' by N. Gibbs (1995) and then some other popular books, i.e

1. **Executive EQ** : emotional intelligence in leadership and organizations by : —R. K Cooper and A. Swaf. 1997.
2. **The Heart of Parenting** :- How to raise emotionally intelligent child by J. Gottman 1997.
3. **The Whole Intelligence** : the emotional quotient (EQ) by J. G. Salerno. (1996)
4. **Raising Your Emotional Intelligence–by Jeanne** Segal (1997).

Emotional Intelligence In the Indian Context

Anjum Sibia; Girishwar Misra; Ashok Srivastava (2004) suggested that EI in the Indian context cannot be viewed as a homogenous trait, or amount as ability devoid of social concerns like respecting elders, concern for others, fulfilling one's duties. These along with moral values of Ahimsa (non-violence), kindness, benevolence, provide the very basis of emotional expression and responsivity. They are built in ways an individual deals with situations emotional, social or otherwise. These culture specific ways of behaving, therefore, are basic to the notion of EI.

The responses of parents, teachers and children regarding desirable, and successful emotional qualities related to the category of pro-social values (respecting others, being cooperative, sincere etc), social sensitivity (which include social concern, control of negative emotion and showing empathy to others), action tendencies (such as perseverance, helpful, punctual and disciplined) and affective states (such as happiness, creativity and optimism).

Cognitive intelligence or IQ refers to the ability to concentrate and plan, to organize material, to use words and to understand, assimilate and interpret facts. it is essentially a measure of an individuals personal information bank – one's memory, vocabulary and visual motor coordination. Some of these skills contribute to doing well in life. The fact remains however that IQ does not and cannot predict success in life.

As for IQs relevance in the work place, studies have shown that it can serve to predict 20 percent (avg. 6%) of success in a given job.

EQ on the other hand bas been found to be directly responsible for between 27 and 45% of job success depending on which field is under study.

According to a recent survey by Thomas Stanley, the factors responsible for success if people who were multimillionaires, he found that the top 5 factors were

1. being honest with all people
2. being well disciplined
3. getting along with people
4. having a supportive spouse
5. working harder than most people

All these are reflections of EI. Cognitive intelligence or IQ was 21st on the lots of factors and was endorsed by 20% of the millionaires.

Another difference between cognitive and emotional intelligence is that IQ is pretty much set. It tends to peak when a person is 17, remains constant through out adulthood and wanes during old age. EQ however is not fixed. It rises steadily from an average of 95.3 (when you are in your late teens) to an average of 102.7 (where it remains throughout 40s). It tapers off a bit i.e. 101.5 once one is past 50.

Misconceptions about EQ

People confuse EQ with other psychosocial concepts that have made their way into other tests and surveys of human potential.

Some of the misconceptions about EQ are :

1. **EQ is aptitude :** EQ is not an aptitude which concerns a person's ability to perform well in a particular skill or activity or discipline. It isn't achievement, which concerns specific sorts of performance.

   It isn't vocational interest which centres on a person's natural inclination towards a particular field of work.

2. **EQ is not personality :** i.e. a unique set of traits that help form a person's characteristics, enduring and dependable ways of thinking, feeling and behaving, personality is fixed and stable where as EQ is not.

EI is made up of short–term, tactical "dynamic skills that can be brought into play as the situations warrant. Thus the individual building blocks of EI and its overall structure can be improved by means of training, coaching and experience.

Measuring Emotional Intelligence

The ideal E1 test should satisfy the following criteria :

1. **Adequate coverage of content domain :** if the E1 test is to serve as a measure of emotion management, then its developers need to ensure that all major aspects of emotion management are covered by the test items (and in correct proportions). The test should probably cover both managing self – relevant emotions and managing others emotions and should not focus exclusively on one management strategy (eg. using alcohol or drugs) to the exclusion of other management strategies (eg. seeking professional help, meditation, distracting oneself with leisure time activities and so forth.

2. **Reliability :** If a person taking an E1 test gets a below average score on one occasion, then he or she should get a below average score when given the same test again (sometime in the future).

3. **Usefulness :** E1 measure should predict important practical outcomes such as how well people deal with stress, how effective they are at maintaining relationships, and how they are accepted by their peers.

4. **Similarity and Distinctiveness :** An E1 measure should relate to other similar E1 measures but also should not relate too highly on non-E1 measures.

Overview of the E1 Measures

There are two types of measures of E1

1. Self report
2. Performance or ability measures

Self Report Measures

During the last few years, several self report measures have been developed.

1. 1995 Goleman made an attempt to develop a test of E1 which was published in the USA, It was a 10 item test in which the reader had to respond to hypothetical situations portraited in each item.

   Unfortunately, Goleman's scale had a very low reliability (a = 0.18) which can't be accepted. The reported convergent validity was with empathy and emotional control (Davies, Stankov & Roberts, 1998).

2. 1997 Bar–on R. developed a EQ–1 emotional quotient inventory. It is claimed that the EQ–1 is the most comprehensive self report measure of E1 available. It consists of 15 subscales.

   (i) Emotional self awareness
   (ii) Assertiveness
   (iii) Self–regard
   (iv) Self–actualisation
   (v) Independence
   (vi) Empathy
   (vii) Interpersonal relationships

(viii) Social responsibility

(ix) Problem solving

(x) Reality testing

(xi) Flexibility

(xii) Stress tolerance

(xiii) Impulse control

(xiv) Happiness

(xv) Optimism

The EQ 1 yields a measures of the overall E1 as well as scores on each of the sub factors. The EQ 1 also contains four validity scales that measures the extent to which people are responding randomly or distorting their responses to appear favourably or unfavourably to the person administering the test.

The EQ 1 and its subscales have been shown to have high levels of internal consistency (across a wide variety of cultures) as well as high test-retest reliability.

The EQ 1 has been regarded as a useful measure related to peoples employment status, academic success, success at fitting into a culture, prison status and skill at coping with stress (Bar – On R. 1997).

3. 1997 – Cooper also developed the EQ 1 Map to measure EQ and it consisted of 4 aspects.

- **Current environment :** Including life pressures and life satisfactions.
- **Emotional literacy :** Including emotional self awareness, emotional expression and emotional awareness of others.
- **Emotional competencies :** Including intentionality, creativity, resilience, interpersonal connections and constructive discontent.
- **EQ values and attitudes :** Outlook, compassion, intution, personal power and integrated self.

The final EQ outcomes measure general health, quality of life, relationship quotient and optimal performance.

4. EQ Japan Inc (1998) has developed Emotional Quotient inventory (EQI) with sub-scales of

    - Intrapersonal intelligence
    - Interpersonal
    - Judgement abilities

    No alpha and validity were reported.

5. 1998 Schutle et. al developed a unifactor measure of EI with 33 items. It is called as the Schutle–self-report–inventory (SSRI). The scale assesses overall EI as well as 4 EI sub factors.

    - Emotion perception
    - Managing self relevant emotions
    - Managing other's emotions
    - Utilizing emotions.

The test retest reliability was found to be 0.78 over 2 weeks & internal consistent reliability a = 0.87

EI measured by this scale correlated strongly with (i) openness to experience (ii) dlexithy mia (iii) greater attention to feelings (iv) greater clarity of feelings (v) more mood repair (vi) greater optimism, and moderately with (vii) less depression and (viii) less impulsivity.

6. Boyatzis, Goleman and Hay/McBer (1999) developed emotional competence inventory (ECI) to measure factors given by Goleman (1998). The Coefficient alpha ranges from 0.55 to 0.82 for self assessment (N = 628 to 670). However except emotional self awareness and empathy, the remaining factors are undoubted by beyond the construct of emotion and intelligence.

7. **Two Self report scales to Assess Meta Mood Cognitions Have Been Employed** : trait scale Salovey et al (1995) and state scale (Mayer & Stevens, 1994). Former is the 30 item Trait Meta Mood Scale (TMMS) which taps into peoples belifs about their propensity to attend with clarity to their own mood states and to engage in mood repair. The psychometric properties of this scale are quite good and some empirical findings have been generated from its use (Goldman, Kraema & Salovey, 1996; Salovey et al

1995). The Scales have been shown to possess adequate reliability.

8. Taylor G.J; Bagby R. M. & Parker J. D. (1994) developed the 20 item self report. Toron to alexithymia Scale (TAS) the TAS – 20 is one of the most commonly used EI measure, however it was originally designed to measure a clinical syndrome known as alexithymia. The scale consists of 3 sub scales
   - Difficulty in identifying feelings
   - Difficulty in describing feelings.
   - Externally oriented thinking.

The over all alexithymia score and the first two scale score tend to be highly reliable. However, the third scale has sometimes been found to be some what less reliable than is desirable (Bogby, Parker, paylor 1994), Importantly the TAS 20 has been shown to be availed instrument across disparate cultures and different types of populations. (eg. Students & psychiatric patients) (Taylor 2000).

There are many other self report measures that are related to EI.

9. Rogers D & Nagarian B (1989) developed the emotional control questionnaire–it measures peoples ability to control emotion in trying circumstances and consists of scales for measuring "aggression control" rehearsal "benign control " and emotional inhibition.

10. Weinberger D. A. Schwar G. E. & Davidson R. J. (1979) used the repression – sensitisation scale which assesses the extent that people defensively avoid aversive emotions and stimuli. Repression tendency has predicted how accurate people are at identifying emotions.

11. Nolen Hocksema S & Morrow J. (1991) used the response styles questionnaire which measures the tendency to experience behaviours and thoughts that focus on one's depressive symptoms.

12. Miller S M, Brody D. & Summer Ton J. (1998) used the Monitoring –blunting scale which measures the extent that people seek out (or avoid) information when faced with a stressful situation.

13. Carver C. S. Scheier M. F. & Weintaub J. K. (1989) used the COPE inventory which measures how people generally cope with stressful events and includes subscales that measures active coping denial, turning to religion, and seeking social support.

Attempts have been made to develop EI scales in India too.

14. Dr. N. K. Chadha (1998) prepared the emotional intelligence test for the Indian population. This test has been standardized on Indian managers, business men, bureaucrats and industrial workers.

15. Thingujan and Ram (2000) made an attempt at Indian adaptation of emotional intelligence scale (Schutte et al 1998) but no item modification was made. The internal consistency of the Indian adaptation was 0.89. They mode a classification of the individual status on EI ranging from below average to very superior, which is based on general intelligence classification, women were scoring significantly higherthan men.

16. Singh S. (2004) developed and standardized the measure of EI. This scale has followed Goleman's 1998 model of EI competencies, i.e. self awareness, self regulation, motivation, empathy, and social skills. The scale was validated against other measures like organizational commitment, emotional expression, and quality of life. The 5 dimensions were found to positively correlate with the above measures.

17. Bhatta Charya M. J. Dutta . A. K; Mandal. M. K. (2004) developed the Indian adaptation of emotional intelligence scale by drawing items from the scales developed on the western population, the psychometric properties ensure the relevance of the construct EI with the Indian Cultural context.

Emotional Intelligence can be do a lot

E1 is proved to be important and related to many other phenomenon eg. Leadership (Ashforth and Humphrey, 1995), group performance (Williams & sternbery, 1988) individual performance, interpersonal change, managing change and conducting performance evaluation (Goleman, 1995). According to Goleman (1995) "Emotional intelligence, the skills that help people harmonize, should become increasingly valued as a workplace asset in the year to come.

Peter Salovey (2001) found that appropriate regulation of emotions is an important predictor of good health and a key to investing money wisely.

David R. Caruso and Charies J. Wolfe (2001) explained how E1 can be important in career development, selection, training and management development.

Maurice J. Elias, Lisa Hunter, Jeffrey S. Kress (2001); and Ellas, MJ; Zins J; Weissberg, R.P., & Associates (1997) proposed that to be educated involves being knowledgeable, responsible, and caring and being non violent. It means that the traditional focus on intellectual skills IQ must be supplemented by a strong concern with social and emotional skills – 'EQ' the skills of emotional intelligence (E1). Further National Centre for innovation and education (1999) found that a primary principle of E1 is that caring relationships form the foundation of all genuine and enduring learning.

Judith Flury and William Ickes (2001) examined several aspects of E1 and empathic accuracy as they relate to friendships and dating relationship and found a strong relationship between perception of emotions in others and empathic accuracy.

Julie Fitness (2001) investigated the relevance of E1 for marital success and found both to be related.

It is also found that low levels of E1 is related to different mental illnesses in people.

Jeanne Segal (2000) EQ provides a critical edge in work family, social, romantic and even spiritual settings, emotional awareness brings our inner world into focus. It enables us to make good choices about what to eat, whom to marry, what job to take, and how to strike a mutually healthy balance between our own heads and the head of others.

Brackett et al (2004) demonstrated that high E1 was more predictive of life space (self care, behaviour, leisure, pursuits, academic activities, interpersonal relationships). Low E1 was associated with inability to perceive emotions and to use emotions to facilitate taught and therefore negative outcomes including; drug and alcohol use, deviant behaviour and poor relationship with friends.

Spence, Codes & Caputi (2004) found that trait E1 and goal self integration are related to emotional well–being.

Mc. Haught A., (2004) demonstrated that E1 can enhance the positive effects of promoting alternative thought strategies and learning skills.

Schuttle et al (2002) found that high E1 is associated with positive mood, and well being and high self esteem.

Palmer etal (2002) found that high scores on TAS – 20 was associated with high life satisfaction.

Hence from above evidence it is understood that high E1 is required for efficient functioning in different aspects of life.

Caruso R.D., Wolfe, C.L. (2001) demonstrated through their case studies that it may be possible for a person to enhance their knowledge about emotions and to bolster their emotional skills.

The results of emotional literacy programme carried out in different schools also found that through the emotional literacy programmes the children's emotional and social competence, for their behaviour in and out of the classroom, and their ability to learn improved (Goleman, 1995).

Being trained through the emotional literacy programmes children improved in the following areas :-

Emotional Self–Awareness

- Improvement in recognizing and naming own emotions.
- Better able to understand the causes of feelings
- Recognizing the difference between feelings and actions

Managing Emotions

- Better frustration tolerance and anger management
- Fewer verbal put – downs, fights, and classroom disruptions.
- Better able to express anger appropriately without fighting.

- Fewer suspensions and expulsions
- Less aggressive self destructive behaviour.
- More positive feelings about self, school and family.
- Better at handling stress.
- Less loneliness and social anxiety.

Harnessing Emotions Productivity

- More responsible
- Better able to focus on the task at hand and pay attention
- Less impulsive, more self – control
- Improved scores on achievement tests
- Empathy : reading emotions
- Better able to take another person's perspective
- Improved empathy and sensitivity to other feelings
- Better at listening to others

Handling Relationships

- Increased ability to analyze and understand relationships
- Better at resolving, conflicts and negotiating disagreements
- Better assertive and skilled at communicating
- More popular and outgoings, friendly and involved with peers
- More sought out by peers
- More concerned and considerate
- More "pro social" and harmonious in groups.
- More sharing, cooperation, and helpfulness
- More democratic in dealing with others

How to Improve Ones' Emotional Intelligence

W.T. Grant consortium (1992) developed a emotional literacy programme. This emotional literacy programme can help us to understand and raise EQ, one needs to learn how to consolidate ones emotional, cognitive and behavioural skills to effectively deal with the difficult situations in life.

The key ingredients of effective programs include.

Emotional Skills

- Identifying and labelling feelings
- Expressing feelings
- Assessing the intensity of feelings
- Managing feelings
- Delaying gratification
- Controlling impulses
- Reducing stress
- Knowing the difference between feelings and actions

Cognitive Skills

- Self talk-conducting an inner dialogue as a way to cope with a topic or challenge or reinforce one's own behaviour.
- Reading and interpreting eg. Reorganizing social influences on behaviour and seeing one self in the perspective of the larger community.
- Using steps for problem – solving and decision making eg. Controlling impulses, setting goals, identifying alternative actions, anticipating consequences.
- Understanding the perspective of others.
- Understanding behavioural norms (what is and is not acceptable behaviour).
- A positive attitude towards life.
- Self awareness eg. Developing realistic expectations about one self.

Behavioural Skills

- **Nonverbal :** Communicating through eye contact, facial expressiveness, tone of voice gestures, and so on.
- **Verbal :** Making clear requests, responding effectively to criticism, resisting negative influences, listening to others, helping others participating in positive peer groups.

Stone, K.F. & Dillehunt, H.Q. (1978) developed the self science curriculum which was carried out in schools concentrated on the following components making up the E1.

- **Self–awareness :** Observing yourself and recognizing your feelings; building a vocabulary for feelings; knowing the relationship between thoughts, feelings and reactions.
- **Personal–decision Making :** Examining your actions and knowing their consequences, knowing if thought or feeling is ruling a decision; applying these insights to issues such as sex and drugs.
- **Managing Feelings :** Monitoring self – talk to cash negative message such as internal put downs; realizing what is behin feelings (eg. the hurt that underlies anger) finding ways to handle fears and anxiety, anger and sadness.
- **Handling Stress :** Learning value of exercise, guided imagery, relaxation methods.
- **Empathy :** Understanding others feelings and concerns and taking their perspective, appreciating the differences in how people feel about things.
- **Communications :** Talking about feelings effectively; becoming a good listener and question asker; distinguishing between what someone does or says and your own reactions or judgements about it, sending 'I' message instead of blame.
- **Self disclosure :** Valuing openness and building trust in a relationship; knowing when its safe to risk talking about your private feelings.
- **Insight :** Identifying patterns in your emotional life and reaction, recognizing similar patterns in others.
- **Self–acceptance :** feeling pride and seeing yourself in a positive light; recognizing your strengths and weakness, being able to laugh at yourself.
- **Personal–responsibility :** taking responsibility, recognizing the consequences of your decisions and actions, accepting your feelings and moods, following through commitments (eg. to studying).
- **Assertiveness :** Stating your concerns and feelings without anger and passivity.

- **Group Dynamics :** cooperation; knowing when and how to lead, when to follow.
- **Conflict Resolution :** how to fight fair with other kids, with parents, with teachers, the win / win model for negotiating compromise.

Seagel J. (2000) proposed a 10 – step curriculum for raising ones EQ. It is as follows.

- Caring for ones body–relaxation and exercise.
- Understanding ones feeling by being aware of the bodily changes.
- Building ones emotional competence by taking time of focus on ones emotional experiences in day to day life.
- Be accepting of all that one feels.
- Open ones heart to others.
- Take actions–do things that make one feel useful and relevant.
- Listen to others with empathy.
- Tell them how you feel.
- Use change as an opportunity to grow.
- Take a dose of humor with you wherever you go.

Caruso, D.R. & Walfe, C.J. (2001) provided techniques that can help us to learn more about emotions and provide for more effective emotion management strategies.

Reading peoples emotions is a skill and can be improved (i) One must attend to ones emotions (ii) learn to read between the lines when dealing with others.

Generating an emotion to solve a particular problem also can be learnt through following techniques :

Relaxation techniques include breathing and progressive muscle relaxation. Visualization imagery and self statements can assist you in becoming more upbeat and existing.

Some people are able to understand emotions but they fail to pay attention to them. One can learn about emotions, what causes them, and what their functions are.

If you have read the emotional situations accurately and understand the underlying emotional dynamics, then you will need to effectively manage the emotional situation.

Mayer and Salovey identified 4 major ways in which most of us handle our emotional situations.

1. **Defensive Reactions :** i.e. distracting. This strategy is fine in the short term. However this may not be effective in long term.
2. **Acknowledge and Delay :** initially recognize the emotion but does not process it. This is useful in some situations where you need to simply acknowledge a problem or a feeling.
3. **Social convention :** Expressing awareness of the emotional component of a situation.
4. **Emotion Management :** The most effective way to manage emotions, begins with recognition of thc cmotions and then using them to solve the problem.

Attempts to improve El in schoolchildren have been increasing. Schilling (1996) recommended units in self awareness, managing feeling decision making, managing stress, personal responsibility, self concepts, empathy communication, group dynamics and conflicts resolution.

Many of the school–based interventions designed to promote El are better classified under the more general label as social and emotional learning (SEL) programs (Choen 1999a; Elias e al 1997).

There are over 300 curriculum based programmes in the US purporting to teach social and emotional learning. These range from programs based on very specific social problem – solving skills training (Elias & Toblas 1996) to more general conflict resolution strategies (Lantieri & Patti 1996) to very broad programs organized around themes like character development (Lickona, 1991).

Possible interventions to increase emotional intelligence also can be found in the work place (Caruso, Mayer & Salovey; cherniss & Goleman 1998; Goleman 1998). Many of these work place El programs are really old and familiar training sessions on human relations, achievement motivation, stress management, and conflict resolution.

Further Directions for Research

Investigation is needed in helping to refine the ability based assessment of emotional intelligence and subsequently, studying the predictive validity of E1 in accounting for important outcomes in school, workplace, family and social relationships (Salovey, Mayer & Lasuro 2002).

There should be steps taken towards developing intervention programmes designed to improve E1, performance, relationship quality and general well being (Furhham, Petcides 2003).

Simmons, S & Simmons J (1997) suggested that there are 3 absolutely vital areas still to be addressed.

1. Precise measurement of E1–without proper measurement of E1 it is difficult to identify which areas are sound and which need improvement, which are compatible with others, which are not.
2. The full range of E1 while others have discussed upto five aspects of emotional intelligence, we have 13 distinct areas.
3. Application : There is a need to teach how to relate to others based on E1, how to develop E1, and how to apply knowledge of E1 to the world of work.

References and Further Reading

1. Anastasi, A & urbina, S. (1997). Psychological testing. New Jersey : Simon & Schuster.
2. Ashforth, B.E. & Humphrey, R.H. (1995) Emotion in the work place : A reappraisal. Human relations, 48 (2), 97 – 125.
3. Aristotle (1984). The complete works of Aristotle : The revised oxfored translation (J. Barners, Ed.) Princeton : Princeton university press.
4. Bade, M., Lamba, S & Ram, U. (2000) Emotional intelligence, anger and irrationality. Paper accepted for presentation at the XXVII International congress of psychology, Stockholm, Sweden, July 23 – 27.
5. Bagby. R.M., Parker, J.D. & Taylor, G.J. (1994). The twenty item Toronto Alexithymia scale – 1. Item selection and cross – validation of the factor structure. Journal of Psychosomatic Research. 38, 23 – 32.
6. Bar – On, R. (1997) Emotional Intelligence quotient inventory : A measure of emotional intelligence. Toranto Canada. ON : Multi – Health Systems Inc.

7. Barth, J & Bastiani, A (1997) A longitudinal study of emotion recognition and preschool children's social behaviour. Merril – Palmer Quarterly, 43, 107 – 128.

8. Bhattacharya, M; Dutta, A.K.; Mandal. M.K. (2004). Factor structure of emotional intelligence in India; Psychological studies vol 49 Number 2-3, Pg. – 142 – 146.

9. Boyatzi, R.E., Goleman, D., & Hay / McBer (1999). E-motional competence inventory. Hay group.

10. Brackett, M., & Mayer, J.D. (2003). Convergent, discrimnant and incremental validity of competing measures of emotional intelligence. Personality and social psychology Bulletin, 29, 1147 – 1158.

11. Brackett, M.A.; Mayer J.D., Warner, R.M., (2004) Emotional intelligence and its relationship to the everyday behaviour Personality and individual differences Apr. 2004, Vol – 36 (6) pp. – 1387 – 16p.

12. Buck, R., (1984) The communication of emotion, New York Guilford.

13. Caruso, D.R., Mayer, J.D., & Salove, P. (in Press) Emotional intelligence and emotional leadership. In R. Riggo & S. Murphy (Eds.), Multiple intelligences and leadership, Mahwah, NJ: Erlbaum.

14. Caverm, C.S., Scheier, M.F., & Weintraub, J.K.(1989). Assessing coping strategies : A theoretically based approach. Journal of Personality and Social Psychology 56, 267 – 283.

15. Cassidy, J., Parke, R., Butkobsley, L., & Braugart, J., (1992), Family and peer connections : The roles of emotional expressiveness within the family and children understanding of emotions. Child development, 63, 603 – 618.

16. Chadha, N.K., (1998). Indian Prime ministers and their EQ (unpublished).

17. Charbonreau, D., & Nicol, A.A.M, (2002). Emotional intelligence and prosocial behaviours in adolescents Psychological reports, 90, 361 – 370.

18. Cherniss, C., & Goleman, D. (1998). Bringing emotional intelligence to the work place. Technical report issued by the consortium for Research on emotional intelligence in organizations (available at www.eiconsortium .org)

19. Ciarrochi, J., A., & Bajgar, J, (2000). Measuring emotional intelligence in adolescents. Manuscript submitted for publication.

20. Ciarrochi, J., Chan, A., & Caputi, P. (2000). A critical evaluation of emotional intelligence construct. Personality and individual differences 28, 539 – 561.

21. Ciarrochi, J. Chan, A., Caputi, P., & Roberts. R. (2001) Measuringemotional intelligence E1. In J.V. ciarrochi J.P. Forgas & J.D. Mayer (Eds). Emitional intelligence in everyday life : A scientific inquiry. Philadelphia Psychology Press.

22. Ciarrochi, J., Deanne, F. & Anderson, S. (2000). Emotional intelligence moderates the relationship between stress and psychological adaptation, as measured by depression hopelessness and suicidal ideation. Manuscript submitted for publication.
23. Cohen, J. (Ed.) (1999). Educating minds and hearts social emotional learning and passage into adolesence New York : Teachers College Press.
24. Cooper, R.K. (1997). EQ map. San Francisco : AIT & Essi system.
25. Cooper, R.K., & Sawaf, A. (1997). Executive EQ : Emotional intelligence in leadership and organizations New York Grosset / Putnam.
26. Costa, P.T. Jr., & Mc Crae, R.R. (1992). Revised NEO Personality inventory (NEO – PI – R) and NEO five factor Inventory (NEO – FFI). Oolessa, FL : Psychological assessment resources.
27. Dabrowski, K., & Piechowski, M.M. (1977). Theory of levels of emotional development (Vol. 1) Oceanside. NY : Dabor science publications.
28. Darwin, C, (1965). The expression of the emotions in man and animals. Chicago : University of Chicago Press (original work published 1872).
29. Davies, M., Stankov, L., & Roberts, R.D. (1998). Emotional Intelligence : In search of an elusive construct Journal of personality and social psychology, 75, 989 – 1015.
30. Dawd, D. & Hart, S.D. (2000). Assessing emotional intelligence : Reliability and validity of the Bar – on emotional Intelligence Inventory (EQ – 1) in university students. Personality and individual differences, 28, 797 – 812.
31. Elias, M.J., & Tobias, S.E. (1996). Social problem solving interventions in schools in schools. New York : Guilford.
32. Elias, M.J., Zins, J.E., Weissberg, R.P., Frey, K.S., Greeberg, M.T, Haynes, N.M., Kessler, R., Sohwab – stone, M.e., & Shriver., T.P. (1997). Promoting social and emotional learning : Guidelines for educators. Alexendria VA : Association for supervision and curriculum Development.
33. Ellias, M.J., Hunter, L. & Kress.J.S. (2001) Emotional intelligence and education. In J.V. Liarroch; J.P. Forgas, & J.D. Mayer (Eds). Emotional intelligence in every day life : A scientific inquiry. Philadelphia Psychology press.
34. Ellis, A. (1962) Reason and emotion in psychotherapy Secaucus, NJ: Lyle staurt.
35. Field, T.M. & Walden, T.A. (1982). Production and discrimination of facial expressions by preschool children, child development, 53, 1299 – 1311.
36. Flury, J. & Ickes, W. (2001) Emotional Intelligence and empathic accuracy, IN J.V. Ciarrochi, J.P. Forgas & J.D. Mayer (Eds) Emotional

intelligence in everyday life : A scientific inquiry. Philadelphia Psychology Press.

37. Forgas, J.P. (2001). Affective intelligence : Towards understanding role of affect in social thinking and behaviour. IN J.V. ciarrochi, J.P. Forgas, J.D. Mayer (Eds). Emotional intelligence in everyday life : A scientific inquiry. Philadelphia. Psychology Press.
38. Freud; S. (1962). The ego and the id. (J. Strachey, Ed; J. Riviere, Trans) New york : Norton. (Original work published 1923).
39. Friedman, H.S., & Milla – Herrigner, T. (1991). Non – verbal display of emption in public and in private : Self – monitoring, personality and expressive cues. Journal of Personality and social psychology, 61, 766 – 775.
40. Friedman, H.S., Riggio, R.E., & Casella, D. (1988) Nonverbal skill, personal charisman, and initial attraction Personality and social psychology Bulletin, 14, 203 – 211.
41. Friedman, H.S; Riggo, R. (1999). Individual differences in the ability to encode complex affects, Personality and individual differences, 27, 181 – 194.
42. Gardner, H. (1983). Frames of mind. New york : Basic Books.
43. Gibb, N. (Oct. – 1995). Time. New York : Time Warner Goleman, D. (1995). Emotional intelligence. New York Bantam Books.
44. Goldman, S.L., Kraemer, D.T., & Salovey, P. (1996). Beliefs about mood moderate the relationship of stress to illness an symptom reporting Journal of psychosomatic research, 41, 115 – 128.
45. Goleman, D. (1995). Emotional intelligence. New York Bantam Books.
46. Goleman, D. (1995b) what is your EQ ? The utne Lens, Utne reader (on – line). Available : http//www.utne.com/lens/bms/eq.html.
47. Goleman, D. (1998). Working with emotional intelligence New York : Bantam.
48. Gottman, J. (1997). The heart of parenting : How to raise an emotionally intelligent child. New York : Simon & Schuster.
49. Graves, J: (1999) Emotional intelligence and cognitive ability : Predicting performance in the job stimulated activities. Unpublished Phd. Thesis. California school of professional psychology, San Diego.
50. Dume, D. (1948). A treastise of human nature. In H.D. Aiken (Ed), Hume : Moral and political philosophy (pp – 1 – 169) New York : Hafner Press. (Original work published 1739).
51. Izard, C.E. (1971). The face of emotion. New York : Appleton – Century – Crofts.
52. James, W.(1950) The principles of psychology (Vol. – 2.). New York : Dover. (Original work published 1890).

53. Lare, R.D., Quinlan, D.M., Schwartz., G.E., Walker, P., & Zeutlin, S.B. (1990). The levels of emotional awareness scale : A cognitive – developmental measure of emotion, journal of personality Assessment, 55, 124 – 134.

54. Lane, R.D., Rei man, E.M., Axelrod, B., Yun, Lang – Sheng, Homes, A., & Schwarz., G.E. (1998). Neural correlates of levels of emotional awareness. Evidence of an interaction between emotion and attention in the interior cingulated cortex. Journal of cognitive.

55. Lantieri, L., & Patti, J. (1996). Waging peace in our schools. Boston : Beacon.

56. Leeper, R.W. (1948). A motivational theory of emotions to replace "emotions as disorganized response." Psychological review, 55, 5 – 21.

57. Leible, T., Shell, Jr. W.E. (2004) Boarder line personality disorder and multiple aspects of Emotional intelligence Personality and individual difference, Vol – 137 (2) P- 393.

58. Lesser, I.M (1985) Alexithymia. New England Journal of medicine, 312, 690 – 692.

59. Lickona, T. (1991). Educating for character : How our schools can teach respect and responsibility New York : Bantam.

60. Lolas, F. & Van Rad, M. (1989). Alexithymia. In S. Cheren (Ed), Psychosomatic medicine : Theory, physiology , and practice, Vol. – 1. Madison, CT : International University Press, PP.189 – 237.

61. Marlowe, H.A. (1986). Social intelligence : Evidence for multidimensionality and construct independence Journal of Educational psychology, 78, 52 – 58.

62. Mayers, J.D. (1986). How mood influences cognition. In N.E. Sharkey (Ed), Advances in cognitive science (pp. – 290 – 314) Chichester, West – Sussex : Ellis Harwood.

63. Mayer, J.D., Carlsmith, K.M. & Chabot, H.F. (1998). Describing the persons external environment : Conceptualising and measuring the life space. Journal of research in personality, 32, 253 – 296.

64. Mayer, J.D., Caruso, D. & Salovey, P. (2000). Emotional intelligence meets traditional standards for an intelligence. Intelligence, 27 : 267 – 298.

65. Mayer, J.D., & Salovey, P. (1993). The intelligence of emotional intelligence. Intelligence, 17 (4), 433 – 442.

66. Mayer, J.D. & Salovey P., Caruso, D. (in Preparation) Mayer, Salovey and Caruso emotional intelligence test (MSCEIT). Toranto, Ontario : Multi – Health Systems.

67. Mayer, J.D., Salovey, P. & Caruso, D. (in preparation) The Mayer, Salovey, Caruso emotional intelligence Test : MSCEIT Version – 2 : Toronto, ON : Multi – Health Systems.

68. Mayer, J.D., & Stevens, A. (1994) An emerging understanding of the reflective (meta) experience of mood, journal of Research in Personality, 28, 351 – 373.

69. McCrae, R.R. (2000). Emotional intelligence from the perspective of the five – factor model of personality. In R. Bar – on & J.D.A. Parker (EDs), The Handbook of emotional intelligence : Theory, Development, Assessment and application at home, school and in the workplace. San Franscisco – Jorsey – Bas Wiley.

70. McNaught, A. (2004). Stepping out of shells. Times educational supplement 7 / 23 / 2004. Issue 45 93, P 22.

71. Miller, S.M., Brody, D.S., & Sumerton, J./ (1988). Styles of coping with threat : Implications for health. Journal of personality and social psychology, 34 (1), 142 – 148.

72. Mowrer, O.H. (1960). Learning theory and behaviour New York : Wiley.

73. Nemiah, J.C. (1977). Alexithymia: Theoretical considerations. Psychotherapy and psychosomatics, 28, 199 – 206.

74. Newsome, S., Day, A.L., and Catano, V.M. (2000) Assessing the predictive validity of emotional intelligence, Personality and individual differences, 29, 1005 – 1016.

75. Nolen – Hoeksema, S & Morrow, J. (1991). A prospective study of depression and distress following a natural disaster : The 1989 Loma Prieeta earthquake. Journal of personality and social psychology. 61, 105 – 121.

76. Palmer, B, Donaldson, C. Stough. C, (2002). Emotional intelligence and life satisfaction. Personality and individual difference, 33 (7) p – 1091.

77. Paulhus, D.L., Lysy, D.C., & Yik., M.S. (1998). Self report measures of intelligence : Are they useful as proxy IQ tests ? Journal of personality, 66, 525 – 554.

78. Petrides, K.V. & Funham, A(2000). On the dimensional structure of emotional intelligence. Personality and individual difference 29, 313, 320.

79. Petrides, K.V., Perez, Furhham A (2003) Trait E1 questionnaire (TEIQue) A measure of emotional self efficacy. In E.J. Austin & D+S Saklofske (Chairs) E1 symposium conducted at the 11th Beinniel meeting of the international society for the study of the individual difference. Tiraz. Austria.

80. Petrides; K.V. Fredreckson, N. & Furnham A (in Press) The role of trait E1 in academic performance and deviant behaviour at school. Personality and individual differences.

81. Rice, C.L. (1996) A quantitative study of emotional intelligence and its impact on team performance, unpublished masters thesis, Pepperdine university.

82. Riley. H., Schutte, N.S., (2003) Low E1 as a predictor of substance use problem. Journal of drug education, 33 (4), P 391.

83. Roberts, R.D. Zeidnes, M. & Mathews G (2001). Does emotional intelligence meet traditional standards for an 'intelligence' ? Some new data and conclusion Emotions, 1., 196 – 231.

84. Roger, D., & Nagarian, B. (1989). The construction and vaiidation of a new scale for measuring emotion control. Personality and individual differences, 1, 845 – 8458.

85. Roiser, R.H. (1994, 1995). The competency Model Handbook volume one and two Boston.

86. Rovenger, J. (2000). Role of literature on enhancement of child emotional intelligence. School. Library Journal 46 (12) p – 40.

87. Rubin, M.M. (1999). Emotional intelligence and its role in mitigating aggression : A correlatioal study of the relationship between emotional intelligence and aggression in urban adolescents unpublished manuscripts, Immaculata college, Immaculata, P.A.

88. Ruesch, J. (1948). The infantile personality. Psychosomatic medicine, 10, 134 – 144.

89. Saarni, C. (1988) Emotional competence : How emotional relationships become integrated. In R.A. Thompson (Ed), Nebraska symposium on motivation (vol. 36, p 115 – 182). Lincoln : University of Nebraska Press.

90. Saarni, C. (1999). The development of emotional competence. New York. Guilford.

91. Saklofske, D.H., Austin, E.J. & Minski, P.S. (2003). Factor structure and validity of a trait emotional intelligence measure. Personality and individual differences, 34, 707, 721.

92. Salerno, J.G. (1996) The whole intelligence : emotional quotient (EQ). Oakbank, South Australia : Noble House of Australia.

93. Salovey, P. (2001). Applied emotionai intelligence : Regulating emotions to become healthy, wealthy, and wise. In J.V. Ciarrochi, J.D. Forgas, & J.D. Mayers (Eds), Emotional intelligence in everybody life : A scientific inquiry. Philadelphia : Psychology. Press.

94. Salovey, P., Bedell, B.T., Detweiler, J.B., & Mayer, J.D. (2000) current directions in emotional intelligence research. In M. Lewis & J.M Havi land – James (Eds.) Handbook of emotions (2nded, p 504 – 520). New York Guilford.

95. Salovey, P. & mayer, J.D. (1990) Emotional intelligence Imagination, cognition and personality, 9, 185 – 211.

96. Salovey, P. Mayer, J.D., Goldman, S.L., Turvey, C & Palfai, T.P. (1995). Emotional attention, clarity and repair : Exploring emotional intelligence

using the Trait – meter – mood scale. In J.W. Pennebaker (Ed), Emotion, disclosure, and health (p – 125 – 154). Washing ton, DC : American Psychological Association.

97. Salovey, P., Mayer, J.D., Caruso, D. (2002) The positive psychology of emotional intelligence. Handbook of positive psychology. Snyder CR, ed, Lopez shane Jed Oxford, Oxford university press.

98. Schaffer, L.F., Gilmer, B., & Scheen, M. (1940). Psychology. New York : Harper.

99. Schwarz, N. (1990). Feeling as information : Informational motivational function of affective states. In E.T. Higgins & E.M. Sorrentino (Eds), Handbook of motivation and cognition : Foundations of social behaviour (vol. 2 p 527 – 561). New York Guilford Press.

100. Schwarz, N., & Clore, G.L. (1983). Mood, misattribution and judgemetn of well – being : Informative and directive functions of affective states. Journal of personality and social psychology, 45, 513 – 523.

101. Schilling, D. (1996). Fifty activities for teaching emotional intelligence : Level I : Elementary Torrance, CA : Inner choice publishing.

102. Schutte, N.S., Malauff, J.M., Hall, L.E., Haggerty, D., Copper, J.T., Golden, C.J., & Dorhneim, L. (1998) . Development and validation of measure of emotional intelligence. Personality and individual differences, 25, 167 – 177.

103. Schutte, N.S., Malouff, J.M., Bobik, C., Coston, TD., Greeson, C., Jedlicka, C., Rhodes, E., & Wendorf, G., (2001). Emotional intelligence and interpersonal relations. The Journal of social psychology, 141, 525 – 526.

104. Schutte, N.S., Malouff, J.M., Stimunek, M., McKenley, J.S. & Hollander, S. (2000) characteristics of emotional intelligence and emotional well – being cognition and emotion, 16, 769, 785.

105. Segal, J. (1997) Raising your emotional intelligence New York : Holt.

106. Segal, J. (2000) Raising your emotional intelligence A practical guide. Magna Publishing Co. Ltd.

107. Sibia, Mishra, G., Srivastava, A.K. (2004) Towards understanding emotional intelligence in the Indian context : Perspectives of parents, Teachers and children, Psychological studies, 49, 114.

108. Simmons, S., & Simmons, J.C. (1997), Measuring emotional intelligence. Arlington, TX : Summit.

109. Sifneos, P.E. (1967). Clinical observations on some patients suffering from a variety of psychosomatic diseases. Acta Medicina Psychosomatica, 21, 133 – 136.

110. Singh, S. (2004) Development of a measure of Emotional Intelligence. Psychological studies, 49, p 136.

111. Spinoza, B. (1677). Ethics. In E. Curley (Ed.), The collected works of spinoza. Princeton : Princeton University press.

112. Stein, S. & Book, H. (2000). The EQ edge : North York ON. Stoddart.

113. Sternberg, R.J. (1988). The triarchic min : A new theory of human intelligence. New York : Viking.

114. Stone, K.F. Dillehunt. H.Q. (1978) Self science : The subject is me. Santa Monica : Good year publishing Co.

115. Taylor, G.J. (2000) Recent developments in Alexithymia theory and research. Canadian Journal of Psychiaky 45, 134 – 142.

116. Taylor, G.J., Bagby, R.M., & Parker, J.D.A. (1991). The alexithymia construct. A potential paradiagm for psychosomatic medicine. Psychosomatics, 32 153 – 164.

117. Taylor, G.J., Bagby, R.M. & Parker, J.D.A. (1997) Disorders of affect regulation : Alexithymia in medical and psychiatric illness – Cambridge : Cambridge University Press.

118. Taylor, G.J., and Taylor, H.L. (1997). Alexithymia : In M.Mc. Callum & W.E. Piper (Eds). Psychological mindedness : A contemporary understanding (p 77 - 104) Mahwah, N.J. Lawrence Erlbaum Associates.

119. Ten Houten, W.D.,Hopper, K.D., Begen, J.E. & Walter, D.O. (1986). Alexithymia : An experimental study of cerebral commissurotomy patients and normal control subjects. American Journal of psychiatry 143, 312 –316.

120. Terman, L.M. (1921) second contribution to "Intelligence and its measurement : A symposium Journal of education psychology, 12, 127 – 133.

121. Thinguja, N.K.S & Ram, U. (1999). Emotional intelligence, trait – anxiety, coping with stress, and belief in social relation. Paper presented at 5th International and 36th Indian Academy of Applied Psychology(IAAP) conference, Bangalore, India, Dec. 27 – 29.

122. Thingujam, N.K.S. & Ram, u (2000). Emotional intelligence scale : Indian norm. Journal of Education and Psychology, 58, 40 – 48.

123. Thorndike, E.L. (1920) Intelligence and its uses Harper's Magazine, 140, 227 – 235.

124. Tomkins, S.S. (1962). Affect, imagery and consciousness (Vol. 1 : The positive affects). New York; Springer.

125. Trinidad, D.R., & Johnson, C.A. The association between emotional intelligence and early adolescent tobacco and alcohol use. Personality and individual differences.

126. W.T. grant consortium on the school – based promotion of social competence, "During and alcohol Prevention Curricula," in J. David Hawkins et al, communities that care (San Francisco : Jassey – Bass, 1992).

127. Weinberger, D.A., Schwarz, G.E. & Davidson, R.J. (1979) Low anxious high anxious and repressive coping styles : Psychometric patterns and behavioural and physciological responses to stress. Journal of abnormal psychology, 88.

128. Williams, W.M. & Sternberg, R.J. (1988). Group intelligence : why some groups are better than others. Intelligence, 12, 351 - 377.

129. Wood worth, R.S. (1940). Psychology 4th (Ed) New York. Holt.

130. Young, P.T. (1936). Motivation of behaviour : New York Wiley.

20

Stress and Health Related Consequences

Ivancevich and Matteson define stress simply as "the interaction of the individual with the environment," but then they go on to give a more detailed working definition, as follows: "an adaptive response, mediated by individual differences and/or psychological processes, that is consequence of any external (environmental) action, situation, or event that places excessive psychological and/or physical demands upon a person."

Beehr and Newman define job stress as "a condition arising from the interaction of people and their jobs and characterized by changes within people that force them to deviate from their normal functioning."

1. **Stress is Not Simply Anxiety.** Anxiety operates solely in the emotional and psychological sphere, whereas stress operates there and also in the physiological sphere. Thus, stress may be accompanied by anxiety, but the two should not be equated.
2. **Stress is Not Simply Nervous Tension.** Like anxiety, nervous tension may result from stress, but the two are not the same. Unconscious people have exhibited stress, and some people may keep it "bottled up" and not reveal it through nervous tension.
3. **Stress is Necessarily Something Damaging, Bad, or to be Avoided.** Eustress is not damaging or bad and is something people should seek out rather than avoid. The key, of course, is how the person handles the stress. Stress is inevitable; distress may be prevented or can be effectively controlled.

The Background of Stress

Hans Selye is the father of stress. He gave a phenomenon called the general adaptation syndrome (GAS).

The GAS has Three Stages: alarm, resistance, and exhaustion. In the alarm stage an outside stressor mobilizes the internal system of the body. There are a number of physiological and chemical reactions such as increased pituitary and adrenaline secretions; noticeable increases in respiration, heart rate, and blood pressure; and a heightening of the senses. If the stressor continues, then the GAS moves into the resistance stage, during which the body calls upon the needed organ or system to deal with the stressor. However, while there may be a great deal of resistance to one stressor during this second stage, there may be little, if any, resistance to other, unrelated stressors. This helps explain why a person going through an emotional strain may be particularly vulnerable to other illness or disease. Finally, if the stressor persists over a long period of time, the reserves of the adaptive mechanisms during the second stage may become drained, and exhaustion sets in. When this happens, there may be a return to the alarm stage, and the cycle starts again with another organ or system, or the "automatic shutoff valve" of death occurs. This GAS process, can be very hard on the person and takes its toll on the human body.

Besides the physiologically oriented approach to stress represented by the classic GAS model, psychological and behavioral dimensions are important to the understanding of job stress and coping strategies in modern organizations (Davis, 1998).

Response To Stress

Researches have identified three major categories of possible responses to stress, physiological, psychological and behavioural. The physiological responses included cardiovascular symptoms such as increased blood pressure and cholesterol level, biochemical measures such as catecholamines and uric acid, and gastrointestinal symptoms such as peptic ulcers. Faster heart rates have been reported under conditions of role conflict, ambiguity regarding future development on the job, and overall reported stress at work. Levels of catecholamines change very rapidly and respond to a variety of stimuli. Unpredictability at work, loss of control over pace and method, and distracting noise have all been associated with increased levels of catecholamines. Research on gastrointestinal symptoms has shown less consistent results compared to the other two types of physiological response.

There are at least 3 different ways in which stress can affect the immune systems.

1. Stress affects the immune system activation to not only fresh viral onslaught but also tends to reactivate latent viruses. Emotional distress can lower the effects of Hepatitis B vaccination (Glaser et al, 1992); it can reactivate latest virus such as those causing Herpes Simplex. Such effects have been observed in individuals experiencing the pain of a divorce, or tormented by a poor marital relationship, or under examination stress (Bonneau 1994).
2. Stress increases the risk of rheumatoid arthritis. Sternberg et al (1991) have proposed that certain physiological mechanisms associated with depression (a known symptom of stress) may enhance susceptibility to or increase the severity of rheumatoid arthritis.
3. Life stresses affect the immune system function. Researchers on volunteers experiencing negative life events and negative emotions indicate that these people were more likely to have higher rates of infection or contacting colds (Cohen, 1994). Similarly, work by Kiecolt-Glaser et al (1995) confirms a strong link between chronic stress and the immune system function.

Psychological responses to stress at work most typically involve effective variables, with job dissatisfaction being most common. Stress has also been found to influence more intense and aroused affective states such as anger, frustration, hostility, and irritation. More passive, but perhaps no less negative responses include boredom, burnout, fatigue, and depressed mood. The psychological effects of work related stress have been found to produce lowered self-confidence and self-esteem.

Behavioural responses to stress at work have not been studied as frequently as psychological responses. However, five broad categories of behavioural responses have been examined: the work role (job performance, accidents, drug use at work), oppressive behaviour at work (theft, purposeful damage), flight from the job (absenteeism, turnover), degradation of other life roles (spouse & child abuse), and self damaging behaviours (alcohol and drug abuse).

Direct behaviors that may accompany high levels of stress include undereating or overeating, sleeplessness, increased smoking, drinking, and drug abuse.

There is some research evidence indicating the relationship between stress and especially absenteeism and turnover. For example, workers may experience stress and react by getting drunk and staying home from work the next day with a hangover. They then feel bad about this drinking. They may feel that they are letting everyone down "the morning after" and eventually quit or be fired from the job. In the meantime the absenteeism rate climbs, and subsequently the turnover rates increase, both of which are very costly to the organization in terms of filling in for absent workers and replacing those who have left. Staying away from a job that is causing stress or quitting the job is a "flight" reaction to the situation. Actually, this may be a healthier reaction than a "fight" reaction, which the person may stay on the stress-producing job and become angry and/or aggressive (Agarwal, 2001;Luthans, 1992; Muchinsky, 2000).

Burn Out

It's a personal energy crisis due to exhaustion of our adaptation energy. The chief cause of burn out is unrelieved work stress. It is a situation in which employees are emotionally exhausted, become detached from their clients and their work and feel unable to accomplish their goals. When workers become burned out, they are more likely to complain, to attribute their errors to others and to be highly irritable. The alienation they feel drives many of them to think about having their jobs, to seek out opportunities to become trained for new careers and actually to quit. In addition to higher turnover, burnout also leads to increased absenteeism and decreased quality and quantity of job performance. A tragic product of burnout by workers in Japan is called Karoshi or sudden death at work. This is believed to be triggered by overload, culminating in a fatal heart attack or stroke (Davis, 1998).

Emotional Consequences: Anger, Anxiety, Depression

Emotions refer to the feeling aspect of behaviours such as mild irritation, rage, despair, sadness, love and liking. Whereas the physiological effects of stress can be clearly pinpointed, observed and measured, emotional changes are highly subjective. One can experience them, but one cannot express them in words. Often a person may be seething with anger with in, but maintains a cool exterior, clearly indicating that emotions are not always observable. In general, emotions are internal states, which are often short lived, and can even be experienced in combination. Three identifiable emotions that are a fairly regular outcome of stress are anxiety, anger and depression.

Anxiety : Generally an unpleasant emotional state accompanied by physiological arousal and cognitive aspects like apprehension, guilt and a sense of impending disaster. It is different from fear which is an emotional reaction to a specific or identifiable object.

Depression : A reaction characterized by apprehension, self-devaluation and feelings of guilt and worthlessness, defection and a pervasive pessimistic outlook.

Anger : This is one of the offshoots of stress. It may be manifested in a variety of forms. One may express anger, bottle it up, or distort it till it becomes something else.

Expressing anger may develop into a bad habit, leading to poor emotional control and unnecessary temper tantrums. It may grow out of proportion, be inappropriate to the situation and may sour many a relationship. It may also lead to strong feelings of guilt on one's part and retaliation from the person on whom the anger was vented.

Bottling up anger may be unhealthy. It may cause somatic symptoms such as headaches, ulcers, bowel problems, skin problems, high BP & heart attacks. Suppression of anger may also lead to self-hatred.

Neither untimely expression nor suppression provides the answer. It is not wrong to be angry. Anger can be a strong motivation. It is the force which makes one agitated when one is wronged. The problem is learning how to discharge our anger in a way which is not only acceptable to society but also healthy for us (Agarwal, 2001).

First Aid for Depression

1. Turn to friends or family for support. Don't isolate yourself.
2. Initiate an exercise program or sport. Take a walk during your lunch break with a friend.
3. Reduce alcohol consumption. Alcohol is depressant.
4. Avoid overeating. Especially your sugar and fat intake.
5. Avoid financial overload.

Anxiety Busters

1. Learn how to set limits. Say "no" to certain activities and people. Put down your agenda so that you have more time for activities meaningful to you.

2. Delegate or share responsibilities or workload when appropriate. Recognize that you cannot do everything.
3. Learn how to prioritize.
4. Take enough "space" or time alone – in nature, if possible.
5. Allow time for personal creative expression especially through writing, art, music or dance.
6. Give yourself permission to relax, by reading, daydreaming, playing games or cards, etc.
7. Revise your expectations of yourself and of others. Be realistic, so that you don't feel guilty or agitated when a project isn't completed by an arbitrary or unrealistic deadline.
8. Cut down on caffeine. Consumption of only two cups of coffee contributes to feelings of anxiety, more than two cups creates feelings/symptoms of anxiety (O'Hara, 1995).

Properties of the Persons As Stress Mediators/Personality

Individual differences in resistance to stress have long been recognized. Two personality characteristics have been clearly identified as mediating the effects of stress. The first is personality type.

Friedman and Rosenman define the Type A personality as "an action-emotion complex that can be observed in any person who is aggressively involved in a chronic, incessant struggle to achieve more and more in less and less time, and if required to do so, against the opposing efforts of other things or other persons." They are the ones who:

1. Work long, hard hours under constant deadline pressures and conditions for overload.
2. Often take work home at night or on weekends and are unable to relax.
3. Constantly compete with themselves, setting high standards of productivity that they seem driven to maintain.
4. Tend to become frustrated by the work situation, to be irritated with the work efforts of others, and to be misunderstood by superiors.

At first, because of Rosenman and Friedman's studies, it was generally thought that Type A's were much more prone to the worst outcome of stress: heart attacks. More recently, however, a number of studies have been unable to confirm their findings.

The most recent studies seem to indicate that it is not so much the impatience that is closely associated with Type A's, but rather anger and hostility that lead to heart problems. Besides the debate surrounding the impact of Type A personality on health is the question of the success of Type A's versus Type B's. It is pretty clear that Type A's are typically on a "fast track" to the top. They are more successful than Type B's. However, at the very top they do not tend to be as successful as Type B's, who are more patient and take a broader view of things. The key may be to shift from Type A to Type B behavior, but, of course, most Type A's are unable and unwilling to make the shift and/or to cope with their Type A characteristics.

Type A is a personality type that intensifies the effects of various job stressors. Type A people walk, eat and talk rapidly. They are aggressive and competitive and constantly feel under time pressure. Type B people are less concerned about time; they play for fun, not to win, and they can release without guilt. Type A people have a higher pulse rate than type B people and are twice as likely to develop heart disease. Berking and Boswell (1995) identified an irritability dimension to Type A behaviour that adversely affects health and concentration. Wright (1988) concluded that Type A people have a high possibly insatiable need for achievement. They experience early (no later than adolescence) success, which seems to breed and greater than usual sense of hope that striving efforts will eventually pay off. Type A individuals cannot control themselves when exposed to work related stimuli. In assessing the proclivity of Type A individuals to feel stress from work, Wright said, "what is needed are ways of training ourselves and others to maintain diligence with pacing – that is to run the race of life like a marathon and not a series of 100 yard dashes."

The second personality characteristic that mediates stress is locus of control. LOC differentiates people who believe that they themselves are primarily responsible for what happens to them from those who believe that major events in their lives are determined mainly by other people or forces beyond themselves. People whose LOC is primarily internal respond to stress differently from those whose LOC is external. Those who are internally oriented are more likely to take action against the source of the stress itself, or to mitigate its effects in other ways.

Those who are externally oriented are more at liberty to see effective actions as beyond their powers and thus endure rather than act. Some researches have also identified a personality construct associated with the capacity to endure negative life events, including job stress. This personality construct has been called ego resilience or hardiness (Kinicki, McKee, & Wade, 1996; Luthans, 1992; Muchinsky, 2000).

Coping Strategies

The strategies used to deal with distressing events are examples of coping. Coping refers to the ways we try to change circumstances, or our interpretation of circumstances, to make them more favourable and less threatening (Lazarus, 1993, Folkman & Lazarus, 1991).

Coping tends to be a dynamic, ongoing process. We may switch our coping strategies as we appraise the changing demands of a stressful situation and our available resources at any given moment. We also evaluate whether our efforts have made a stressful situation better or worse and adjust our coping strategies accordingly. When coping is effective, we adapt to the situation and stress is reduced. Unfortunately, coping efforts always help us adapt (Lukoff & others, 1989; Paykel & Dowlatshahi, 1988). Maladaptive coping can involve thoughts and behaviours that intensify or prolong distress or that produce self-defeating outcomes (Bolger & Zuckerman, 1995).

Adaptive coping responses serve many functions. Most important, adaptive coping involves realistically evaluating the situation and determining what can be done to minimize the impact of the stressor. But adaptive coping also involves dealing with the emotional aspects of the situation. In other words, adaptive coping often includes developing emotional tolerance for negative life events, maintaining self-esteem, and keeping emotions in balance. And third, adaptive coping efforts are directed toward preserving important relationships during stressful experiences (Lazarus, 1993; Lazarus & Folkman, 1984).

Psychologists Richard Lazarus & Susan Folkman (1984) have described two basic types of coping, each which serves a different purpose. Problem - focused coping is aimed at managing or changing a threatening or harmful stressor. If we think there is nothing that can be done to alter a situation, we tend to rely on emotion – focused coping: We direct our efforts toward relieving or regulating the emotional impact of the stressful situation. Although emotion –

focused coping does not change the problem, it can help one feel better about the situation.

Problem–focussed Coping Strategies: Changing the Stressor

Problem – focused coping strategies represent actions that have the goal of changing or eliminating the stressor. When a person who is aggressive or risky efforts to change the situation, he is engaging in confrontive coping. Ideally, confrontive coping is direct and assertive without being hostile. When it is hostile or aggressive confrontive, coping may well generate negative emotions in the people being confronted, damaging future relations with them (Folkman & Lazarus, 1991).

In contract, planful problem solving involves efforts to rationally analyze the situation, identify potential solutions, then implement them. In effect, you take the attitude that the stressor represents a problem to be solved. Once you assume that mental stance, you follow the basic steps of problems solving like trial & error, algorithm, heuristic, insight and intuition.

Trial & Error : A problem solving strategy that involves attempting different solutions and eliminating those that do not work.

Algorithm : A problem solving strategy that involves following a specific rule, procedure, or method that inevitably produces the correct solution.

Heuristic : A problem solving strategy that involves following a general rule of thumb to reduce the number of possible solutions.

Insight : The sudden realization of how a problem can be solved.

Intuition : Coming to a conclusion or making a judgment without conscious awareness of the thought processes involved.

Emotion-focused Coping Strategy: Changing or Reaction to the Stressor

When the stressor is one over which we can exert little or no control, we often focus on dimensions of the situation that we can control-the emotional impact of the stressor on us (Thompson & others, 1994). All the different forms of emotion – focused coping share the goal of reducing or regulating the emotional impact of a stressor.

When you shift your attention away from the stressor and toward other activities you are engaging in the emotion-focused coping strategy called escape-avoidance. The basic goal is to escape or avoid the stress or and neutralize distressing emotions. Simple examples of using escape-avoidance to deal with a stressful situation might include escaping into fantasy (also called wishful thinking), exercising, or immersing yourself in your work, studies, or hobbies. Maladaptive forms of escape-avoidance include drug use or excessive sleeping.

By focusing your attention on something other than the stressor, escape–avoidance tactics tend to provide emotional relief in the short run. Thus avoidance strategies can be helpful when facing a stressor that is relatively brief and has limited consequences. But avoidance strategies like wishful thinking tend to be counterproductive when the stressor is severe or long lasting (Stanton & Snider, 1993). Escape – avoidance strategies are also associated with increased psychological distress in facing other types of stressors, such as adjusting to college (Aspinwall & Taylor, 1992).

On the long run, escape–avoidance tactics are associated with poor adjustment and symptoms of depression and anxiety (Stanton & Snider, 1993, Folkman & Others, 1986). If the problem is one that needs to be dealt with promptly, such as pressing medical concern, the delays caused by escape avoidance strategies can make the stressful situation worse.

Seeking social support is the copying strategy that involves turning to friends, relatives, or other people for emotional, tangible, or informational support. Having a strong network of social support can help buffer the impact of stresses. Confiding in a trusted friend gives us an opportunity to vent our emotions and better understand the stressful situation. (Lepore & others 1996).

When you acknowledge the stressor but attempt to minimize or eliminate its emotional impact, you are imaging in the coping strategy called distancing. A relatively common example of distancing is the person who tries to change the meaning of the stressor by claiming that is "no big deal" or "not that important". Making jokes about the stressful situation is another form of distancing. And sometimes people emotionally distance themselves from a stressor by discussing it in a detached, depersonalized, or intellectual way.

In certain high-stress occupations, distancing can help workers cope with painful human problems. Clinical psychologists, social workers, rescue workers, police officers, and medical personnel often use distancing to some degree to help them deal with distressing situation without falling apart emotionally themselves.

In contrast to distancing, denial in a refusal to acknowledge that the problem even exists (Goldberger, 1983). Like escape-avoidance strategies, denial can compound problems in situation that require immediate attention.

Perhaps the most constructive emotion – focused coping strategy is positive reappraisal. The person who uses positive reappraisal not only tries to minimize the negative emotional aspects of the situation but also tries to create positive meaning by focusing on personal growth. (Folkman & others, 1986). People sometimes use positive reappraisal to help them make sense out of a stressful experience. This is especially true when people have experienced a tragedy, disaster, or catastrophic loss.

People who can find some sense of personal meaning in the stressful event – sometimes through their religious faith tend to cope better with loss than those who see it as senseless (Meichenbaum & Fitzpatrik, 1993; Wortman & others, 1992).

Most people use multiple coping strategies in stressful situation often combining problem – focused and emotion-focused forms of coping. (Lazarus, 1993; Dunkel – Schetter & others, 1992). Different coping strategies may be used at different stages of dealing with a stressful encounter. In the initial stages of a stressful experience, we often rely on emotion-focused strategies to help us step back emotionally from a problem. Once we have regained our emotional equilibrium, we may rely more on problem focused coping strategies to identify potential solutions to the situation (Hockenbury, Hockenbury, 1998).

Conclusion

Stress is usually coceptualized in negative terms. But stress is not always bad. A certain amount of stress can lead a person to perform better in his work. Maladaptation of stress can include physiological, psychological and behavioural symptoms. A person's personality can also lead to stress. Usually it is thought that Type A personality leads to more stress than Type B personality. But more recent research suggests that these findings are questionable. Stress can lead to anxiety, anger, depression, and in extreme cases, causes burnout in the individual. Coping strategies are aimed at reducing the stressors.

Problem–focused copying strategy involves changes the stressor. Emotion–focused coping strategy involves reducing the emotional impact of a stressor. Everybody at some point experiences stress. The key is to deal with it effectively.

References and Further Reading

1. Agarwal Rita (2001). "Stress in life and at work." New Delhi: Response Books.
2. Davis Keith, Newstrom John W (1998). "Organizational Behaviour." New Delhi: Tata McGraw–Hill Publishing Company Ltd.
3. Hockenbury Don H, Hockenbury Sandra E (1998). "Discovering psychology." New York: Worth Publishers.
4. Kaila HL (2004). Indian Women Managers: Their Stress, Health, and Coping Behavior - A Survey in Mumbai, Special issue on Occupational Health Of Women, The Journal of Health Management, 6:2, 2004.
5. Luthans Fred (1992). "Organizational Behaviour." Singapore: McGraw Hill International Editions.
6. Muchinsky Paul M (2000). "Psychology applied to work." Bangalore: Eastern Press.
7. O'Hara Valerie (1995). "Wellness at work. Building resilience to stress." Oakland: New Harbinger Publications Inc.

21
Stress and Social Resources

Social/Family Support–An Important Mediator of Stress

The experience of stress and its consequences depend upon one's ability to tolerate and manage stress. Several factors contribute to this ability. These factors function through interaction with the person's environment specially the social environment which has been built through ages to safeguard against the various stressors a person encounters in his life. The significance of social environment becomes evident from the fact that man and his ancestors have lived in close-knit informal social groups. These close-knit social groups comprise of individuals who are simultaneously members of several groups which serve different functions in their life.

Through such multiple memberships groups form a network of social relationships and as a consequence every individual becomes a member of a social network which becomes a part of his personal life. His behavior is regulated by the demands put by the groups in the network, the role he plays in them and the succour he seeks from them. Once a person becomes a member of a network he strives to maintain it at some cost. This desire to build and maintain a social network serves a special function in the survival of a person.

When humans arrive in this harsh unpredictable world, they need close personal contact to go through the harshness of a strange world. It is through the care and nurture provided by the first and the primary social group (the family) he belongs to, that his survival is made possible. Gradually he is able to fend for himself but the need for others and the desire 'to belong' becomes so ingrained in him that he is willing to pay for maintaining the relations that form a part of his network of inter-relationships.

Some people experience stress because they are detached from the world around them; they lack warm interpersonal relationships. Individuals with a driving ambition and a strong need for independence may fail to develop close attachments to friends and colleagues. To achieve their success, they often sacrifice fulfillment of their social needs. Their lack of social attachments may result in anger, anxiety, and loneliness- all producing stress in their lives.

A powerful antidote to this problem lies in the presence of social support at work. Social support is the network of helpful activities, interactions, and relationships that provides an employee with the satisfaction of important needs. There are four types of support in a total network: instrumental, informational, evaluative, and emotional. Social support can come from family, friends, coworkers, or supervisors. Its focus may be on either work or social exchanges and may even take the form of games, jokes, or teasing. Research suggests that when employees have at least one person from whom they can receive social support (especially emotional support), they will experience lower stress. Females, in particular, not only place more value on social support but also seem to feel more comfortable (and capable) in providing it to others. Supervisors- male or female- need to develop the capacity to play this role for their employees when support is needed. An alternative option is to simply provide opportunities for social support and encourage it to develop among a group of workers. Managers may need to allow time for employees to develop and nurture their social support networks at work.

Family

It is generally recognized that a person's family has a big impact on personality development. A family situation–either a brief crisis, such as squabble or the illness of a family member, or long-term strained relations with the spouse or children – can act as a significant stressor for employees. Also, recent trends have made it increasingly difficult for employees to adequately balance the responsibilities of their jobs and their families. As employees are working longer hours and bringing more work home at night, more and more pressure is being placed on work-family relationships and more emphasis on the coordination of work and vacation schedules, and the search for elder and child care options has become prominent and very stressful.

Relocating the family because of a transfer or a promotion can also lead to stress. For most people in recent years, their financial situation has also proved to be a stressor. Many people have been forced to take a second job, or the spouse has had to enter the workforce to make ends meet. This situation reduces time for recreational and family activities. The overall effect on employees is more stress on their primary jobs.

Social Inter-relationships and Social Support

Social support is a special condition of inter-relationships which makes one feel worthy of someone's concern and also generates the feeling that the other persons too feel for him the same way. The supportive relationships a person can rely upon at any particular time emerges out of social network of which he is a member. Since a person's social network comprises of all attachments he has, it includes all of his social resources and his support system which may comprise of his friends and relatives and also some professionals. It may however be noted that at the time of stress he seeks support only from a few chosen ones and not from all those who constitute the network of his social resources.

What is Social Support?

Social support is a special condition of mutual relationship. When people come to know that there is someone who is willing to be of some use, they feel supported. Since this condition emerges out of social relationships it has come to be known as social support. Cobb, a pioneer in the study of social support describes it as a set of information which makes him believe that (a) he is cared for and loved, (b) he is valued and respected, (c) he is part of a network of mutual obligation and communication. It works like this: from the behavior of the other person one gets the information that there is someone who loves and cares for him, and in return for the love and respect given, the other person puts him under certain obligation. When the other person uses this right he adds to one's sense of self-worth, that is, 'I am important to him'. In this way we can say that social support is a special condition of inter-relationship which is based on mutuality of commitment and communication. When people form any relationship they expect some benefit out of it, more so in supportive relationship wherein some benefit must come to both the parties. In formalized supportive services where one party works for the sake of providing support to the other party that gets direct benefit, there is atleast an expectation of a feedback that its services are appreciated and valued.

Since both giving and receiving of support depends upon communication, mutuality of communication becomes very essential. These communications need not be always verbal as much of the support taking place without the use of words. Gestures, touch, gaze or intonations of statements are more common mode of supportive communication. Whatever be the mode of supportive communication, it should involve genuineness and understanding and these should be made evident from the sharing of thoughts and feelings of those who have gone through the same or similar experiences. Supportive communication involves:

- Genuine information seeking/giving
- Spontaneous problem solving
- Empathy–sensitivity towards other person's thoughts and feelings
- Equality–mutually expressed positive regard and tolerance

Social Support as a Mediator of Stress

There is mounting evidence to show that social support is the most important resource a person has for managing stress. Among adults when people can share their experiences they adapt fast to the losses suffered. Only the lonely and those without having any available support have problems. In other situations also people having strong social support do not show much of after-effects of stress. For instance, in job situations people who are doing highly stressful jobs, if allowed to develop friendship relationship do not suffer from after-effects. Similarly during plant shut down, unemployed youth who belong to a network of relations and friends are able to tide over stress better than those who lack such support.

The most important evidence about the value of social support in stress reduction comes from the researchers in health field. These researchers repeatedly show that, after experiencing major events, availability of social support helps prevent adverse health loss. Absence or loss of support is often predictive of development of serious illness like coronary heart disease (CHD), cancer or depression. Like the migrant population, men and women admitted to old people's homes are deprived of the close bonds with friends and relatives show adverse effects of stress. For these people both the mortality and morbidity rates are much higher than the same age people living in the community. Social support not only helps in prevention of stress related illness, it also helps in recovery from an illness.

Two Ways in Which Social Support Works

There is no doubt that social support is the most important mediator of stress. Whether or not a stressful situation will have an adverse effect depends upon the availability of a number of factors and among these factors social support is the most important. The important question is that how does social support operate that stress does not have any adverse consequences. From the study of scientific literature and also a look around it is found that social support operates through two channels to reduce stress, (a) through creating a positive environment (direct effect) and (b) through being a stress buffer.

The direct effect of stress is best seen when people feel secure and good because they are wanted, loved and liked by others. When we know that there are people we can rely upon, it generates a sense of well being in us. Although such direct effect is not always evident due to several factors operating in our lives at any point of time, yet whatever evidence that is available shows that as the number of friends and relations increases, there is an increase in one's well being.

The positive emotions experienced through contact with others provide an "affect balance" which helps us to go through stressful situation without much damage being caused. The biochemical evidence also suggests that when social support is available stress response occurs at a reduced level. Biochemical analyses of blood during stress response shows that there is a rise in hormones known as corticosteroids.

The other pathway through which social support operates involves the modifying of the stressful situation in such a way that stress is not allowed to have any adverse after-effect. This function of social support is known as stress buffering function. Since social support operates between the occurrence of a stressor and its after-effects, the buffering role may be seen as an aid in coping which acts throughout the stress process by (i) reducing the demand and lowering the threat, (ii) getting ready through anticipating the threat, (iii) providing a more objective assessment of a situation so that coping occurs, (iv) providing aid in actual coping, or (v) helping in reducing the stress response through distraction.

Reducing Demand: A supportive person can reduce the demands on a person going through a period of high stress, and thus help in bringing down the stress within the tolerance limit. Depending upon the exigencies of the situation, different steps can be undertaken to reduce stress.

Anticipatory Preparation: A supportive person decreases severity of stress by providing predictability to the situation. Because an advance warning can help a person make anticipatory preparation, a teacher announces a class test well in advance, a manager explains about the overtime schedule a week ahead of actual implementation.

Provide an Objective View: Since high stress may bring about distortions in perception which interferes with correct assessments of the situation, a supportive person may help in making a more objective assessment of the situation so that source of stress is correctly identified and tackled.

Help in Coping: Support can come in the form of actual coping, when the supportive person takes over the responsibilities of the person under stress temporarily. In this stage, encouragement, persuasion and even coercion may be helpfully used.

Keeping the Arousal Level Low: Finally, the supportive person can help create a situation in which a very severe stress is not experienced. Various tension reduction techniques are used for this purpose. Cheering, joking, distracting or being available and building faith are some of the ways of providing support. The calm and confident way of facing a problem is also unconsciously adopted by the person under stress. Sharing of thoughts and experiences is helpful though it is an elementary supportive situation.

Social support helps to reduce stress as well as to prevent its adverse effects. Presence of social support safeguards one's physical and mental health. However, there are situations when social support rather than reducing stress may add to one's stress. The increase in stress may be in several ways, i.e. by adding to the cost of support, by adding to the stress or through a mismatch between the need and the support. All supportive relationships involve mutuality and whatever the donor does in order to help a person, puts the recipient under some obligation. If the cost of meeting the obligation is more than what a person can afford, it may add to one's stress.

Because support involves closeness of relationships it may be regarded as an intrusion upon one's privacy since by sharing of thoughts one has to open up about one's anxieties, worries and other negative thoughts. At the same time knowing about the other person's affairs, problems and achievement adds to one's own burden e.g. when a good friend's family is going through hard times it becomes difficult to ignore it and friend's problems add to one's own problems. Problem may come from over-enthusiastic support also. If the supporting person is over-imposing it can deprive a person of the sense of control which is very essential for a person's survival. Sense of control comes from successful mastery of a difficult situation through active coping. When a person makes active efforts to cope with a problem he takes an overview of the situation, takes into consideration several strategies and chooses one. But when other person makes this choice for him, he loses the sense of mastery or the feelings that he is the master of the situation. Such a situation of over-support brings about dependence. In extreme cases it develops a sense of helplessness in a person.

Rational choice and support seeking: The support system comprises of all the resources a person has access to, and this is built through active effort of the individual over the years. The process of support building starts almost from the beginning of life. Very early in life infants have to send through their gestures, actions or words, a message which will invoke a positive response in other individuals. These behaviors gradually develop into special modes of coping with stressful situations. Turning to others, sharing of thoughts and feelings are examples of coping modes adopted when no other solution to a problem is in sight.

However people do not seek support indiscriminately. Before seeking support from anyone people make a cost benefit analysis of the support. Only when the benefit from the support is likely to be greater or equal to the cost that support will be sought or given. Besides the cost consideration, discretion is used in choosing the support since different types of support serve different purposes.

Ego support/emotional support is required when people are feeling demoralized and disheartened. Cognitive support is needed when stress so overwhelms a person and he lacks the means to cope with the problem.

Several things are seen here: (1) support systems do not emerge spontaneously; they have to be built with efforts over the years, (2) once support systems have been built they remain there and become operational during times of stress, (3) out of network of relationships, discretion has to be used in choosing the source and the type of support that is needed, i.e. who can provide which type of support.

Who Can Provide Support

Every individual living in a society has at least some capacity to provide support. Support giving is built in our nature very early in life. All it needs is some degree of empathy or ability to see things from others point of view. Empathy is a perceptual ability which comes with experience while interacting with other people. When we interact with others we realize that meaningful interaction is possible only if we are able to see things from the other person's point of view, in other words, without being a participant in the experiences we should be able to live through the other person's joys, sorrows, worries and successes. Possibility of empathy increases if we are aware of the other person's circumstances.

The other important ability required is to get the other person convinced of the genuineness of one's intents. Both research and clinical observation show that if we can reveal a little of our own self, the other person will be able to have confidence in us. Perhaps some self-disclosure on the part of the donor makes the receiver of support feel that the donor is also human being with emotions and weaknesses, therefore it is okay to rely on him. People who avoid self-disclosure are seen as secretive and untrustworthy. Such people are not good at providing support.

Besides being trustworthy, appearing trustworthy is also important. Similarity in experiences makes people more acceptable as supporting. Many professional persons are specially trained to provide support to people in need. Various well defined systems which have been recognized as sources of support are: (a) organized community groups such as religious groups, schools, clubs, trade unions and various voluntary organizations, (b) self-help groups like alcoholic anonymous and PTA, (c) formalized supportive services like foster homes and old age homes. Other agencies in a society that provide support are police, judiciary and healthcare systems although their help is sought only as a last resort.

People can be made to desire social interaction through pleasurable encounters with others. Since much of our behavior depends upon the reinforcements we get, a positive tendency towards support seeking can be built through rewarding such behaviours reinforcements like smiling or patting. It has been observed that when people are put in congenial groups they gradually shed their inhibitions and start interacting. Such interactions can initiate the building up of a supportive relationship (Davis,1998; Luthans, 2002; Robbins, 2003; Srivastava, 1998).

Organizational Culture

Social culture creates the wide ranging context in which organizations operate. It provides the complex social systems of laws, values, and customs in which organizational behaviors occur. Employee behavior, according to social psychologist Kurt Lewin, is a function of the interaction between personal characteristics and the environment around the person. Part of that environment is the social culture in which the individual lives and works, which provides broad clues as to how a person with a given background will behave.

Inside the organization lies another powerful force for determining individual and group behavior. Organizational culture is the set of assumptions, beliefs, values, and norms that are shared by an organization's members. This culture may have been consciously created by its key members, or may have simply evolved across time. It represents a key element of the work environment in which employees perform their jobs. This idea of organizational culture is intangible, for we cannot see it or touch it, but it is present and pervasive. It surrounds and affects everything that happens in an organization. Because it is a dynamic systems concept, culture is also affected by almost everything that occurs within an organization.

Organizational cultures are important to the firm's success for several reasons. They give an organizational identity to employees- a defining vision of what the organization represents. They are also an important source of stability and continuity to the organization, which provides a sense of security to its members. At the same time, knowledge of the organizational culture helps newer employees interpret what goes on inside the organization, by providing an important context for events that would otherwise seem confusing. Cultures help stimulate employee enthusiasm for their tasks. Cultures attract attention, convey a vision, and typically honor high-producing and creative individuals as heroes.

Organizational culture refers to a system of shared meaning held by members that distinguishes the organization from other organizations. This system of shared meaning is a set of key characteristics that the organization values. There are seven primary characteristics that capture the essence of an organization's culture.

1. Innovation and risk taking. The degree to which employees are encouraged to be innovative and take risks.
2. Attention to detail. The degree to which employees are expected to exhibit precision, analysis, and attention to detail.
3. Outcome orientation. The degree to which management focuses on results or outcomes rather than on the techniques and processes used to achieve those outcomes.
4. People orientation. The degree to which management decisions take into consideration the effect of outcomes on people within the organization.
5. Team orientation. The degree to which work activities are organized around teams rather than individuals.
6. Aggressiveness. The degree to which people are aggressive and competitive rather than easygoing.
7. Stability. The degree to which organizational activities emphasize maintaining the status quo in contrast to growth.

Each of these characteristics exists on a continuum from low to high. Appraising the organization to these seven characteristics, then, gives a composite picture of the organization's culture.

If organizations are to consciously create and manage their cultures, they must be able to communicate then to the employees, especially the newly hired ones. People are generally more willing to adapt when they want to please others, gain approval, and learn about their new work environment. Similarly, organizations are anxious to have new employees fit in, and therefore an intentional approach that helps make this happen is used by many firms.

Cultural communication acts can be lumped under the term organizational socialization, which is a continuous process of transmitting key elements of an organization's culture to its employees. It consists of both formal methods and informal means. All these methods help shape the attitudes, thoughts, and behavior of employees. Viewed from the organization's perspective, organizational socialization is like placing an organization's fingerprints on people or stamping its own genetic code on them. From the employee's viewpoint, it is essential process of "learning the ropes" to survive and prosper within the firm. The important point is that socialization can be functional for both workers and their employees.

A reciprocal process emerges when changes occur in the other direction. Employees can also have an active impact on the nature of the organization's culture and operations. Individualization occurs when employees successfully exert influence on the social system around them at work by challenging the culture or deviating from it. The interaction between socialization and individualization is seen, which shows the types of employees who accept or reject an organization's norms and values, while exerting various degrees of influence. The two extremes – rebellion and total conformity – may prove dysfunctional for the organization (and the individual's career) in the long run. Isolation is seldom a productive course of action. If it is assumed that the culture of a certain organization invites its employees to challenge, question, and experiment while also not being too disruptive, then the creative individualist can infuse new life and ideas for the organization's benefit (Davis,1998; Luthans, 2002; Robbins, 2003).

Organizational Culture and Conflict

Every organization has its own culture. Organizational culture is the product of all the organization's features – its people, its successes, and its failure. Organizational culture reflects the past and shapes the future. It is the job of HR specialists to adjust proactively to the culture of the organization. For example, objectives can be achieved in several acceptable ways. This idea, called equifinality, means there are usually multiple paths to objectives. The key to success is picking the path that best fits the organization's culture.

In every organization, a few core values or beliefs shape its culture. 'Get the best people and set them free' was the spirit of the late J.R.D. Tata and this belief shaped the culture of the Tata conglomerate. L&T is known for its professional approach, while competitive spirit is imbibed by every executive and employee of the Reliance Industries. IBM is known for service, whereas product innovation is the hallmark of GM. Effective HR practitioners identify the core beliefs or values of their organizations and strive to further those values.

There is often conflict between organizational culture and employee's attitudes. Conflict arises because of the following dualities:

- Personal goal vs organizational goal
- Personal ethics vs organizational ethics
- Rights vs duties
- Obedience vs self-respect
- Discipline vs autonomy
- Self-confidence vs arrogance
- Authority vs accountability
- Leadership vs followership
- Delegation vs abdication
- Participation vs anarchy
- Feedback vs abuse
- Cleverness vs wisdom
- Grooming vs pampering
- Doing vs becoming
- Material benefit vs spiritual loss
- Change vs stability
- Greed vs renunciation
- Short-term vs long-term

The above are not hypothetical conflicts, they occur daily in organizations. HR departments are expected to develop and enforce policies in these areas (Aswathappa, 2002).

Stress and Health

Good and Bad Stress

Stress is an essential part of life. Experts like Hans Selye equate stress with life and its absence with death itself. Even if we do not agree with such an extreme view we know that the stress has a positive value in life. There are innumerable occasions when stress leads to an improved sense of well being. That is called as 'good stress'. We can differentiate between the good stress and the bad stress. So long as a person can successfully handle a situation it leads to good stress. When stress provides 'opportunities' to try out new solutions to life's problems and leads to new insights which are useful in future it is good stress. It is also considered good stress when successful handling of a situation is ego boosting. Such stress is experienced in situations which arc apparently beyond one's control.

Situations which can be easily handled do not cause stress, situations which are somewhat difficult, need some extra effort, but do not upset a person's functioning cause 'good stress' since they provide a challenge. But situations which are uncontrollable and cannot be handled easily even with an all-out effort cause 'bad stress' since under such circumstances stress tends to persist.

Good stress is a 'must' for life. It acts as a motive force which helps people to explore, to grow and to test their own capacities. Even when the situation is highly stressful and people handle it well, they come out of it healthier, since they provide a sense of mastery. Such encounters with situations which cause good stress are frequent. Our lives are full of problems. In normal course of life crises come, and are overcome, and individuals come out of these situations more mature and wiser. Such evidences prove that when a stressful situation is utilized as an 'opportunity' rather than as an occasion for self-denigration and self-pity, it causes good stress.

Occasionally people convert bad stress into good stress by redefining a situation i.e., they perceive a positive meaning in a stressful situation. The best example for such transformation of bad stress into good stress can be obtained from the warfield, where soldiers who consider their injuries as 'good wounds' do not complain of pain. These soldiers see their wounds as an opportunity to get relieved from the active duty and to go home.

But stress is good upto a certain limit after which it becomes bad stress. It can cause damage to the health and well being if stress goes beyond that limit. The negative consequences of stress may range from mild psychological distress symptoms to serious illness depending on the severity of stress experienced. However, it must be said that the impact of stress may range from increased well being to serious illness depending on whether it is coped effectively or continues uncontrolled. When stress continues unabated it can result in ill health – the extent and nature of which depend upon the presence of other factors, the most important among them are biological vulnerability and the environmental conditions under which an individual is going through a stressful experience (Srivastava, 1998).

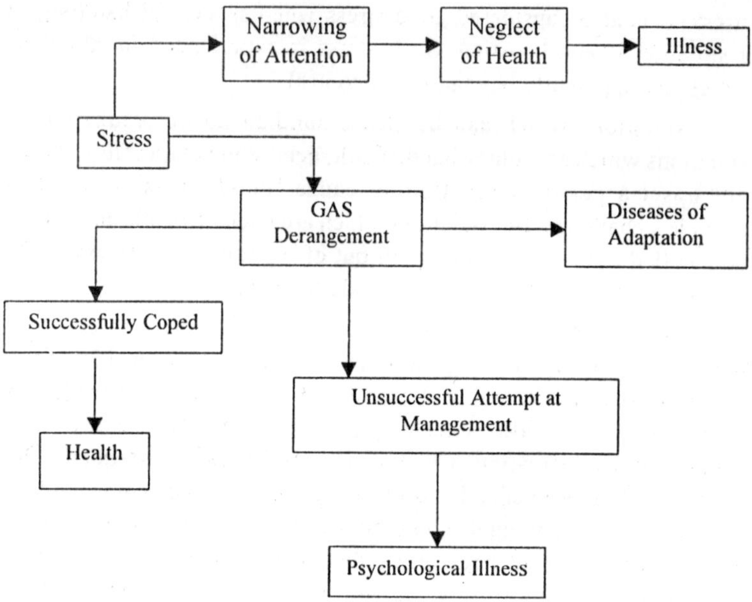

Fig. A Model relating stress and health

Stressor

Stress and Psychosomatic Disease

There is a general agreement that a high percentage of diseases afflicting mankind are psychosomatic and that their primary causes are our thoughts, attitudes and beliefs. When we speak of psychosomatic nature of a disease, we basically mean that the major source of the disease lies in one's emotional, mental or perceptual and behavioral habits. In other words, the way that we have been conditioned to react to our environment has resulted in internal physiological changes which either evolve into disease or allow disease states to exist. Brown (1977) pointed out that which disease occurs and which internal process is involved, is the consequence of a very complex interaction of psychological, constitutional or genetic and environmental factors. The pattern will be unique for each individual. However, even though the development of the specific psychosomatic disease is unique to each individual, the underlying principles are the same. Emotional stress leads to physiological stress and this results in an eventual breakdown (disease) of the target organ system. Udupa (1977) reported that psychosomatic disease appear to progress through four distinct phases:

- **Psychic phase:** This phase is marked by mild but persistent psychological and behavioral symptoms of stress such as irritability, disturbed sleep, loss of appetite, etc.
- **Psychosomatic phase:** If the stress condition continues, these symptoms become more pronounced, along with the beginnings of generalized physiological symptoms such as occasional hypertension and tremors.
- **Somatic phase:** This phase is marked by increased function of the organs, particularly the target, or involved organ. At this stage, one begins to identify the beginnings of a diseased state.
- **Organic phase:** This phase is marked by the full involvement of a so-called disease state, with physiological changes such as ulcerated stomach or chronic hypertension becoming manifest.

Since stress is a state of high physiological arousal there are wide-spread changes in the internal state during stress. When stress is short-lived, the body states and the physiological systems come back to normal but if stress persists for long, the altered body states demand attention and the individual under stress becomes painfully aware of them. The physiological changes are experienced as symptoms and are given the name of an illness. These symptoms can be varied and can be experienced in relation to any of the body systems. The possible symptoms related to various body parts are:

Muscular symptoms: tension and pain.

Gastrointestinal symptoms: dyspepsia, indigestion, vomiting, heart burn, constipation, and irritable colon.

Cardiac symptoms: palpitation and chest pain.

Respiratory symptoms: dyspnoea and hyperventilation.

Central nervous system: neurotic reactions, insomnia, weakness, faintness and headaches.

Genital symptoms: dysmenorrhoea, frigidity and impotence.

These symptoms are genuine experiences of a person undergoing stress. Since they are perceived as a danger signal signifying some disease, the well being of an individual is disturbed. The symptoms listed above though innocent in their own right can be a danger signal on several counts. (a) Firstly because they indicate that the individual is going through a very high level of stress. In fact they could be the body's 'cry for help' so that something can be done to reduce stress. (b) Secondly because the symptoms could be the first signs of some serious illness which occurs due to stress. The symptoms of many serious illnesses are similar to an exaggerated stress response e.g. chest pain could be the beginning of a heart attack, pain in the abdomen could be the first signs of gradually developing depression. In short, the disturbed well being due to stress could be in the form of some of the psychosomatic symptoms or could be a real full-blown somatic disease. Although stress is not the only reason for the loss of health and well being and presence of stress may not invariably lead to illness, stress does not play a vital role in causing damage to a person's well being, specially when a person fails to cope with it in an effective way.

Stress and Psychological Problems

Although considerable attention has been given to the relationship between stress and physical health, especially within the medical community, not as much has been given to the impact of stress on mental health. The psychological problems resulting from stress are just as important to day-to-day job performance as the physical problems.

High levels of stress may be accompanied by anger, anxiety, depression, nervousness, irritability, tension, and boredom. One study found that stress had the strongest impact on aggressive actions, such as sabotage, interpersonal aggression, hostility, and complaints. These types of psychological problems from stress are especially relevant to poor job performance, lowered self-esteem, resentment of supervision, inability to concentrate and make decisions, and job dissatisfaction. These outcomes of stress can have a direct cost effect on the organization.

Of even greater significance, the outcomes of stress can have a subtle, but very real, effect on the styles and effectiveness of managers in key positions. For example, managers who are under constant stress may become very moody, and their subordinates soon learn not to disturb them, even with important information, because they will just "bite your head off." Such managers may also realize, at times, that they are acting this way; they may feel that they are not living up to the expectations of their important position and suffer a loss of self-esteem. In this state they may also procrastinate and continue to put things off and not make needed decisions. And, finally, they may resent their boss for trying to get them back on track and begin to hate the job in general. Coworkers, subordinates, and bosses may become very disgusted with such a manager and explain the behavior away as being the result of stress.

The Stress-illness Relationship

Though the psychosomatic illnesses form a major chunk of the conditions of disturbed well being but there are other ways also in which stress can lead to illness. Three ways in which stress related behavior could facilitate occurrence of illness are:

1. Many serious events put drastic demands and the person has to make an all-out effort to cope with these demands. Happenings like bereavement, unemployment, migration, fall in this category. In case of such events coping has to be prolonged over several years. For example, the struggle of an unemployed person or the grief of parents of a lost child may reach the limits of an obsession so that danger signals coming from the body are neglected till the condition takes the form of full blown illness.
2. Secondly under stress not only are the inner signals but the simple rules of health also ignored. The most commonly neglected rules are also the most important ones. Nutrition, rest, activity, recreation are some of the commonly neglected rules of health. For example, a person may keep awake for long hours, take wrong food, become hyperactive or inactive – all these conditions are likely to facilitate disease conducive conditions within the body.
3. Thirdly people sometimes adopt modes of coping which are health damaging. Among these the most commonly used strategies that have been observed are use of alcohol and other drugs, smoking,

reckless driving. In some rare cases many health damaging events may be brought about to cope with family problems. For example one may get involved in accidents or attempt suicide in the hope of resolving family problems.

Besides the behavioral routes, other most important route through which stress leads to illness is through bio-chemical changes which occur during the stress response in the form of General Adaptation Syndrome. Several hormones are secreted during stress to prepare the body for tackling the threat. Normally the response subsides without any adverse effect but under prolonged or severe stress all the energy is depleted, the stage of exhaustion is reached, and symptoms of alarm stage recur. In other words, the body reacts if a new stressor has appeared. But because the energy that is in reserve is already depleted the stage of exhaustion sets in. it is during this stage that illness occurs because the internal functioning goes topsy tervy. This happens in sequence as shown below.

Recovery

Threat Alarm Resistance & Coping → → ⟨ Recovery / Exhaustion ⟩

Exhaustion

The disturbances that occur during this stage are in the form of either excess or deficits of various hormones. In prolonged stress the disturbed functioning pattern and the system gets conditioned at that level so that the system either continues to function at that level or repeatedly gets into that form of functioning if similar conditions recur. When such disturbed functioning persists, it becomes capable of causing both functional disturbances as well as structural damages.

When several stressful events occur one after the other the activated state is not allowed to come back to normal and the disturbed condition continues with all its adverse effects on health. The vast research in the area suggests that stress has a role in either facilitating or precipitating illnesses like mental illness, gastric ulcers, hypertension, stroke, myo-cardial infarction, sudden cardiac death, influenza, pneumonia, diabetes, cancer and multiple sclerosis. New knowledge about various bio-chemical changes taking place is accumulating and this is helping in understanding how stress can create illness inducing within body systems.

Body During Stress

During stress, as soon as a threat is perceived brain sends signals to the systems to get ready to face the threat, i.e. to either fight or to escape to safety. Several chemicals are poured into the blood stream which carry these signals to the various organs and instruct them to act in a particular way. The most important among these chemicals are hormones released by the adrenal glands so named because they are attached to the kidneys.

Two groups of hormones are called cortico-steriods and catecholamines are secreted by the adrenal medulla or the inner core. Catecholamines play an important role in mobilizing acute adaptive resources during any emergency while cortico-steriods provide a more enduring support during stress. Bio-chemical analysis of urine collected while a person is undergoing stress shows presence of these hormones. But there is a slight difference in the chemical picture if the person is also disturbed. Studies by Marian Frankenaueser show that when a person is performing under stress, adrenaline (a catecholamine) is always high, but if the person is also distressed there is cortisol (a cortico-steroid) also present in urine samples. Thus, two types of stress profiles emerge, stress with distress and stress without distress.

Experimental and other laboratory studies give evidence of the way the raised levels of these chemicals and their after-effects in the form of other chemical changes are associated with various forms of pathology. For example, a high level of cortisol is associated with disturbances in immune system of the body. The importance of immune system in the body is similar to that of a protective army or police in a country. It guards against the various intruders like infections, allergies or any other foreign elements like tumor grafts. This is the reason why people develop allergies or infections while undergoing stress.

High level of adrenaline is associated with raised levels of diastolic and systolic blood pressures. If stress persists high level of blood pressure also persists till the raised level becomes established and the person suffers from hypertension. The bio-chemical insights have helped in understanding the link between stress and illness. They have also provided a support for the theory that stress plays a part in causing illness.

Stress and Hypertension

Both animal and human studies show that subjects working in high stress situations tend to develop hypertension. Air traffic controllers who work in high stress situations develop hypertension and this relationship between stress and hypertension becomes more marked when other factors like increase in age are also operating. As age increases, the effect of stress becomes more evident.

Stress and Coronary Heart Disease

Coronary heart disease (CHD) is a condition in which blood supply to the heart muscles gets reduced due to hardening and thickening of the artery walls. The condition builds up slowly as fatty substances get deposited and is related to the life style and also to the biological factors of the person. When blockage is complete, there may be complete stoppage of blood supply to the heart resulting in the condition called myo-cardial infarction (MI) when severe pain is experienced in the form of angina pectoris.

Researches on stress and CHD relationship show that when stress is high there is an increase in the level of cholesterol due to free fatty acids released by the lever. Cholesterol thickens the blood which makes it difficult for the blood to move freely through the blood vessels specially the coronary arteries resulting in CHD. Enthusiastic researchers have tried to look for the relationship between job stress and CHD. Careful analysis showed that it is not the job requirement per se which is a predictor of stress but the perceived stressfulness of the job which determines the occurrence of CHD. If, despite high demands, a job is perceived to be a 'challenge' it is not health damaging. Perception of the job as highly stressful depends upon a combination of job demands and job satisfaction. A job situation which provides a sense of control is not perceived as highly stressful. The sense of control comes from the job being within one's coping ability combined with autonomy for freedom to make one's own decisions.

To sum up stress from the job is an important factor in CHD specially if it does not provide a sense of control.

Stress and Immune System

Exposure to stress is known to affect immune competence or the ability to monitor, recognize fight and expel foreign intruders in the body. Immuno competence has been found to be decreased when individuals are exposed to stressors like examination, loneliness and overcrowding and such other situations when they are distressed. That is why people under stress become prone to allergies and infections.

Growth of tumor is considered to be an indication of immuno competence. Relay and his associates showed through a series of studies that when animals were exposed to various stresses, there was a rise in secretion of cortico-steroids along with immuno suppression. In these animals there was an acceptance of tumor graft and rapid growth in tumor. Under these circumstances there was also a steep rise in mortality rates specially among female mice.

Human studies also show a positive relation between immuno suppression and tumor growth i.e. cancer after life events like bereavement and separation from near ones. These instances are related to acute stress but the effect of chronic stress is different. When people are exposed to chronic stress there is increase in immuno competence through habituation.

Stress and Gastric Ulcers

Gastric ulcers are a very common form of ailment. It is caused by excessive secretion of stomach acids. These acids help in digestion, but when they are in excess specially with no food inside to digest, they damage the stomach walls. This type of excessive secretion of acids is associated with experiencing of stress in experimental and non-experimental situations. Such conditions are also associated with prolonged emotional activation which tend to get conditioned. Experimental studies with rats show that when they are exposed to continued stress ulcers tend to develop more in animals which make unsuccessful attempts at coping. Human studies also show that people with high emotionality and high stress are more prone to develop ulcers.

Extreme Products of Stress

Stress can be either temporary or long-term, either mild or severe. The effects on an employee depend mostly on how long its causes continue, how powerful they are, and how strong the employee's recovery powers are. If stress is temporary and mild, most people can handle it or at least recover from its effects rather quickly. Resilient individuals often have achieved a balanced life away from work, have learned to set realistic goals, and keep each irritation in perspective. They still face the same amount of stress that others face, but they handle it better.

Burnout

In contrast to temporary stress are some major pressures that result in stress that is sustained for long periods. Problems predictably arise when high-intensity stress continues for an extended duration. According to Hans Selye, the human body cannot instantly rebuild its ability to cope with stress once it is depleted. As a result, people become physically and psychologically weakened from trying to combat it. This condition is called burnout – a situation in which employees are emotionally exhausted, become detached from their clients and their work, and feel unable to accomplish their goals. Some jobs, such as those in the helping professions (counselors, health care professionals, and social workers) and those with continuous high stress (air-traffic controllers, customer service representatives, and stockbrokers) are more likely than others to cause burnout.

When workers become burned out, they are more likely to complain, to attribute their errors to others, and to be highly irritable. The alienation they feel drives many of them to think about leaving their jobs, to seek out opportunities to become trained for new careers, and actually quit. In addition to higher turnover, burnout also leads to increased absenteeism and decreased quality and quantity of job performance.

Organizations need to identify both the jobs that lead to early burnout and the employees who exhibit some of the burnout symptoms. Sometimes it may be possible to change the parts of a job that contribute to burnout, such as reducing the frequency or intensity of interpersonal contacts. In other cases the firm can help employees learn how to cope better with the stressful work situations.

Trauma

Another severe product of stress, called trauma, occurs following a major threat to one's security. The event could be a natural disaster, an organizational crisis, dramatic employee abuse by the employer, or personal job loss.

One problematic disorder is called workplace trauma, which is the disintegration of employees' self-concepts and beliefs in their capabilities. It can arise from harassment at work, wrongful termination, discrimination, or an employee's perceived incapacity to meet evolving performance expectations. Attitudes clues to workplace trauma include severe moodiness, concentration difficulties, and alienation, in addition to the more distinctive behaviors of tardiness, absenteeism, and accident proneness. A common source of workplace trauma is sudden job loss, with its potentially crushing effect on one's self-esteem (Davis,1998; Luthams, 2002; Pestonjee, 1999; Robbins, 2003; Sahni, 1987; Srivastava, 1998).

Recent Research

Interleukin-6 Levels Increased With Chronic Stress

Researchers at Ohio State University have discovered a link between chronic stress and a body chemical that is associated with the development of serious and even deadly medical conditions.

Dr. Janice Kiecolt-Glaser and colleagues studied a group of 119 men and women who were dealing with the stress of caring for a spouse with dementia. These individuals were compared with a control group of 106 individuals of similar age and health status who did not serve as caregivers. Over the six-year study, blood tests showed that a chemical known as interleukin-6 (IL-6) dramatically increased in the caregivers as compared to the non-caregivers. IL-6 is a chemical known as a cytokine that is involved in the body's immune system. Overproduction of IL-6 has been associated with the development or progression of a number of medical conditions, including heart disease, type 2 diabetes, certain types of cancer, osteoporosis, arthritis, and functional decline. Even if the spouse of the caregivers died, the increased levels of IL-6 persisted for several years in the group of caregiving spouses.

Why does stress increase levels of a chemical associated with disease progression? One possible explanation is that persons under chronic stress tend to engage in behaviors that are known to increase IL-6 production, such as smoking or gaining weight. In contrast, healthy practices such as exercise and regular sleep patterns can help lower IL-6 levels.

These data, published in the July 2, 2003 issue of the Proceedings of the National Academy of Sciences (USA) offer one possible explanation for the link between stress and illness, suggesting that stress may increase the risk of many typical age-associated diseases by altering the immune response. The data also underscore the need for stress management and control of chronic stressors.

(Kiecolt-Glaser J, Preacher KJ, MacCallum RC, Atkinson C, Malarkey WB, Glaser R. Chronic stress and age-related increases in the proinflammatory cytokine IL-6. Proceedings of the National Academy of Sciences (USA) 2003 Jul 2.)

Friends and Family could be the Cure for Work Related Stress

Posted By: News-Medical in Medical Study News Published: Tuesday, 26-Oct-2004

On-the-job stress can increase your blood pressure, adding to your risk of having a heart attack or stroke, according to evidence from two new studies by Heart and Stroke Foundation researchers.

One of the studies suggests that a happy marriage may offset some of the negative effects, and the other has found that social solidarity among workers goes some way to lessening stress.

"Dealing with stress is important to protect your heart health," says Dr. George Honos, Heart and Stroke Foundation spokesperson. "These studies give us valuable information about what helps people manage their stress."

Employees from a large Toronto teaching hospital and from public organizations in Quebec City offered up their working lives – and blood pressures–for detailed analysis. The results were presented at the Canadian Cardiovascular Congress 2004, hosted by the Heart and Stroke Foundation of Canada and the Canadian Cardiovascular Society.

The findings come from Heart and Stroke Foundation researcher Dr. Sheldon Tobe of Sunnybrook and Women's College Health Sciences Centre, Toronto.

Dr. Tobe says that feelings of helplessness and lack of decision making powers in the face of escalating demands by supervisors and employers is a significant contributor to workers' high blood pressure.

Dr. Tobe enrolled 248 full-time Toronto hospital workers in his study. All were married or with partners. The subjects wore an ambulatory blood pressure monitor for 24 hours – at work, and at home with their spouses. One hundred and thirty-five of the subjects were women, 113 were men. Mean age was 50.8 years. All filled in questionnaires designed to evaluate job stress and marital cohesion.

Over the 24 hour period, job stress was associated with increased systolic blood pressure.

"But we also found that spouses who enjoy each other's company actually modulate their blood pressure down when they are together, away from work," says Dr. Tobe.

Dr. Alain Milot of Laval University presented, on behalf of his colleagues, Dr. Chantal Brisson, Dr. Chantal Guimont and others, results from a seven-year study on workers of 22 public organizations in Quebec City. Between 1991 and 1993, 7,485 white-collar workers were recruited for the study. At follow-up, 7.6 years later, 6,206 (85% of the initial group) were reevaluated. They were 18-65 years old, without cardiovascular disease or hypertension, not pregnant, and worked 20 hours or more per week.

The authors found that although stress resulting from job strain makes a significant contribution to high blood pressure and heart disease, companionship of fellow workers significantly reduces stress levels.

"Job strain is a combination of high levels of psychological demand at a rapid pace coupled with low decision latitude - a feeling of having no control, no empowerment, no opportunity to use one's skills," says Dr. Milot.

"But sometimes things are made worse because workers may have a perception of their job that adds to the stress level. We have found that the social support of colleagues or supervisors can significantly modify this," he says. "The worst situation to be in is a combination of high demand, low latitude and low social support."

Dr. Milot says the study suggests that preventive intervention that would make a more worker-friendly environment could reduce heart disease risk.

The Heart and Stroke Foundation is a leading founder of heart and stroke research in Canada. Our mission is to improve the health of Canadians by preventing and reducing disability and death from heart disease and stroke through research, health promotion and advocacy.

Age differences in Stress, Social Resources, and Well-being in Middle and Older Age

Martin M, Grunendahl M, Martin P. German Centre for Research on Ageing, Heidelberg, Germany. (mmartin@dzfa.uni-heidelberg.de)

The present study examines the interrelationships among the constructs of social resources, stress, and well-being in middle-aged and older adults. Two samples of 489 middle-aged adults (41-43 years) and 449 older adults (61-63 years) from the Interdisciplinary Longitudinal Study of Adult Development were compared with respect to the availability of social resources, levels of stress, and well-being. The data were used to construct separate structural equation models explaining the influence of stress and social resources on well-being in the two groups. The results indicate higher levels of health-related stress and similar levels of social resources in the older group. Structural equation models and examination of total and indirect effects confirmed that a stress-suppression model has the best fit in explaining the interrelationships between stress, social resources, and well-being. There was a strong effect of stress on well-being, no direct effect of social resources on well-being, and a mediating effect of stress on well-being. The relative contributions of stress and resources to well-being were comparable between age groups (J Gerontol B Psychol Sci Soc Sci. 2001 Jul;56(4):P214-22.)

Summary

Some people experience stress because they are detached from the world around them; they lack warm interpersonal relationships. Individuals with a driving ambition and a strong need for independence may fail to develop close attachments to friends and colleagues. To achieve their success, they often sacrifice fulfillment of their social needs. Their lack of social attachments may result in anger, anxiety, and loneliness- all producing stress in their lives.

A powerful antidote to this problem lies in the presence of social support at work. Social support is the network of helpful activities, interactions, and relationships that provides an employee with the satisfaction of important needs. There are four types of support in a total network: instrumental, informational, evaluative, and emotional. Social support can come from family, friends, coworkers, or supervisors. Its focus may be on either work or social exchanges and may even take the form of games, jokes, or teasing. Research suggests that when employees have at least one person from whom they can receive social support (especially emotional support), they will experience lower stress. Females, in particular, not only place more value on social support but also seem to feel more comfortable (and capable) in providing it to others. Supervisors- male or female- need to develop the capacity to play this role for their employees when support is needed. An alternative option is to simply provide opportunities for social support and encourage it to develop among a group of workers. Managers may need to allow time for employees to develop and nurture their social support networks at work.

Stress is an essential part of life. Experts like Hans Selye equate stress with life and its absence with death itself. Even if we do not agree with such an extreme view we know that the stress has a positive value in life. There are innumerable occasions when stress leads to an improved sense of well being. That is called as 'good stress'. We can differentiate between the good stress and the bad stress. So long as a person can successfully handle a situation it leads to good stress. When stress provides 'opportunities' to try out new solutions to life's problems and leads to new insights which are useful in future it is good stress.

Our lives are full of problems. In normal course of life crises come, and are overcome, and individuals come out of these situations more mature and wiser. Such evidences prove that when a stressful situation is utilized as an 'opportunity' rather than as an occasion for self-denigration and self-pity, it causes good stress.

But stress is good upto a certain limit after which it becomes bad stress. It can cause damage to the health and well being if stress goes beyond that limit. The negative consequences of stress may range from mild psychological distress symptoms to serious illness depending on the severity of stress experienced. However, it must be said that the impact of stress may range from increased well being to serious illness depending on whether it is coped effectively or continues uncontrolled. When stress continues unabated it can result in ill health – the extent and nature of which depend upon the presence of other factors, the most important among them are biological vulnerability and the environmental conditions under which an individual is going through a stressful experience.

References and Further Reading

1. Aswathappa K. (2002). Human Resource and Personnel Management (3rd ed). New Delhi: Tata McGraw-Hill Publishing Company Limited, 32-33.
2. Davis K; Newstrom, J.W.(1998). Organizational Behavior. Human Behavior at Work (10th ed). New Delhi: Tata McGraw-Hill Edition, 101-103, 430-434, 442.

3. Kaila HL (2002). Stress Is A Way of Life For Mumbai Workers' Psychology International, Vol. 13, No. 3, Fall 2002.
4. Luthans F.(2002). Organizational Behavior (9th ed). New Delhi: Mc Graw-Hill International Edition, 122-124, 397-399, 411-414.
5. Pestonjee D.M. (1999). Stress and Coping. The Indian Experience (2nd ed). New Delhi: Sage Publications India Pvt. Ltd., 35-56.
6. Robbins S.P. (2003). Organizational Behavior. New Delhi: Prentice Hall Inc.,524-525, 582-586.
7. Sahni A. (1987). Stress and Health of Executives and Professionals. Bangalore: Indian Society of Health Administrators, 7-11, 135-139.
8. Srivastava S. (1998). Understanding Stress. A Multidimensional Approach. New Delhi: Regency Publications, 59-74, 127-144.
9. http://www.heartandstroke.ca/
10. http://www.news-medical.net/
11. http://clk.about.com/?zi=18/17a & sdn=health_stress & tm=10 & gps = 39_56_0_0 & f=10 & su=p313.1.140.ip_ & zu=http%3A//stress. about. com/cs/ medicalconditions/a/aa071003a_p.htm

22

Problem Behaviours at Work

1. Absenteeism
2. Job stress

Absenteeism

'The satisfied, worker is a productive worker' paradigm doesn't work. It is much more complicated than that - Glenn Bassett.

There is abundant evidence that indicates that the financial cost of absenteeism incurred by organizations is significant. - Joseph J Martocchio.

In work situations, attitudes are a major potential source of performance differences – of variations in quantity and quality of output, absenteeism, turnover and other aspects of performance. (John Miner,1992). When attitudes are negative, they are both a symptom of underlying problems and a contributing cause of forthcoming difficulties in organizations. Declining attitudes may result in wildcat strikes, work slowdowns, absences and employee turnover. (Keith Davis; 1998).

In almost all jobs, employees who are often absent are judged as performing worse than others, all other factors being equal. However, the measurement and interpretation of absenteeism are not clear–cut. Absences can be "excused" or "unexcused" depending on many factors pertaining to both the individual and the job. (Muchinsky, 2000).

Absenteeism is a condition that exists when an employee fails to come to work even though he is properly scheduled to work. Normally, the rate of absenteeism is around 5 per cent. But in many industries we come across excessive absenteeism that constitutes considerable loss to the business unit even absentee worker may not receive pay. Work schedules are upset or delayed. It may result in confusion. It may lead to hasty transfers, overtime or even failure to meet delivery dates of orders. When the workers are ill and sick, pay is authorized, the costs of absenteeism mount up more rapidly. (Sherlekar,1987)

Absenteeism can be measured in different ways; it is always a function of definition, regulations and policies established by the employing organization. To the extent that these vary, absenteeism rates will vary as well. Thus absenteeism is an objective index, but with imprecise bases for measurement.

Companies use a variety of formulas to indicate absence rates (Miner, 1992). One common approach is:

Number of person – days lost through job absence during period

Average number of employees * number of work days

It has been posited that dissatisfied employees are more likely than satisfied employees to be absent from workplace. Many recent studies support this conclusion, but not strongly (Hackett, 1989), (Miner, 1992). Fig 1 shows that those employees who have low job satisfaction tend to be absent more often. The connection is not always sharp, for a couple of reasons. First, some absences are caused by legitimate medical reasons. Second, dissatisfied employees do not necessarily plan to be absent, but they seem to find it easier to respond to the opportunities to do so. These voluntary absences often occur with high frequency among a certain cluster of employees and usually occur on Mondays or Friday. These involuntary absenteeism can sometimes be predicted and often be reduced through the use of pre-employment physical exams and work history record checks, different approaches are needed for absences caused by poor attitudes.(Keith Davis,1998).

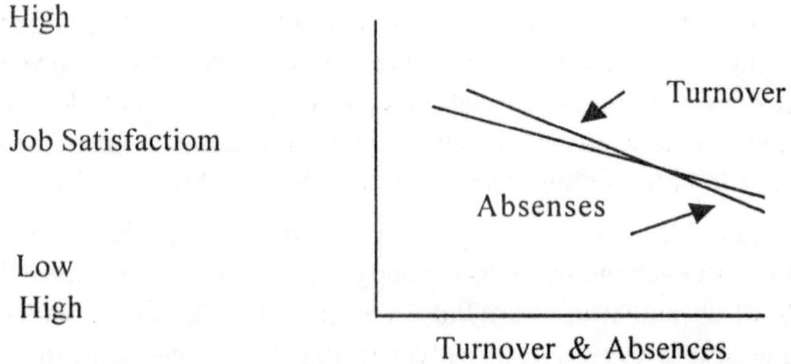

Fig. 1: Relationship of job Satisfaction to Turnover & Absences

Reasons for Absenteeism

1. **Absence Prone Persons:** 10 to20 per cent of the total number of employees are absence -prone persons. Such persons require counseling, a few warnings and ultimately dismissals.
2. **Illness:** It accounts for more than 50 per cent of all absences.
3. **Age and Sex**: Younger employees show more absenteeism. Women employees also show more absenteeism.
4. **Date:** Mondays and Fridays are vulnerable days showing high rates of absenteeism. Days before and after holidays also show absenteeism. Similarly, days after payday also indicate tendency of absenteeism. This cause of absenteeism is really due to lack of responsibility on part of the employees and we can remove this cause only when the workers realize their responsibilities and show self-discipline.
5. **Miscellaneous Reasons:** Transfer difficulties, duty accidents, care of children, or family member, etc., are other reasons of absenteeism.
6. **Alcoholism:** Drinking has become a major cause of absenteeism in many countries, 22 days per year absenteeism is attributed to alcoholism.
7. **Adverse Conditions of Work:** Excessive hours of work, natural fatigue, monotonous job, poor supervision, adverse working conditions, poor production control, all these reasons contribute to absenteeism, indicating the feeling of irresponsibility among employees. These causes of absenteeism of course, can be removed by the management, which is responsible for providing favorable working conditions and particularly providing preventive measures of industrial fatigue.

Program for reducing absenteeism may include discipline, counseling, rewards for good attendance, contests, flexible working hours, particularly for female employees and part-time work schedules. (Sherlekar,1987)

A study of absenteeism revealed that men who felt they should be receiving more pay showed significantly more absences than those who felt their pay was fair. However, the actual pay had no relation to absences [Patchen, 1960], [Norman Maier, 1965].

Absenteeism is often referred to as withdrawal behavior because they reflect the employee withdrawing from a noxious employment condition, either temporarily (absence) or permanently (turnover). The relationship between how much you like your job and whether you withdraw from it has attracted interest among industrial psychologists. The correlation between job satisfaction and absence is considerably less, approximately 0.25 (Johns, 1997), [Muchinsky, 2000].

The annual cost of absenteeism has been estimated at over $40 billion for U.S. organizations and $12 billion for Canadian firms. At the job level one-day absence by a clerical worker can cost an employer up to $100 in reduced efficiency and increased supervisory workload. These figures indicate the importance to an organization to operate smoothly and to attain its objectives if employees fail to report to their jobs. The work flow is disrupted and often important decisions must be delayed. In organizations that rely heavily on assembly-line technology, absenteeism can be considerably more than a disruption – it can result in a drastic reduction in quality of output, and in some cases, it can bring about a complete shutdown of the production facility. But levels of absenteeism beyond the normal range in any organization have a direct impact on the organization's effectiveness and efficiency.

Are all absences bad? Probably not! While most absences impact negatively on the organization, we can conceive of situations where the organizations may benefit by an employee voluntarily choosing not to come to work. For instance, fatigue or excess stress can significantly decrease an employee's productivity. In jobs where an employee needs to be alert -surgeons, air pilots are obvious examples. The cost of an accident in such jobs could be prohibitive. Even in managerial jobs, where mistakes are less spectacular, performance may be improved when managers absent themselves from work rather than make poor decision under stress. For the most part, we can assume that organization benefits when employee absenteeism is reduced. (Stephen Robbins, 1996)

Some employees have successfully used incentives to control absenteeism as the following example shows.

Statistically, Drakenfeld Colors Corporation, did not have an overall absenteeism problems (0.89%). As a matter of fact, almost (44%) of its 250 employees had perfect record. However a small handful of employees missed several days per year and they were perceived to be taking advantage of company and its working colleagues. Drakenfeld attacked this problem by offering small cash bonuses for those with perfect attendance every six-months, a sweepstakes opportunity featuring an all expenses paid trip for two to a resort for the perfect record winner of a drawing and a progressive disciplinary procedure for abuses of the attendance policy. The results? Absenteeism fell to 0.35%, the number of significant abuses fell by 90% and the proportion of employees with perfect attendance increased to 62%. This case demonstrates that absenteeism can be controlled. (Keith Davis, 1998)

Controlling Absenteeism

A measurement of the effectiveness of training may often be obtained from records of absenteeism. This method is illustrated here. During each group's first thirty days of work there was an average of 5.1 days absent among the seventy operators who were trained on the floor, in contrast with an average of only 2.5 days absent among seventy operators who had vestibule training. (Joseph Tiffin & McCormick, 1960)

To the extent that the job does not provide satisfaction at every level, today's employee will usually look elsewhere for significant need satisfaction. This explanation helps to account for some problems management is facing such as turnover & absenteeism. Mc Gregor acquires that these problems can be avoided. Management is interested in work and work according to Gregor is as natural and can be satisfying for people. (Hersey & Blanchard, 2001).

Absence from work, like turnover, is an index of employee stability. Although some degree of employee turnover is good for organization whereas employee absenteeism always has bad consequences. Rhodes and Steers (1990) and Martocchio and Harrison (1993) reviewed many studies on why people are absent from work. Absence appears to be the product of many factors, including family conflicts, feelings of job dissatisfaction, alcohol and drug abuse, and personality. However, as John (1994) noted, employees are likely to give self-serving justification for their absence.

Absenteeism is a pervasive problem in industry; it costs employees billions of dollars a year in decreased efficiency and increased benefit payments and payroll costs. Absenteeism has social, individual, and organizational causes, and it affects individual, companies and even entire industrial societies (Muchinsky, 2000).

Job Stress

Stress is costly business expense that affects both employee's health and company profits.

—Susan L. Lind and Fred L. Otte.

Job stress is a consequence of two key ingredients: a high level of job demands and little control over one's work.

—Paul Froiland.

Stress has been defined in many ways, but most definitions say that stress is caused by a stimulus, that the stimulus can be either physical or psychological and that the individual responds to the stimulus in some way. [Griffin, 2000].

Stress is an adaptive response, mediated by individual characteristics and/ or psychological processes, that is a consequences of any external action, situation or event that places special physical and or psychological demands upon a person. [Ivancevich & Matteson, 1980], [Miner, 1992].

Stress is the general term applied to the pressures people feel in life. The presence of stress at work is almost inevitable in many jobs. However, individual differences account for a wide range of reactions to stress; a task viewed as challenging by one person and may produce high levels of anxiety in another person. When stress becomes excessive, employees develop various symptom of stress that can harm their job performance and health, and even threaten their ability to cope with the environment. Stress also leads to physical disorder because the internal body system changes to try to cope with the stress. Therefore, it is important that stress, both on and off the job, be kept at a level low enough for most people to tolerate without developing either emotional or physical disorders. (Keith Davis and Newstorm, 1998).

In one study of over three thousand of business executives aged between thirty nine and fifty and employed in eleven Northern California Corporations, it was reported that the hard –driving manager with a pressing sense of the urgency of the time is likely to suffer a heart attack in his middle years than his more complacent colleague

Longitudinal studies, using the Minnesota Multiphasic Personality Inventory [MMPI] and one temperament Schedule, found that those who developed coronary heart disease fourteen years later had originally held higher scores on "hypochondriasis", "masculinity", and "activity." [B. Gilmer,1971]

Extreme Products of Stress

Stress can be either temporary or long term either mild or severe. The effects on an employee depend mostly on how long its causes continue, how powerful they are, and how strong the employees recovery powers are.

Problems predictably arise when high intensity stress continues for an extended duration. According to the theory developed by Hans Selye, the human body cannot instantly rebuild its ability to cope with stress once it is depleted. As a result, people become physically and psychologically weakened from trying to combat it. This condition is called BURNOUT – a situation in which employees are emotionally exhausted, become detached from their client and their work, and feel unable to accomplish their goals.

Some jobs, such as those in the helping profession (Counselors, Health case professionals, and social workers) and those with continuous high stress (air traffic controller, customer service representatives and stock brokers) are more likely than others to cause burnout. In addition to higher turnover, burnout also leads to increased absenteeism and decreased quality of job performance.

Another severe product of stress, called trauma, occurs following a major threat to ones security. The event could be a natural disaster, an organizational crisis, dramatic employees abuse by the employer, or personal job loss.

One problematic disorder is called workplace trauma, which is the disintegration of employees self-concept and beliefs in their capabilities. It can arise from harassment at work place, wrongful termination, discrimination. A common source of workplace trauma is job loss, with its potentially crushing effect on ones self-esteem. This phenomenon became widespread in the 1990's as a consequence of the wave of corporate downsizing. Another source of trauma and product of stress is to witness workplace violence. (Keith Davis & Newstorm, 1998).

The Model of Stress

The model of stress was developed by Kahn and Byosiere (1992). It deals with stress in organizations in terms of seven major categories. There are numerous linkage among the categories. This reflects one of the primary research findings about stress. There are complex associations among the antecedents of stress.

The Inverted U Relationship Between Stress and Performance

This hypothesis claims that up to a point, stress serves to a person and increase attention to the job, thus improving performance. Beyond that optimum level of stress, however, performance falls off. A good deal of laboratory research focused on decision making seems to confirm this view and there are other supporting studies as well.

An example of how stress may help to improve performance comes from a study in which participants in a management development program filled out a personal life–events checklist and an index of their information–search activities. Results showed that the more extensive was their information search, presumably as a way of finding help in coping with a changed environment (Weiss, Ilgen & Shanbaug, 1982).

Performance–whether measured by supervisor ratings, organizational perception of effectiveness or job performance decrease with increasing levels of stress (Jamal, 1984, Motomidlo, Packard, & manning, 1986). In special situation this may not be true, but in general low performance can be anticipated where stress is high.

—(John B. Miner, 1992)

Sources of Occupational Stress

There are innumerable factors which may be broadly classified into the following groups:

1. Job demands and role characteristics.
2. Organizational characteristics and processes.

1. **Job Demands:** Certain jobs are more stressful than others. The more responsibilities one is required to shoulder the greater are the chances of stress experience. Managers and executives experience stress more than the blue collar employees experience more strain but not stress. That is why the percentage of individuals with heart attack and hyper-tension is generally higher among the executives than among the lower level employees.

2. **Role Ambiguity or Arbitrariness:** Why do managers and top executives experience more stress? Is it because of the large number of responsibilities. The answer is 'No'. The most appropriate answer probably is that they do not know what their responsibilities are and their nature. The roles become more ambiguous and one rises to higher and higher position. At the topmost level the roles are maximally ambiguous. Only those persons who have high tolerance for ambiguity may become successful in the higher positions. These jobs are so much unstructured that any responsibility can be included in their responsibility bag.
3. **Role Conflict:** This factor may lead to the experience of stress at any level in the organization. The supervisor is generally the victim of role conflict. He being a link between the management and the employees, is often torn between conflicting expectations. However, this is not the only position where the impact of role conflict is maximally felt. In a modern organization, multiple boss is a common phenomenon. When the subordinate is faced with conflicting expectations from two or more bosses he is in a state of indecision.
4. **Work Overload and Underload:** Generally it is believed that work overload i.e. excessive work is primarily responsible for stress. But probably work under load contributes towards stress more than the overload. Even if the employee is underburdened with work, he has to create the impression that he is either overburdened or at least adequately loaded with work. For this purpose, he has always to be in search of excuses to show that he is busy. Making a show of being busy is more stressful than actually being busy. Having adequate or more work has greater status in the society. Therefore comfort-oriented persons may experience stress under the conditions of work under-load as they are required to create the impression that they are busy. Development oriented persons also experience stress under such conditions. But their stress experience is the consequence of trying to pretend being busy, such people either may seek more and more responsibilities or if it is not possible, may migrate to some other organization where their potentialities could be put to use.

5. **Nonfulfilment of Responsibilites:** This is very important factor contributing towards stress. It includes employers or supervisors as well as employees or subordinates. Whoever doesn't fulfill his/ her responsibilities, experiences stress and also leads to stress in others. The responsibilities of superiors and subordinates are to fulfill the expectations of each other for the attainment of the organizational goal, within the constraints imposed by the organization. Such expectations may be in the form of salary, nature of work, participation, responsibility etc.

6. **Organizational Characteristics:** It is extremely difficult to describe every organizational characteristic in relation to stress. The factors just described among the most important sources contributing towards stress. The very knowledge that performance is being evaluated is stressful for some individuals. Inadequate evaluation real or perceived may create a feeling of injustice in the employee which is stressful in nature.

   - Poor Communication: Communication is a vital process for smooth functioning of the organization. But this process is maximally uncared for. Multidirectional communication in an atmosphere of trust and confidence is maximally conducive to healthy growth and development of the organization. But right from the top to the bottom almost every one is afraid of such multidirectional communication. Generally, what prevails in most of the organizations is down-ward communication with scant attention paid to upward communication. Feedback and self-disclosure are the two processes through which effectiveness of communication may be increased. These two processes simply mean that in order to increase the effectiveness of an organization, individuals or groups in interaction with each other should give expression to their perception of others without any inhibitions and also disclose information about themselves in an atmosphere of trust and confidence.
   - Opportunity for Growth and Advancement: As every individual joins the organization for himself/herself, it is necessary that organizations should fulfill the egoistic motive of every individual. Any disparity between expectation and availability may result in the experience of

stress. Growth and advancement oriented persons are likely to experience stress from lack of opportunity, whereas comfort oriented persons may experience stress when subjected to growth and advancement oriented organizational climate. One experiences stress when opportunity is denied whereas the other does so because the opportunity is provided. Promotion is generally believed to be a motivator and a satisfier. But when it is given to a person who is not mature enough to shoulder the responsibilities of the higher position, he may experience stress. Emphasis on specialization and division of labor also may be considered under this heading as a source of stress. Excessive emphasis on specialization amounts to the use of limited capacities of an individual. Several other capacities remain unutilized preventing the growth and advancement of an individual. An individual may experience the feeling of monotony, which may result in the feeling of stress.

Utilization of multiple aptitudes may make the job more challenging and result in reduced stress. We should not be under the impression that challenging work is always stress producing. To a stability prone individual it may be stress producing, but a change prone employee may enjoy the challenge in such a type of work.

Responsibility for People

One may be working in the production department, another in marketing, and still another may be is the personnel or human resources department. It has been observed that those who are required to shoulder the supervisory responsibilities for other people experience stress more than those shouldering other responsibilities. Supervising products and supervising people require different skills. Responsibility for other people requires an accurate understanding of their motives, attitudes, problems and personality. In addition to such understanding, one's own understanding of oneself is also equally important. Clash of interests, attitudes, personality orientation etc. may lead to emergence of various problems. That is why dealing with other is most difficult responsibility leading to stress. At the lower of the hierarchy the only skill that is predominantly required is the muscular skill, but as we move to higher and higher positions, human relations skill becomes more and more important, and the top managers and executives require human relations only.

Frustration

Another cause of stress is frustration. It is a result of a motivation (drive) being blocked to prevent one from reaching a desired goal. One of the most common reactions to frustration is aggression. Whenever people are aggressive, it is likely that they are reflecting frustrations that are upsetting them. Additional reactions to frustration include apathy, withdrawal, regression, fixation, physical disorders, and substitute goals. Another reaction is withdrawal, such as asking for a transfer or quitting your job. Regression to less mature behavior, such as self-pity also is possible.

Management is only one of several sources. Another major source is coworkers who may place barriers in the way so goal attainment. Perhaps they withhold inputs to you, thereby delaying your work. Or their poorly done inputs prevent you from doing quality work. You also can be frustrated by the work itself, such as a part that does not fit or a machine that breaks down. A source of frustration rarely recognized is you, yourself. Perhaps your goals are higher than your present abilities. (Keith Davis, 1998)

Life Stressors

Stress in organizational settings also can be influenced by events that take place outside the organization. Life stressors generally categorized in terms of life change and life trauma.

Thomas Holmes and Richard Rahe first developed and popularized the notion of life change as a source of stress. Life change is any meaningful change in a person's personal or work situation. Holmes and Rahe reasoned that the major changes in a person's life can lead to stress and eventually to disease.

Holmes and Rahe argued that a person can handle a certain threshold of LCUs (Life Change Units), but beyond that level problems can set in. In particular, they suggest that people who encounter more than 150 LCUs in a given year will experience a decline in their health the following year. A score of between 150 and 300 LCUs supposedly carries a 50 percent chance of major illness, while the chance of major illness is said to increase to 70 percent if the number of LUCs exceeds 300.

These ideas offer some insight into potential impact of stress and underscore our limitations in coping with stressful events. However, research on Holmes and Rahe's proposals has provided only mixed support. An avenue that does seem promising, however, is based on the notion of hardiness.(Keith Davis, 1998)

Type A and Type B Personality Profiles

As we noted earlier, not everyone responds to stress in the same way. In fact, virtually every aspect of stress, from what triggers it to its consequences, can vary from person to person. One line of thinking about systematic differences among people is in terms of Type A and Type B personality profiles.

The Type A and Type B profiles were first observed by two cardiologists, Meyer Friedman and Ray Rosenman. The idea started when a worker repairing the upholstery on their waiting room chairs noted that many chairs were worn only on the front. This suggested the two cardiologists that many heart patients were anxious and had a hard time sitting still.

Using this observation as a starting point, and based on their own clinical practice, Friedman and Rosenman concluded that their patients' exhibited two very different types of behavior patterns. Their research led them to conclude that the differences were personality based.

The Type A individual is extremely competitive, is very devoted to work, and has a strong sense of time urgency. Moreover, this individual is likely to be aggressive, impatient, and highly work oriented. He or she has lot of drive and wants to accomplish as much as possible in as short a time as possible.

The Type B person, in contrast, is less competitive, is less devoted to work, and has a weaker sense of time urgency. This person feels less conflict with either people or time and has a more balanced, relaxed approach to life. She or he has more confidence and is able to work at a constant pace. Finally, the Type B person is not necessarily any more or less successful than the Type A individual.

Friedman and Rosenman point out that people are not purely Type A or Type B; instead, people tend toward one or the other type. For example, an individual might exhibit marked Type A characteristics much of the time but still be able to relaxed once in a while and even forget about time in a few situations.

Early research by Friedman and Rosenman on Type A and Type B profile differences yielded some alarming findings. In particular, it was argued that Type A were much more likely to experience coronary heart diseases than Type B. in recent years, however, follow up research by other scientists suggest that the relationship between Type A behavior and the risk of coronary heart diseases is not that straight forward.

Although the reasons are unclear, recent findings suggest that Type A are much more complex than originally believed. They not only exhibit the traits noted, but are also likely to be depressed and hostile. Any one or a combination of these feelings can lead to heart problems. Moreover, different approaches to measuring Type A tendencies have yielded to different results.

Finally, in one study that found Type A's to actually to be less susceptible to heart problem than Type B, The researchers nevertheless offered an explanation consistent with earlier thinking: Because Type A's are compulsive, they seek treatment earlier and are more likely to follow their doctors orders!(Keith Davis, 1998)

Consequenses of Stress

May be more energy, enthusiasm, and motivation. Of more concern are the negative consequences of stress.

We should first note that many factors listed are obviously interrelated if the category for the A number of consequences can result from stress. If the stress is positive then the result consequences seem somewhat arbitrary, be aware that each consequences is categorized according to its primary constituent.

Individual Consequences

Individual consequences of stress, then, are those outcomes that mainly affect the individual. The organization also may suffer, either directly or indirectly, but it is the individual who pays the real price. Three categories of the individual consequences of stress are behavioral, psychological, and medical.

Behavioral consequences: Behavioral consequences of stress are responses that may harm the person under stress or others. One such behavior is smoking. Research has clearly documented that people who smoke tend to smoke more when they experience stress. There is also evidence that alcohol and drug abuse are linked to stress, although this relationship is less documented.

Other possible behavioral consequences are accident proneness, violence, and appetite disorders.

Psychological Consequences: Psychological Consequences of stress relate to an individuals mental health and well being. When people experience too much stress at work, they may become depressed or may find themselves sleeping too much or not enough. Stress may also lead to family problems and sexual difficulties.

Medical Consequences: Medical Consequences of stress affect a persons physical well-being. Heart diseases and stroke among other illnesses have been linked to stress. Other common medical problems resulting from too much stress include headaches, backaches, ulcers and related stomach and intestinal disorders and skin conditions like acne and hives.

Organisational Conseqnenses

Still other consequences of stress have even more direct consequences for organizations. These include decline in performance, withdrawal, and negative changes in attitude.

Performance: One clear organizational consequences of too much stress is a decline in performance. For operating workers, such a decline can translate into poor quality work or drop in productivity. For managers, it can mean faulty decision making or disruptions in working relationship as people become irritable and hard to get along with.

Withdrawal: Withdrawal behaviors can also result from stress. For the organizations, the two most significant forms of withdrawal behavior are absenteeism and quitting. People who are having a hard time coping with stress in their jobs are more likely to call in sick or consider leaving the organization for good. Other, subtler forms of withdrawal can also be from stress. A manager may start missing deadlines or taking longer lunch breaks. An employee may withdraw psychologically by ceasing to care about the organizations and the job.

Attitudes: Another direct organizational consequences of employee stress relates to attitude. Job satisfaction, morale, and organizational commitment can also suffer, along with motivation to perform at high levels. As a result, people may be more prone to complain about unimportant things, do only enough work to get by, and so forth.

Burnout

A final consequence of stress has implications for both people and organizations. Burnout is a general feeling of exhaustion that develops when an individual simultaneously experiences too much pressure and too few sources of satisfaction.

Burnout generally develops in the following way. First people with high aspirations and strong motivation to get things done are prime candidates for burnout under conditions. They are especially vulnerable when the organization suppresses or limits initiative while constantly demanding that they serve the organizations for own ends.

The most likely effects of this situation are prolonged stress, fatigue, and helplessness under the burden of overwhelming demands. The person literally exhausts his or her aspirations and motivations, much as a candle burns itself out. Loss of self-confidence and psychological withdrawal follow. Ultimately, burnout results. (Keith Davis, 1998)

Managing Stress

Given that stress is widespread and so potentially disruptive in organizations, it follows that people and organizations should be concerned about how to manage it more effectively. And in fact they are. Many strategies have been developed to help manage stress in the workplace. Some are strategies for individuals and others are geared towards the organizations.

Individual Coping Strategies

Many strategies for helping individuals manage stress have been proposed.

Exercise: One method by which individuals can manage their stress is through excercise. People who excercise regularly are known to be less likely to have heart attacks than inactive people are. More directly, research has suggested that people who exercise regularly feel less tension and stress, are more self-confident, and show greater optimism. People who do not exercise regularly feel more stress, are more likely to be depressed and so forth.

Relaxation:A related method individuals can use to manage stress is relaxation. It can take many forms. One way to relax is to take regular vacations. A recent study found that peoples attitudes toward a variety of workplace characteristics improved significantly following a vacation. People can also relax while on the job.

Time Management: Somewhat related to time management is the idea of role management, in which the individual actively works to avoid overload, ambiguity, and conflict. For example, if you do not know what is expected of you, you should not sit and worry about it. Instead, ask for clarifications from your boss.

Another role management strategy is to learn to say no. As simple as saying no might sound improper, a lot of people create problems for them selves by always saying yes. Besides working in their regular jobs, they agree to serve on committees, volunteer for extra duties, and accept extra assignments. Sometimes, of course, we have no choice but to accept an extra obligation. In many cases, however, saying no is a viable option.

Support Groups: A final method for managing stress is to develop and maintain support groups. A support group is simply a group of family members or friends with whom a person can spend time. Going out after work with a couple of coworkers to a basketball game, for example, can help relieve the stress that built up during the day. Supportive family and friends can help people deal with stress on an ongoing basis.

Support groups can be particularly useful during times of crisis. For example, suppose an employee has just learned that she did not get the promotion she has been working towards for the month. It may help her tremendously if she has good friends to lean on, be it to talk or to yell at.

Organizational Coping Strategies

Increasingly, organizations are realizing that they should be involved in managing their employees stress. There are two different rationales for this view. One is that because the organization is at least partly responsible for creating the stress, it should help to relieve it. The other is that workers experiencing lower levels of harmful stress will be able to function more effectively. Two basic organizational strategies for helping employees manage stress are institutional programs and collateral programs.

Institutional Programs: Institutional programs for managing stress are under-taken through established organizational mechanisms. For example, properly designed jobs and work schedules can help ease stress. Shift work in particular can cause major problems for employees, as they constantly have to adjust their sleep and relaxation patterns. Thus, the design of work schedules should be a focus of organizational efforts to reduce stress.

The organizations culture also can be used to help manage stress. In some organizations, for example, there is a strong norm against taking time off or going on vacation. Thus, the organization should strive to foster a culture that reinforces a healthy mix of work and non-work activities.

Finally, supervision can play an important institutional role in managing stress. A supervisor is a potential major source of overload. If made aware of their potential for assigning stressful amounts of work, supervisors can do a better job of keeping workloads reasonable.

Collateral Programs: In addition to their institutional efforts aimed at reducing stress, many organizations are turning to collateral programs. A collateral stress program is an organizational program specifically created to help employees deal with stress. Organizations have adopted stress management programs, health promotion programs, and other kinds of programs for this purpose. More and more companies are developing their own programs or adopting existing programs of this type.

These kinds of programs attack stress indirectly by encouraging employees to exercise, which in turn is presumed to reduce stress. On the negative side, this kind of effort costs considerably more than stress management programs, because the firm must invest in physical facilities. Still, more and more companies are exploring this option.

Finally, organizations try to help employees cope with stress through kinds of program. For example, existing career development programs, like that at General Electric, are used for this purpose. Other companies use programs promoting everything from humour to massage as antidotes to stress. Of course, there is little or no research to support some of the claims made by advocates of these programs. Thus, managers must take steps to ensure that any organization effort to help employees cope with stress is at least reasonably effective. (Keith Davis, 1998)

Summary

Organizational Psychology is concerned with the application of the theories and researches of psychological science. It aims at solving the problems of human organizations and for the benefit of human resources in the organizaion / institutions.

Organzational Psychology deals with various aspects of work and people performing the work. Some of them are absenteeism, job satisfaction, stress, quality and quantity of output and many more.

Absenteeism is a topic which has been studied for a long time by many Psychologists. It has been posited that dissatisfied employees tend to be more absent than the satisfied ones. Absenteeism affects the overall performance and output of the company as well as the employee.

Some absenteeism is considered to be good also. For instance, absence can reduce the stress and fatigue so that the employee can perform better work. Comparatively, the negative impacts are more serious and need to be dealt with by the organization.

There are different ways in which the company measures absenteeism depending on the policies and regulations.

There are various reasons for absenteeism by employees. Some are like absence prone persons, illness, age and sex, alcoholism or dugs, adverse conditions at work and many more.

There are many ways and tactics by which organizations can reduce the absenteeism rate among employees. Companies can provide with rewards or bonus to employees who have the least number of absences or can give recognition or praise in front of all the other employees. Different methods can be used as per the convenience and creativity of the organizations.

Stress is another problem that the organization needs to handle among its employees. Stress can be defined as the pressure of time or workload on an individual. As far as stress at work is concerned; it is something that is inevitable. Individual differences come into account as far as the intensity of stress is concerned, one person for whom a task is very stressful can be a normal task for the other person.

Excessive stress can lead various kinds of problems in an employee. These problems are not just work related but may also affect his personal life. Many studies show that stress can create physiological problems in an individual such as heart diseases, hypertension, anxiety and many more of such kinds.

It has been found that small amount of stress is required for the employee to work better and give his best but excessive stress can lead to a severe decline in his productivity. This relationship between stress and performance is called inverted "U" relationship.

There are many sources of stress such as job demands, role conflict, work-overload and under-load, non-fulfilment of responsibility, poor communication in organization and many more.

Various strategies have been developed to cope with stress such as personal and organizational strategies. Exercise, relaxation, time management, role management and support groups are some individual strategies to overcome stress. The management can help its employees to reduce stress by developing health programs and stress management programs within the organization. Counselors can also be appointed to help employees deal with their work and to overcome emotional problems and various kinds of personal problems that can hinder the performance of the worker.

References and Further Reading

1. B.Von Haller Gilmer: Industrial and Organizational Psychology.1971.McGraw Hill Kogakusha,Ltd. Tokyo
2. Bhagwatwar P.A.: Psychology of Industrial and Organizational Behavior. 1993 (3d edition) Sheth Publishers Pvt. Ltd.
3. John Miner:Industrial-Organizational Psychology. 1992. McGraw Hill International Edition.
4. Kaila H.L. (2005). Human Factors in Organisations: New Paradigms. Mumbai: Himalaya Publishing House.
5. Moorhead and Griffin: Organizational Behavior. Managing People and Organization. 2000 (3rd edition). Jaico Publishing House. Mumbai.
6. Newstorm and Keith Davis: Organizational Behavior- Human Behavior at Work. 1998.(10th edition). Tata McGraw Hill Publication.
7. Norman R.F.Maier: Psychology on Industry. 1965 (3rd edition) Oxford and IBH Publishing Co.
8. Paul Hersey and Blanchard: Management of Organizational Behavior. 2001 (7th edition). Prentice Hall of India Pvt Ltd. New Delhi.

9. Paul.M.Muchinsky: Psychology applied to work. 2000 (6th edition). Wadsworth Publishing, Thompson Asia Pte Ltd. Mumbai.
10. Sherlekar S.A. and Sherlekar V.S.: Modern Business Organization and Management. 1987 (4th edition). Himalaya Publishing House.
11. Stephin Robbins: Organizational Behavior. 1996 (7th edition). Prentice Hall of India Pvt. Ltd., New Delhi.
12. Tiffin and McCormick: Industrial Psychology. 1960 (4th edition). Asia Publishing House, Bombay.

23

Performance Management System

Introduction

Performance management is the process of creating a work environment or setting in which people are enabled to perform to the best of their abilities. The performance management process begins with analysis and description of the job. The performance manager identifies essential functions in the job description and the strategic mission and goals of the department or organizational unit. Standards of minimum acceptable performance are developed for the position with the employee. Additionally, standards for performance, which exceeds expectations, may be set to encourage the employee to strive for even better results. Throughout the appraisal period (typically one year), the performance manager observes and provides behavioral feedback on the performance of the employee, focusing on helping the employee to achieve successful performance. At the end of the appraisal period, and in collaboration with the employee, the performance manager prepares, writes, delivers and then produces a final copy of the written performance appraisal. At any point in the process, the employee and performance manager may identify needs and create a plan for employee education, training or development in job- or career-related areas.

This chapter highlights the working of performance management system in ABB Ltd, Marketing office only. It starts with introducing the concept of performance management, ABB profile, AIM as a process of performance management, and later documents the survey details and analysis. It also gives insight into the system and suggestions to improve.

About The Company- ABB

ABB is a global leader in power and automation technologies that enable utility and industry customers to improve their performance while lowering environmental impact. ABB is present in more than 100 countries.

ABB is headquartered in Zurich, Switzerland. ABB Ltd. shares are traded on the stock exchanges in London /Zurich, Stockholm, Frankfurt and New York. More than half of ABB's revenues come from European markets, nearly a fifth from Asia, the Middle East and Africa, while about a quarter of the revenues come from North and South America markets.

ABB has approximately 160,000 employees in more than 100 countries. ABB ranks number one, two or three in almost all its operations.

Company's History

The ABB Group was formed in 1988, when the Swedish Asea and Swiss BBC Brown Boveri merged in the name of ABB. Asea's history dates back to 1883. BCC Brown Boveri was founded in 1891.

In India, the Company was incorporated on 24th December 1949 as Hindustan Electric Company Limited. In 1965, the company's name was changed to Hindustan Brown Boveri Limited (HBB). Pursuant to the Scheme of Amalgamation of Asea Limited with HBB with effect from 1st January 1989, the name was further changed to Asea Brown Boveri Limited (ABB) with effect from 13th October 1989.

Jörgen Centerman is the President and CEO of ABB Ltd. and Ravi Uppal is the Managing Director of ABB Ltd., India. In India, the corporate office is at Bangalore and the registered office is at Mumbai.

Core Business Segments

ABB has four divisions, which serve utilities, process industries, manufacturing and consumer industries, and oil, gas and petrochemicals sectors. Two ABB divisions provide power and automation technology products via internal and third party channel partners as well as direct sales. The group's financial services division serves ABB companies, ABB customers and third party customers.

The company's business segments are organized around customers on industry and product lines. End user customer segments are utilities, process industries and manufacturing and customer industries. The product segments are power technology and automation technology which supply products to the customers as also sell directly to channel partners.

ABB's long-standing commitment to India and extensive manufacturing and market presence has helped to establish a vast and proven installed base. The complete range of offering helps deliver added value for the customers through locally focused products, services and solutions.

The business segments of ABB are:

- **Utilities:** The utilities division offers a portfolio of products, services and systems to the electric, gas and water utilities – whether state-owned or private, global or local, operating in liberalized or regulatedîmarkets. The division's main aim is to improve the competitiveness of the customers worldwide, and to set industry benchmarks in customer responsiveness, ease of collaboration and ease to use and sustainability. The division has approximately 16,000 employees worldwide.

  In India, the transmission equipment manufactured and supplied by the companies has formed an integral part of the power systems spread across the country. ABB delivers complete solutions and plays a key role in the electrification and energy projects for urban and rural utilities as well as industrial and commercial customers. The entire offering is supported by a strong countrywide after-sales and service network.

- **Process Industries:** The process industries division serves the chemical, Pharmaceutical, Petroleum, gas, marine, metals, minerals, mining, cement, pulp, paper and printing industry. Process industry has a strong domain expertise and uses its automation, power and supply chain and service portfolio to create Industrial IT automation and information solutions for customers in that area. The division employs approximately 16,000 worldwide.

  In India, ABB provides a compete range of products, systems and services to industries as diverse as paper and pulp, metals, mining, cement, chemicals, petrochemicals and refineries. ABB is also a major supplier of turbochargers to the locomotive, power and marine sectors of India.

Manufacturing and consumer industries: The manufacturing and consumer industries division sells products, solutions and services to improve customer productively and competitiveness in areas like automotive industries, telecom, consumer goods, products manufacturing, electronics, airports, parcel and cargo distribution, public, and commercial buildings. It also provides air-handling solutions for industrial and environmental processes. The division employs approximately 31,000 employees worldwide.

In, India, ABB offers an entire spectrum of power technology products and services for manufacturing and consumer industries to improve productivity and competitiveness in sectors like automotive, telecom, consumer goods, electronics, airports, etc. ABB offers turnkey solutions in terms of design, supply, installation, commissioning and service support for a wide range of infrastructure, industrial and commercial applications.

- **Power Technology:** The power technology products division produces transformers, switchgear, breakers, capacitors, cables and other products and technologies for high and medium voltage applications and sold through ABB end-user divisions as well as through external partners – original equipment manufacturers (OEMs), system integrators, distributors. The division employs approximately 29,000 employees worldwide.

  In India, ABB offers an entire spectrum of power technology products and services for transmission and distribution sectors as well as industry. This includes a complete range of HV and MV switchgear, live tank breakers, instrument transformers, network and protection control, and other substation equipment supported by a focused after sales and services network.

- **Oil, Gas and petrochemicals:** The oil, gas and petrochemicals division focuses on systems, technologies, products and services for oil and gas exploration and development, gas processing, refineries and petrochemical plants worldwide. The division employs approximately 13,000 employees worldwide.

- **Automation Technology:** The automation technology division provides products, systems, software and services for the automation and optimization of industrial and commercial processes. Key technologies include measurement and control, instrumentation, process analysis, drives and motors, power electronics, robots and low voltage products. These technologies are served to customers via internal and third party channel partners, through ABB's direct sales force and electronically over the Internet. The division employs approximately 41,000 employees worldwide.

In India, ABB provides automation and optimization technologies for discrete, process and batch manufacturing operations and business related aspects. The offering includes process analytics, PLC's, motors and machine, drives, power electronics, metering, robotics, instrumentation, control systems, transducers, distribution and protection relays and complete range of low voltage products.

- **Financial Services:** The financial services division creates value for its customers with innovative financial solutions in structured finance, leasing, project development and ownership, financial consulting, insurance and treasury activities. The financial services division started with no staff and no business but a good idea- to help ABB finance its business ventures and customers. Today it is one of the top contributors of earnings in the ABB Group. The division employs approximately 1,200 people worldwide.

Concept of Performance Management

Performance Management is the process of creating a work environment or setting in which people are enabled to perform to the best of their abilities. Performance management begins when a job is defined. It ends when an employee leaves the company.

Performance management is a means of getting better results from the organization, teams and individuals by understanding and managing performance within an agreed framework of planned goals, standards and competence requirements. It is a process for establishing shared understanding about what is to be achieved, and an approach to managing and developing people in a way that increases the probability that it will be achieved in the short and longer term. It is owned and driven by line management.

Definitions

Performance Management is a systematic, data oriented approach to managing people by arranging conditions for positive reinforcement in individual and group performance. Grounded in the science of Applied Behaviour Analysis, PMS employs measurement, feedback and positive consequences (recognition and reward) for achieving the specific behaviors that bring about desired results.

Performance Management, is an ongoing communication process that involves both the performance manager and the employee in:

1. Identifying and describing essential job functions and relating them to the mission and goals of the organization.
2. Developing realistic and appropriate performance standards
3. Giving and receiving feedback about performance.
4. Writing and communicating constructive performance appraisals.
5. Planning education and development opportunities to sustain, improve or build on employee work performance.

Performance Management can be defined as a strategic and integrates approach to delivering sustained success to organizations by improving the performance of the people who work in them and by developing the capabilities of teams and individual contributors – (Armstrong and Baron, 1998).

Performance Management is critical to key human resources transactions. The compensation program of many employers includes performance-based or merit pay, in which past performance, as documented in a performance appraisal, is a key determinant of the size of an employee's pay increase. Promotional decisions are often based in part on past performance as documented in a performance appraisal. And performance appraisals often serve as a critical tool in validating an employer's selection process.

But more importantly, performance management can serve as a key transformation tool for the employer. It can help transform the employer's stated mission, vision and values into specifics for employees- specific results expected or specific behaviors required.

Difference between Performance Appraisal and Performance Management:

Performance appraisal as an informal process has no doubt existed among employers since the point at which the first employee began working. It can be defined as "the process of establishing written standards of performance criteria and telling employees about those standards and frequently informing them how they are performing in relation to the standards"— (Myers 1992).

Performance Management can be defined as all of those processes, led by managers, which help employees, perform as effectively as possible. Included are defining responsibilities, setting expectations, providing the necessary resources, giving ongoing feedback, periodically appraising performance, and utilizing information.

Uses include making human resources decisions, solving individual and organizational systems. The appraisal of performance is but one aspect of the broader process of performance management. Performance appraisal looks back and asks the question: "How well was the work done?" Follow up issues might include what can be done to improve future performance.

Performance Management, by contrast, asks a future oriented question: "What can be done to help employees perform as effectively as possible".

The Performance Management Cycle

The process of performance management is summarized in the performance management cycle, which incorporates the major components involved.

1. **Define the Job:** Relate to Employer Goals, Values, and Customer Expectations. The process of performance management begins with ensuring that each individual's activities are aligned and organized to effectively accomplish the goals and objectives of the employer. Effective performance management requires the proper organizational structure so that the effort of both individuals and groups is positioned to achieve organizational ends. Job analysis and job descriptions can serve to capture and summarize the broad parameters of expected employee activities, but they have often hindered an employer's ability to properly direct employee effort.
2. **Set Expectations:** Paint a Picture of a Good Job. Perhaps the most significant component of the performance management cycle is to "set expectations". Performance management requires, therefore, that performance planning occur. There must be a meeting of the minds between each employees and her or his manager about the expected duties and norms for performing

those duties. Setting expectations requires the following steps:

- Review organizational and unit goals and individual performance expectations.
- Identify objectives, duties, and projects.
- Describe performance measures and standards.
- Identify performance factors.
- Develop a monitoring plan.

Review Organizational and Unit Goals and Individual Performance Expectations

Organizational goals serve as the stating point for individual performance planning by describing the specific areas in which the organization expects accomplishment. Department or unit goals, and ultimately individual goals all serve to support the accomplishment of the employer's goals. These larger organizational and departmental goals must be reviewed to identify individual and team accomplishments necessary for their achievement. When individual and/or team performance expectations are established, they must be checked against employer goals to ensure that they served to support those goals.

Identify Objectives, Duties, and Projects

The manager of a department is responsible for accomplishing the goals of that department. Therefore, for those individuals higher in the organization hierarchy, setting unit expectations serves to establish individual expectations at the same time. Because others within the organization may find themselves directly responsible for some portion of the unit's goals, a review of the organizational and unit goals is essential in performance planning for all employees.

Relevant duties and tasks for which the employee is responsible can be identified from the job description. Any special projects to which the employee has been assigned must also be identified.

Describe Performance Measures and Standards

Performance measures provide ways of describing a "good job" on each objective, duty, or project. As part of the process of setting expectations, agreement must be reached on measures that will be used to appraise how well the employee did with regard to each objective, duty or project.

Where feasible, it is helpful to focus on objective, quantifiable measures rather than subjective ones. Often, however, quantifiable measures are difficult or costly to obtain. The cost of measuring must not exceed the value added from measuring. Effective objectives and measures are consistent with and support the organization's mission and goals as well as the mission and goals of the relevant department or unit. Effective objectives and measures should reflect the more important, or key responsibility areas of the employee and should be specific in stating end results and the timing expected. In other words, good objectives are SMART.

- Specific.
- Measurable.
- Aligned with organizational and unit goals.
- Realistic and results oriented.
- Time limited.

When developing objectives and measures, active involvement of the employee leads to greater employee commitment to accomplishing the objectives.

Performance levels or standards conclude the process of describing a "good job". Standards communicate in advance to the employee what must be accomplished to achieve each rating level. Standards usually define and describe the performance level that meets expectations.

Identify Performance Factors

A process of setting expectations that includes the identification of specific and measurable performance objectives and the communication of expectations about how those objectives are to be accomplished implies that "the ends justify the means". This is rarely the case in organizations. If an employer, through its strategic planning process, has identified important organizational values, then that employer's performance management process should require and support employees behaving in line with those values. Performance factors provide this direction through identification, discussion, and agreement on the methods by which objectives are to be attained. Ideally, the performance management process includes the identification of specific behavioral examples to describe any relevant performance factors.

Develop a Monitoring Plan

The final phase of setting expectations is developing a plan to monitor employee performance. Monitoring requires discussion and agreement on the methods and tools for tracking employee performance. The development of a monitoring plan allows the employee as well as the manager to track employee progress and take corrective actions throughout the performance period.

Conduct Review: Appraise Performance and Hold Period Review: The performance cycle includes a periodic, scheduled review of performance; a discussion with the employee; the rating or appraising of the employee's performance if required. Organizational planning and goal setting generally occur on a regular cycle, most often annually. Because goal and objectives have expected completion dates, it is important to review the performance of individuals in attaining those goals on a regular cycle in line with those completion dates.

The most frequent cycle used by employers for conducting performance reviews is annually. Some employers use a shorter cycle, quarterly or semi-annually. In any case, the periodic review session should be in addition to, not in lieu of, regular discussions about employee performance.

Conducting the Performance Appraisal Interview: In many respects the key to a successful performance feedback session relates more to what occurs before the interview than during it. If the manager and employee have not reached a clear understanding of performance, constant feedback is the key to a good review session and improved performance.

In preparing the review session, the supervisor should also arrange for a private, comfortable meeting place. Moving out from behind a desk often contributes to more open communication. Better review sessions are conducted from a coaching or helping approach, rather than a judgmental one. The appraiser must concentrate on active listening and encouraging feedback from the employee. Finally, because most employees are performing well in more areas than those in which they are performing poorly, a balanced session would normally include more discussion of strengths and accomplishments than areas in need of improvement.

In conducting the session, the attitude of the appraiser is critical. If she or he sincerely views the session as a helpful opportunity to discuss the employee's accomplishments and areas in need o improvement relative to the employer's goals, this attitude is likely to be translated to the employee, leading to a more positive interview. The session should begin with a review of the purposes of the session:

- To discuss employee accomplishments and areas in need of improvement relative to organizational and unit goals.
- To discuss ways in which the supervisor and organization can be more supportive in helping the employee perform.
- To develop performance improvement strategies where required.
- To begin to discuss expectations for the upcoming performance period.

Common Rating Errors

There are a number of common biases that affect the rating process.

- **Halo**—the tendency to rate appraisee highly in many performance areas because of good performance in one area.
- **Horns**—the tendency to rate appraisee poorly on most performance areas because of one or a few areas in which he or she performs poorly.
- **Recency**—the tendency to let recent events (performance or behavior) unduly affect the appraisal.
- **Lenience/Severity**—the tendency toward "easy" or "tough" ratings.
- **Central Tendency**—the inability of the rater to distinguish different levels of performance, so everyone gets rated as average.
- **Similarly**—rating people high who are like the appraiser or do things in the same way as the appraiser.
- **Stereotypes**—viewing people with certain characteristics the same way.
- **Contrast Effect**—comparing an employee to other employees rather than to a standard.
- **Selective Perception**—the tendency to see and hear what we want to see and hear.

Principal Goals of Performance Management

The major goals of performance management are discussed in the following sections:

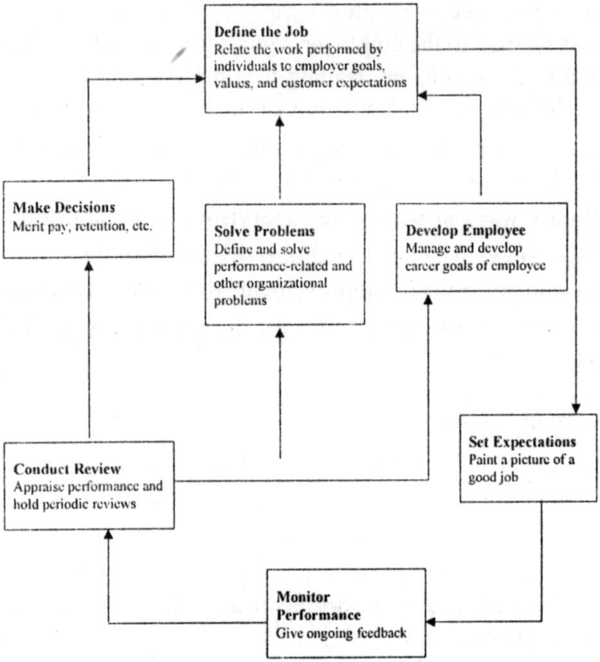

Figure: Performance Management Cycle

Improve Employee Performance

Most employers adopt performance management processes primarily to help employees perform more effectively in their current positions and to be more successful in accomplishing organizational goals. Traditional performance appraisal methods have performed poorly against this goal by taking a "rearview mirror" approach to management. They focus more attention on past performance than on the present and future. Performance management processes include a future orientation designed to paint a clear picture of what is expected from employees and how the employer will support them in their efforts.

Develop People for promotional Opportunities

Neither traditional performance appraisal nor performance management processes are well suited for achieving a goal of identifying employees for promotional opportunities. Past performance is no guarantee of success on a new job assignment involving duties that require a different skill set. Identifying candidates for promotion or new organizational assignments is a selection decision that requires a thorough look at the extent to which a candidate possesses the necessary competencies to perform well in the new job. Past performance may provide a good indication of likely success where the required competencies are very similar, but will likely provide little guidance if different competencies are necessary. Performance management processes can serve to help develop people for new assignments and promotional opportunities.

Meet Employee's Need for feedback

Most agree that the majority of employees want to know how they are doing on the job. They would like positive feedback from their employer about their accomplishments and suggestions on how they can improve. A well-designed and well-implemented performance management process helps accomplished this goal, by providing the tools with which employees can monitor their own performance and engage in self-feedback.

Ensure That Employees Are Working Toward Organizational Goals

Some traditional performance appraisal programs ask the question, "Are you performing well?" More effective performance management approaches rephrase it as "Are you performing well on the right things?" Performance Management programs can serve to link the organization's strategic planning process to individual efforts.

Provide the Information Needed to Make and Defend Important Human Resources Decisions

At its core, the process of making job-related or valid human resources decisions involves assessing the extent to which the decision made actually predicted success on the job. Performance appraisal results often provide the dependent variable for determining the validity of the hiring or promotion processes. The performance appraisal usually serves as the information source when an employer chooses to use performance or merit as a basis for allocating salary increases. The performance appraisal can serve as essential information source documenting not only past employee performance, but also that the employee had been made aware of her or his performance and the consequences of not improving.

Key Benefits of Performance Management (PM)

PM focuses on Results, Rather than Behaviors and Activities

A common misconception among supervisors is that behaviors and activities are the same as results. Thus, an employee may appear extremely busy, but not be contributing at all toward the goals of the organization. An example is the employee who manually reviews completion of every form and procedure, rather than supporting automation of the review. The supervisor may conclude the employee is very committed to the organization and works very hard, thus, deserving a very high performance rating.

Aligns Organizational Activities and Processes to the Goals of the Organization

PM identifies organizational goals, results needed to achieve those goals, measures of effectiveness or efficiency (outcomes) toward the goals, and means (drivers) to achieve the goals. This chain of measurements is examined to ensure alignment with overall results of the organization.

Cultivates a System-wide, Long-term View of the Organization

Richard A. Swanson, in Performance Improvement Theory and Practice (Advances in Developing Human Resources, 1, 1999), explains an effective performance improvement process must follow a systems-based approach while looking at outcomes and drivers. Otherwise, the effort produces a flawed picture. For example, laying off people will likely produce short-term profits. However, the organization may eventually experience reduced productivity, resulting in long-term profit loss.

Produces Meaningful Measurements

These measurements have a wide variety of useful applications. They are useful in benchmarking, or setting standards for comparison with best practices in other organizations. They provide consistent basis for comparison during internal change efforts. They indicate results during improvement efforts, such as employee training, management development, quality programs, etc. They help ensure equitable and fair treatment to employees based on performance.

Other Benefits of Performance Management

Literature indicates that, Performance Management (PM):

1. Helps you think about what results you really want. You're forced to be accountable, to "put a stake in the ground".
2. Depersonalizes issues. Supervisor's focus on behaviors and results, rather than personalities.
3. Validates expectations. In today's age of high expectations when organizations are striving to transform themselves and society, having measurable results can verify whether grand visions are realistic or not.
4. Helps ensure equitable treatment of employees because appraisals are based on results.
5. Optimizes operations in the organization because goals and results are more closely aligned.
6. Cultivates a change in perspective from activities to results.
7. Performance reviews are focused on contributions to the organizational goals, e.g., forms include the question "What organizational goal were contributed to and how?"
8. Supports ongoing communication, feedback and dialogue about organizational goals. Also supports communication between employee and supervisor.
9. Performance is seen as an ongoing process, rather than a one-time, snapshot event.
10. Provokes focus on the needs of customers, whether internal or external.
11. Cultivates a systems perspective, that is, focus on the relationships and exchanges between subsystems, e.g., departments, processes, teams and employees. Accordingly, personnel focus on patterns and themes in the organization, rather than specific events.
12. Continuing focus and analysis on results helps to correct several myths, e.g., "learning means results", "job satisfaction produces productivity", etc.
13. Produces specificity in commitments and resources.
14. Provides specificity for comparisons, direction and planning.

15. Redirects attention from bottom-up approaches (e.g., doing job descriptions, performance reviews, etc., first and then "rolling up" results to the top of the organization) to top-down approaches (e.g., ensuring all subsystem goals and results are aligned first with the organization's overall goals and results).

Legal Issues In Performance Management

In our increasingly litigious society, employer human resources decisions are more frequently challenged. The many exceptions to the employment-at-will doctrine and the explosion of fair employment practices statutes (Title VII of the Civil Rights Act, the Age Discrimination in Employment Act, the Americans with Disabilities Act, etc.) have forced employees into court to defend their decisions. "Because performance appraisals are often the only tangible evidence by which a jury can determine the employee's worth, appraisals potentially provide either a devastating weapon for the employee or an impenetrable shield for the employer" (Davidson 1995).

The design of our performance management and appraisal process as well as its implementation and use provide critical indicators as to whether the performance appraisal will be an employee weapon or employer shield supporting the employer's performance-based decisions. To develop a feasible performance management and appraisal program, an employer must consider these factors.

Job Related or Valid

The factors being assessed should be relevant, given the tasks and duties expected of the employee. An employer attempting to use the same set of performance criteria for vastly different jobs might have difficulty proving that an individual's performance appraisal is an accurate reflection of his or her performance. As a result, some employers identify not only core performance factors, perhaps reflecting identified organizational values that are required of all its employees, but also individual performance factors unique to each position and/or employee.

Minimum Subjectivity

Defensibility of performance-based decisions is enhanced when performance expectations are clear and unambiguous. Objective standards of performance that are specific, measurable, and with clear timeliness help minimize subjectivity and the possibility of misunderstanding.

Such a clear behavior example of teamwork:

- Treats all team members with respect.
- Supports team decisions even when the decision may not entirely reflect one's own position.
- Tries different approaches to work with people that will create better results and working relationships

Consistent Application/Procedural Fairness

The essence of a discrimination charge is that one was treated inconsistently because of race, sex, age, disability, or some other prohibited characteristic. Unjust dismissal claims in state courts often require establishing that there was an implied employment contract created through an employer did not do what it promised. Employers must be diligent, therefore, in ensuring that the procedures it enunciates in polices and handbooks are scrupulously followed by all appraisers. If required, employees must be notified of performance standards of expectations, must receive feedback about their performance, and must have an improvement plan if their performance is substandard. Required signatures must be provided. Consistency in the administration of the process is critical to employee perceptions of a fair process, which is critical to the process having the desired impact.

Instructions and Training for Appraisers

For a system to be administrated, consistency and in line with its stated objectives, those required to appraise must, at a minimum, receive training on the process. Such training should include not only the mechanics of the particular system, but also performance planning, problem solving, coaching, and feedback skills. Perceptions of fairness are maximized when the employer trains not only appraisers, but also those whose performance is being appraised on the process and their role in it.

Forewarning

Perhaps the most important requirement for developing a defensible performance management process is that those whose performance is to be appraised receive forewarning. Forewarning includes prior knowledge of the results and behaviors expected of them, and of the process and their role in it. Forewarning includes communication of performance or behavior problems early, while there is time for correction. And finally, it includes a clear message that adverse employment consequences (e.g., discipline, dismissal) can result if the employee does not improve within a set time frame.

Ethical Consideration

Performance management should operate in accordance with the following ethical principles as defined by Win Stanley and Suart Smith (1996)

- **Respect for the Individual:** People should be treated as ends in themselves and not merely as means to other ends.
- **Mutual respect:** The parties involved in performance management process should respect each other's needs and preoccupations.
- **Procedural fairness:** The procedures incorporated in performance management should be operated fairly to limit the adverse effect on individuals
- **Transparency:** People affected by decisions emerging from the performance management process should have the opportunity to scrutinize the basis upon which decisions were made.

New Development In Employee Performance Management Criticism

While few argue with the importance of performance planning and feedback for successful individual and organizational performance, employee performance management programs have been criticized on many grounds.

1. The Focus on Ratings and Rewards. By focusing on ratings and rewards, the axiom " You get what you reward" often applies with devastating consequences. Employees and their managers spend too much time arguing over ratings at the expense of productive time directed toward accomplishing employer objectives. The rewards sought are often short term (one year or less), but may have long – term consequences for the employer. Rewards may be achieved in counterproductive ways, i.e., "the ends justify the means."
2. There is Too Much for One Rater to Appraise. Supervisory and management jobs are becoming more complex. It becomes more

difficult to monitor and track what a manager's staff is doing. Remaining managers often find themselves leading a group of employees who are more diverse in their required duties and skills. It becomes more difficult for the manager to assess or appraise the performance of such a diverse team as their duties and skills are often quite different from those of the manager.

3. The System Is Too Top Down. Among the many charges leveled by those being appraised, the complaint that "the system is too heavily controlled by the supervisor without adequate employee participation" is a common one. As a result, general charges of unfairness, favoritism, discrimination, etc. arise.

4. Team-Based Work System. As employers organize their workforces into teams for more effective accomplishment of organizational objectives, the traditional performance appraisal system may not fit. The focus on individual effort and rewards is likely to be incongruent with the team-based structure being utilized. And the supervisor of the team may not be able to appraise the use of the correct teamwork behaviors by team members.

5. Total Quality Management. Total Quality Management proponents argue that traditional performance appraisal programs focus on individual performance, often blaming low-level individuals for errors in organizational systems. In this view, performance appraisal programs are inherently in conflict with achieving product or service quality.

6. Increased Employee Involvement. Consistent with the general trend toward more employee participation in workplace issues that affect them, there has been an increase in employee involvement in the performance management process. Such involvement can include employee participation in the development of his or her performance expectations and measures, more active employee monitoring and initiation of changes during the performance period, and self-appraisal by the employee as part of the review process.

7. Less Focus on Ratings and Rewards. If an employer decides that the major purpose of its performance management program is feedback, rather than making pay or downsizing decisions, then the employer may have no need to affix a rating or label to the

performance of an employee over the performance period. Similarly, if an employer's compensation program calls for skill-based pay, gain-sharing, or simple across-the-board increases, there is little need for an individual rating beyond, perhaps, that the employee is somehow eligible for the increase.

ABB's AIM Process of Performance Management System

People Involved in AIM Process

Key role of Senior Manager is to guide junior Manager, provide assistance and give regular feedback. Senior Managers are the persons with whom managers have a direct line reporting relationship.

Reviewer's role is facilitative in nature. He ensures that performance review has been conducted objectively and also notes any disagreements voiced by manager during the process. H R Department ensures that performance review has been carried out in a valid manner keeping in mind the norms and regulations of the organization.

The AIM process consists of three steps.

A. Performance Planning

Performance planning process takes place in the beginning of AIM cycle after organizational, segment, BA-Business Area and BU-Business Unit targets have been set. The Managing Director (MD) announces the start of the process through a formal mail. Managers are also apprised of the ABB targets, segment targets, BA targets and BU targets through the intranet or manager.

Once this has been done, Managers meet senior manager to discuss their performance plans.

ABB Targets

|

Segments Targets

|

BA Targets

|

BU Targets

During The Performance Planning Meeting

1. **Set targets:** Managers and senior managers jointly cascade organizational/segment/BA/BU targets to individual targets. Although there are provisions for six targets, one can decide to have 5 targets only, but not lesser. However, out of the 5/6 targets, at least one has to be a Developmental Target. A developmental target is one, which focuses on personality Development. It may not have an immediate or direct impact to business results, but it would surely have a long-term impact. Developmental target have to be aligned to both the organization's short and long-term goals and manager's personal objectives.
2. **Write action Plans:** After setting targets, Action plans are written against each. Action plan is a structures approach to realizing our targets. An action helps managers think through the entire process of achieving targets and ensured that they have planned for the resources that they would require in the future. To avoid setting unrealistic targets for the year, one needs to think through the process.
3. **Assign Weights:** It is obvious that not all targets can be equally critical from both the organizations and our personal development perspective. Therefore, each target is assigned weights when manager is discussing with the senior manager.

   The senior manager, with consideration of the below mentioned criteria, assign weights to each target.

   - It must be a collaborative approach to setting Weights.
   - The sum of the weights cannot exceed 100%.
   - The weight is indicative of the priority attached to the target and of the time and effort that its achievement would involve.

4 **Document Baseline Responsibility:** Baseline responsibilities (BRs) are the tasks done on regular basis, not necessarily daily. The focus is on tracking only those BRs that are considered critical to the manager's role, in terms of the time spent on them or the priority accorded to them.

Ending the Performance Planning Meeting: At the end of Performance Planning Meeting, three photocopies of the AIM form are made and each given to manager, senior manager and reviewer and HR department respectively.

B. Periodic Feedback

Time frame: Between the time of setting targets at the beginning of the AIM cycle and the time of reviewing we have 2 formal feedback sessions.

The Period 1 feedback- it takes place 4 months after the performance Planning meeting.

The Period 2 feedback–It takes place four months after the Period 1 feedback.

Informal Feedback: Besides these formal meetings for the specific purpose of providing feedback, seniors are expected to provide informal feedback all the time to managers. Informal feedback cannot replace period feedback meetings, due to its unstructuredness. It tends to be about the immediate past, formal feedback makes one take a longer term, and hence more objective view.

Planning for the Periodic Feedback Meeting: Before the periodic feedback meeting, manager gathers data about their performance and documents their thoughts well in advance of the meeting. Managers analyze their performance for 4 months, and if went wrong, How it could have gone better. They seek guidance from senior manager.

During the Periodic Feedback Meeting: The structured feedback of performance in the last four months, is given only after manager discuss what went well, what did not go well and what could have been gone better. The aim of meeting is to find common solution to our performance and development issues. Senior manager also gives feedback on manager's performance in Baseline responsibility.

Ending the Periodic Feedback Meeting: Targets once set treated as sacrosanct. They are revised in the periodic feedback session only in response to:

1. Significant changes in ABB's business unit strategy
2. Significant changes in your segment/BA goals
3. Significant changes in the business unit/functional priority.
4. Significant changes in manager's role.

C. Performance Review

It takes place at the end of the AIM cycle. During the Performance Review meeting, managers and senior managers do the following:

1. **Score Targets:** Performance on each of the targets is discussed by manager and senior manager, after giving adequate feedback; senior managers score the 5/6 targets using the 4-point rating scale. There is a visual depiction of the scale along with the

description of the four points. Next, the scores are multiplied by the weights that had been decided and we arrive at Weighted Scores.

2. **Score Baseline Responsibilities:** Baseline responsibilities provide detailed feedback on manager's performance. Based on manager's performance, composite score is given using the four point rating scale.
3. **Performance Summary:** It gives us a consolidated picture of performance and tabulates the Total Performance Rating. Weighted scores of all targets are added up and total weighted score is multiplied by corresponding Weight to arrive at the Target Rating. Similar exercise is carried out for baseline responsibilities.
4. **Self-Appraisal:** Managers appraise themselves in other ways as well; need not follow directions in AIM form.
5. **Developmental Plan:** After performance review and own self-appraisal is over, Developmental Plan is created. It refers to a structured plan to help managers enhance performance in current role and prepare for new roles.
6. **Attestations:** The employee attests whether or not the Performance Management Process was conducted to the satisfaction. If satisfied, they need to sign, If not, explain the reasons for dissatisfaction. The senior manager if satisfied, need to sign and in case of dissatisfaction of manager, they need to explain the reasons and express their comments.

The role of Reviewer

The role of the reviewer is essentially quality control. To see whether the performance Review exercise is conducted as per the norms. If he is not satisfied, he may suggest a re-evaluation of performance. After, the reviewer is satisfied with the validity of the scores, he would sign.

We officially end the performance Review process, 3 copies of AIM form are made and original is sent to HR Dept., One photocopy to manager himself and last one to Senior manager.

The Role of HR Department

The HR dept., now defines the linkage of manager's performance to compensation, Career Progress, and to Training and Development.

Compensation-fixed Pay Increase: Project AIM is meant to reward manager's high performance. Performance score of manager feeds in to his increment of the year. Compensation philosophy of ABB, Industry trends and organizational results are taken into consideration while deciding on manager's increment.

Career Development: Based on manager's strength, performance competencies exhibited and interest shown, senior manager and HR Dept, will draw a future growth plan. The growth plan would encompass increasing responsibilities, enhancing job skills and knowledge and increasing your perspective of the organization.

This envisaged growth path, will then tie in with managers training need assessment. Senior manager and HR will have ongoing discussions with manager to evaluate managers needs and balance them with organizational needs and to keep them informed at each stage of their Developmental path.

The performance management system would help identify the consideration set for an internal career movement. The HR dept identifies all the individuals who fulfill the administrative criteria for the job under consideration [experience, qualification etc]. The "Performance Score" of the group of individuals would then be studied. Depending on the size of this group, a certain percentage of the top performers would be identified as the consideration set of employees. This set of employees would then have to be evaluated in terms of skills, attitude, etc.

A Study

Its Objective

To evaluate the functioning of AIM (ABB's performance management system) and its effectiveness.

Sample Description

SIZE: 30

AGE RANGE: 25-60 yrs

Methodology

The objective of the project was to evaluate AIM-Performance management system. A Questionnaire was developed which consisted 14 items and 2 open ended questions of complaints and suggestions. Each statement has three options 'Agree', 'Disagree' and 'Not sure' to choose from.

This questionnaire measures 6 parameters: Awareness, Effectiveness, Targets, Process, Motivation and Rewards.

This questionnaire was administered on 30 marketing office employees from 7 different departments: UT, PT, AT, ATLV, MCBS, FINANCE and HR.

One point was given to every option chosen by employee for each of 14 statements. All department-wise totals were taken and average score was calculated.

Percentages were also calculated for better understanding of each department's stand on each parameter. Complaints and suggestion of employees were compiled in 'Other Findings Section.'

Analysis

Awareness dimension is concerned with employees being aware of performance management system (AIM) operating in ABB; and whether it is taken in right spirit by employees. MCBS and FINANCE department show 100% awareness, followed by PT department with 82%. Moderate awareness was seen in UT and AT department with percentage of 75% each. Only 50% awareness was seen in HR and ATLV department.

Effectiveness dimension, tries to find out whether employees feel that AIM is an effective tool for individual performance. It also tries to find out whether AIM is effective in marketing office. PT, MCBS, FINANCE and HR all departments reveal that AIM is 50% effective in improving individual performance. UT with 37.50% and AT with 44% indicate moderate percentage of effectiveness. ATLV being low in effectiveness with 25%. This suggests that this department employee doesn't consider AIM to be effective tool in improving individual performance.

Target setting dimension, is concerned whether targets are set by employees in consultation with the superiors. It also tries to find out whether targets are not easily achievable and whether group targets are increased with implementation of performance management system. HR department with 100% suggest that, it agrees completely regarding target setting. Moderate percentages are found in department of MCBS, FINANCE with 67% each, UT with 58.30%, PT with 53% and AT with 50%. Lowest being ATLV with 33%.

Process dimension, is concerned whether employees discuss periodically with their subordinates and review their performance; and whether superiors take interest in AIM. As compared to all parameters, process has low percentages indicating that employees do not diligently follow process. FINANCE department with high percentage of 50% indicates that they don't really discuss their performance with subordinates, and superiors don't take enough interest in AIM. Moderate [i.e. less than 50%], percentages were found in PT department with 40%, AT with 44% and MCBS with 33%. Very less percentage were found in UT department- 0.63% and 0% for HR department. This suggests that HR and UT department does not believe in discussing periodically in order to review their performance.

Motivation dimension, is concerned whether feedback given by superiors motivate employees to work hard and whether deficiencies pointed out by superiors encourage employees to improve and fill in the gap. Its also tries to find out whether there was any discrepancy between employees self-appraisal and superior's feedback. FINANCE and HR department shows 100%, suggesting that they are highly motivated by AIM's results and ratings; followed by MCBS with 83 %, AT with 82% and UT with 73%. Comparatively lower percentages were found in department of PT with 48.50% and ATLV with 50%, suggesting that they are not motivated by superior's feedback, and deficiencies doesn't much encourage them to update their skill. And they do find some amount of discrepancy in self-appraisal and superior's feedback.

Reward dimension, is concerned whether rewards given through AIM, makes employees happy and whether AIM recognizes their efforts and hard work. FINANCE department scored high with 75% suggesting that hey are happy with the increments they get, and feel that their efforts are also recognize through AIM. Next following department is ATLV and HR with 50% each. Comparatively low scores were found in UT department with 25%, PT with 23% and MCBS with 25%, suggesting that rewards are not much motivating and AIM fails to recognize their efforts.

Most employees agree on AIM's awareness, its target setting procedure and they do get motivated to some extent. Other 3 parameters of 'effectiveness', 'Process' and 'rewards' having less percentages compared to all, indicate that these areas need improvement, so that all employees, begin to find AIM effective and its process sensible in managing performance. Reward's percentages also suggest that many employees are not happy with incentives given, making AIM a poor performance management system.

An overall analysis suggests that effectiveness of AIM measured with the help of 6 parameters gives insight into employee's view about AIM and how they think about AIM's functioning.

Other Findings

The questionnaire contained 2 open-ended questions regarding complaints and suggestion. Following are findings in this areas.

According to the employees of marketing office, the targets/goals set in the begging of year, do not remain valid in the course of the year. In between employee is busy on some other work (company's demand), but eventually rated on fixed targets.

Few of the employees stated, "Services given to customers, can not be counted in terms of order Booking figure. It is not fair to ignore services given to customers and forces only on figures. One employee reveled that" the AIM System does not take into account differences in customer and products profile. Another employee said its number impact neutralized.

One of the utility department employee stated that AIM is not so proper for utility customer, where team effects are more focused than individual effort.

According to one employee, this AIM system reminds him of targets of the year, but does not recognize the efforts involved in Project Marketing Situations.

Suggestions of Employees Regarding AIM

- Targets should be more objective.
- Feedback should be transparent before and after award.
- Targets need to be made flexible.
- Individual reviewer discussion should be vital in rating.
- In the projects/ systems business, there should be weightage given to process and the efforts of individuals since figures alone do not convey the performance of the individual concerned.
- It needs to be followed religiously to make it a success.
- There should be different schemes for set of customer position / product profile.

- Customer should get benefited and therefore customer satisfaction index should be put in the performance.
- Should be de-linked with incentive for individuals but may be used to improve basic capabilities (except AT).

Suggestions to Improve

1. **Create Awareness about AIM in Organization:** All the employees need to know the process of AIM and how it is being conducted. The new recruits need to be given orientation about AIM Program, as they are new to the organization. Right from target setting to rating performance, employees should know the steps it follows, so that there are no mistakes done by senior manager.
2. **Targets Should Strictly Follow SMART Acronym:** As SMART acronym represents, Simple, attainable, realistic and time bound, it should be checked whether all employees follow it diligently. If not done so, the rating will be difficult for senior manager. The HR Department ought to play vital role of rejecting those targets, which does not follow SMART criteria.
3. **To Make AIM as An online System:** In order to decrease the paper work done, we should introduce AIM online so that all the employees and their managers can feed in the targets and feedback online.
4. **Merger of 360-degree Feedback Concepts into AIM:** 360-degree feedback is a combination upward, downward, peer, colleague, customer or supplier appraisal of an employee. The concept of customer satisfaction should be included in the exiting process of AIM. As customer is an important component in manager's performance. Also the concepts of appraisal by peer and colleague will lead to a better measurement of performance in a team.

Conclusion

The survey objective of evaluation of AIM-Performance Management System of ABB, was conducted to measure effectiveness. The score discussed in analysis section reveal that employees of marketing office are aware of AIM being operating and are also motivated through the ratings done by superiors. But they all are not quite happy with the rewards received through AIM.

On effectiveness parameter all departments have less than 50% agreement, suggesting that it is not absolutely effective tool for performance management, but does a fairly good job.

There were many employees disliking the process of 3 feedbacks and review system, as it is tedious job. Perhaps due to this reason less percentages were seen on ' Process' parameter.

It must be re – emphasized that performance management is not a top down, backward looking form of appraising people. Neither performance management is forward looking and developmental. It provides a framework in which managers can support their team members rather than dictate to them, and its impact on result will be much more significant if it is regarded as a transformational rather than as an appraisal process.

As employees struggle to continually improve their products services and processes, the performance management process can serve as an essential organizational tool. Performance management serves to align the efforts of employees with employer goals and values, help ensure that employees have a clear understanding of what is expected of them, and makes certain that employees receive continuous feedback about their performance.

Finally, this program can serve to develop not only individual but also organizational systems and processes.

References and Further Reading

1. Armstrong, M and B, D (1998) Performance management: the new realities, Institute of personnel and Development, London.
2. Armstrong, M and Baron, D (1998) Relating competencies to pay: the U.K experience, compensation and Benefits Review, May/June, pp 28-29.
3. Bowles, ML and Coates, G (1993) Image and substance: the management of performance as rhetoric or reality? Personnel Review, 22(2), pp 3-21.
4. Boyett, JH and Conn, HP (1995) Maximum Performance Management, Glenbridge Publishing, Oxford.
5. Daniels, AC (1987) What is PM? Performance Management, July, pp. 8-12.
6. Ellen Ernst Kossek, Richard N. Block, Managing Human Resources in the 21st century; South-Western College Publishing-Thomas Learning.
7. Erez, M (1997) Feedback: a necessary condition for the goal-setting performance relationship, Journal of Occupational Psychology, 62(5), pp 624-27.

8. Fletcher, C and Williams, R (1992) The route to Performance Management, Personnel Management, October, pp 42-47.
9. Flower, A (1990) Performance Management: The MBO of the 90's, Personnel Management, July pp 47-51.
10. Grint, K (1993) Whats wrong with Performance Appraisal? A critique and a Suggestion, Human Resource Management Journal, spring, pp 61-77.
11. Hartle, F (1995) Transforming the Performance Management Process, Kogan Page, London.
12. http://www.hr.ucsd.edu/~staffeducation/guide/
13. http://www.p-management.com/
14. IDS Study No. 626 (1997) Performance Management, May, Incomes Data Services, London.
15. IRS Management Review (1996) Performance Management, 1(1).
16. Lawson, P (1995) Performance management: an overview, in M Walters (ed), The Performance Handbook, Institute of Personnel and Development, London.
17. Michael Armstrong, Handbook of Human Resources Management Practice 7th Ed, Kogan Page.
18. Myers, DW (1992) Human Resources Management, 2nd Edition, Chicago: Commerce Clearing House.
19. Rogers Davis, "Choosing Performance Management: A Holistic Approach," CUPA Journal, Summer1995, v.46, No. 2,pp 13-18.
20. Williams, S (1991) Strategy and Objectives, in the Handbook of Performance Management, ed F Neale, Institute of Personnel Management, London.

24

Psychological Tests

1. ASUFA Inventory.
2. Brain Dominance Inventory.
3. Sentence Completion Test.
4. Achievement Motivation
5. General Aptitude Test Battery (GATB)

ASUFA Inventory

Objective

To test how individuals interpret events and to see how this relates to their thinking and behavior and to check the stability and variability of such behaviors.

Introduction

Attribution is the process through which we seek to identify the causes of others behavior and so gain knowledge of their stable traits and dispositions. Heider (1958) was the first to propose a psychological theory of attribution, but Weiner and colleagues developed a theoretical framework that has become a major research paradigm of social psychology. Heider discussed, what he called "naïve" or "commonsense" psychology. In his view, people are like amateur scientists, trying to understand other people's behavior by piecing together information until they arrived at a reasonable explanation or cause.

According to Heider, a person can make 2 attributions:

1. **Internal Attribution:** The inference that a person is behaving in a certain way, because of something about the person, such as attitude, character or personality.

2. **External Attribution:** The inference that a person is behaving a certain way, because of something about the situation he or she is in.

Our attributions are also significantly driven by our emotional and motivational drives. Blaming other people and avoiding personal recrimination are very real self-serving attributions. We will also make attributions to defend what we perceive as attacks. We will point to injustice in an unfair world. We will even tend to blame victims (of us and of others) for their fate as we seek to distance ourselves from thoughts of suffering the same plight. We will also tend to ascribe less variability to other people than ourselves, seeing ourselves as more multifaceted and less predictable than others. This may well be because we can see more of what is inside ourselves (and spend more time doing this).

Various methods have been employed in the measurement and categorization of attributions. Open- ended methods involve the researcher categorizing the oral replies of participants to open-ended questions. Derived score methods require the participant to rate his/ her reasons for. For example, a success or failure on 5- point scales for different elements related to the attribution dimensions. The direct method requires the participant to state his/ her reasons for the event and then map those reasons onto items referring to attribution dimensions.

Attribution theory has been used to explain the difference in motivation between high and low achievers. According to attribution theory, high achievers will approach rather than avoid tasks related to succeeding, because they believe success is due to high ability and effort, which they are confident of. Failure is thought to be caused by bad luck or a poor exam and is not their fault. Thus, failure doesn't affect their self-esteem but success builds pride and confidence. On the other hand, low achievers avoid success related chores because they tend to doubt their ability and / or assume success is related to luck or to other factors beyond their control. Thus, even when successful, it isn't as " whom you know" or to other factors beyond their control. Thus, even when successful, it isn't as rewarding to the low achievers because he/ she doesn't feel responsible, it doesn't increase his/ her pride and confidence.

Despite some uncertainty regarding the dimensions underlying people' unitary attributions, the evidence is clear concerning one point:

after failure, people generally underscore the importance of external causes, while after success, they tend to emphasize the causal impact of internal factor.

The competent persons not only want to have control over the outcome, they should take responsibility for their success or failure. In other words, they attribute the outcome to them selves- their activities and effort. This is called internal locus of control, or internality. Less competent persons attribute the outcome to external factors, called external locus of control, or externality.

Weiner (1974) has added a new dimension to the locus of control paradigm. He has suggested that the locus of control interacts with stability- variability. Internality can be perceived as related to either the stable (ability) or variable factor (luck or chance).

Although the relationships are not clear, we can summarize the effect of attribution as follows: persistence in achievement related activity is likely to be the result of (1) attribution of success to fixed internal (ability), fixed external (task difficulty and opportunity), and variable internal (effort) factors and (2) Attribution of failure to variable internal (effort) and variable external (luck or chance) factors.

We then get both locus of control and attribution of outcome as 2 important variables. If the feeling of internality is higher than that of externality, we may say that the locus of control will result in effectiveness. The term locus competence is defined as the potential effectiveness of the feeling that the causation of outcome is by internal or external factors, and is the ratio of internality or externality scores. Attributional competence is defined as the potential effectiveness of the tendency to attribute failure or success to fixed or variable factors, and is the ratio of variable or stable scores.

Reliability and Validity

Split- half reliability (N=20) was found significant at 0.01 level (0.56).

All variables of Asufa inventory were correlated with the scores on Rotters SRI (1954), indicating external locus of control for a group of 164.

It is worth noting that stables and variables for success and failure as well as their total, and their ratios had no correlation with locus of control. Except for the last 8 dimensions, all other coefficients of correlation were significant at .001 level except for luck in success at.01 level and task difficulty in failure at .004 level.

Description of the Test

Attribution of success and failure inventory assesses the respondents' attribution thinking- to what extent they attribute success and failure (internal or external, and stable and variable)

The inventory contains 12 items for success and 12 items for failure with 2 open ended questions. The respondents check each item by choosing one of the 2 alternatives given. Each of the 4 factors (ability, effort, opportunity and luck) has been paired with each other, thus producing 6 pairs, repeated twice and giving 12 items. The respondents also write down the factors to which they attribute their own success and failure.

Operational Definitions of Variables

1. **Internality/Internal Locus of Control:** It refers to the general orientation of people to attribute the outcomes to their activities and effort or lack of it.
2. **Externality/External Locus of Control:** It refers to the general orientation of people to attribute the outcomes to the external factors.
3. **Variability:** it refers to how a person varies while attributing the causes. Internal variability (effort), External variability (luck or chance).
4. **Stability:** It refers to how stable a person is while attributing the causes. Internal stability (ability); external stability (task difficulty or opportunity.

Materials and Apparatus

1. ASUFA inventory test booklet.
2. ASUFA inventory scoring sheet.
3. Stationery.

Sample

2 Employees.

Sample 1

AGE: 30 yrs.
SEX: Female.
DESIGNATION: Area Manager.

Designation: HR Manager

NAME OF THE ORGANIZATION: Sanofi-Aventis.

Sample 2

AGE: 35 yrs.
SEX: Female.
DESIGNATION: Area Manager.
NAME OF THE ORGANIZATION: Sanofi-Aventis.

Instructions

"Many factors contribute to the success or lack of success of people. Some of these are given below in pairs. Please tick, in each pair, the factor to which you think success can be attributed more. Although both factors may contribute to success or failure, which factor, in your opinion, contributes more than the other in each pair. There are no right or wrong answers, we are only interested in your personal opinion."

Procedure

The administrator arranged all the required materials and then called the employee 1 inside. Rapport was build to make the person feel comfortable. Explaining importance of the test reduced any kinds of fears. Then instructions were delivered. After assuring that the employee had understood the instructions, the test sheet and the answer sheet were given and the signal to start the test was given. After the employee finished responding to all the items, the questionnaire was taken away, even the answer sheet, and the test taker was thanked and asked to leave. Permission to get some time for scoring the test was taken, so that a detailed interpretation could be made available. The same procedure was repeated for the second employee too.

Scoring

Scoring sheet can be used to score the inventory. 8 scores are obtained (4 for success and 4 for failure) from which scores for internality and externality can be calculated. Finally, the locus competence index and the attributional competence index can be obtained.

The reasons mentioned in the 2 open- ended questions can also be classified under 4 factors, and comparisons can be made between these scores and those in the previous section.

Interpretation

Two employees were tested on this inventory (ASUFA), which basically checked onto one's internal / external and stable/ variable causes of attribution. Attribution is the process through which we seek to identify the causes of others behaviors and so gain knowledge of their stable traits and dispositions. When the scores fall in internal and stability block, the attribution is towards the ability. When it falls in external-stability block, it is attributed towards the task difficulty. When, in the internal-variable block, it is towards effort and lastly, when it in external-variable, it is attributed to luck.

The results for the first employee

	Internal	*External*	*Total*
Stability	5	9	14
Variability	3	0	3
Total	8	4	12

In the case of success, this employee scored 9 for stability and 3 for variability, which can be interpreted thus, that her attributing thoughts or behaviors for others are mostly stable and to a very small extent variable across different situations. Whereas her internal score was 8, and external score was 4, this again means that she attributes the cause of others success mostly to internal causes, like personal involvement, hard work, efforts etc and not to external causes like luck, bad climate, and no availability of opportunities.

	Internal	*External*	*Total*
Stability	5	1	6
Variability	4	2	6
Total	9	3	12

In case of failure, her stability score was 6, and variability score was also found to be 6, which means that they are equally balanced. She tends to be stable as well as she could vary in attributing failure as per situational demands. Her internal score was 9, whereas external score was 3. again, even here, it could be said that she attributes others failures also to internal causes as in the case of success attribution too.

	Internal	*External*	*Total*
Stability	10	5	15
Variability	7	2	9
Total	17	7	24

Overall, she scored 15 for internal attribution, 9 for external and 17 for stability and 7 for variability, which means that she tends to attribute both success and failure of others to internal factors and is mostly stable in her attribution.

Even, when told to state 5 factors to which she attributed her own success and failure, what was observed was that she held a very internal locus of control, attributing things to internal causes.

The results of the 2nd employee

	Internal	*External*	*Total*
Stability	4	3	7
Variability	3	2	5
Total	7	5	12

In case of success, she scored 7 for stability and 5 for variability, which can be interpreted thus, that her attributing behaviors or thoughts for others are mostly stable and to a very small extent variable across different situations. Whereas, her internal score was 7 and her external score was 5, this means that she attributes the causes of others success, mostly to internal causes and not to external causes.

	Internal	*External*	*Total*
Stability	4	3	7
Variability	5	0	5
Total	9	3	12

In case of failure, her stability score was 7 and variability score was 5, which means that she is mostly stable across situations, even in case of failure. Her internal score was 9 and external score 3, which would be interpreted thus, that she tends to attribute others failures also to internal causes itself.

	Internal	*External*	*Total*
Stability	8	6	14
Variability	8	2	10
Total	16	8	24

Overall. She scored 14 for stability, 10 for variability, 16 for internal and 8 for external. This means that she tends to attribute both success and failures of others to internal causes more and at the same time, she seems to be much more stable too, in her attribution behavior.

When told to state 5 factors for her own success and failure, she gave 3 internal causes, 1 external and 1 was left blank. Whereas, in case of failure, she was able to list down only 1 factor, which seemed internal to a large extent. That is, she holds an internal locus of control.

Conclusion

Thus, we can conclude by saying that both the employees more or less are internal in their attribution both for others and themselves, as well as tend to be stable across situations (just to give a round about conclusion).

Asufa Inventory

Name:

Date:

Organisation:

Role:

Many factors contribute to the success or lack of success of people. Some of these are given below in pairs. Please tick, in each pair, the factor to which you think success can be attributed more. Although both factors may contribute to success or failure, which factor, in your opinion, contributes more than the other in each pair.

There are no right or wrong answers; we are only interested in your personal opinion.

A. In your opinion, which of the two factors in each pair contributes more towards the success of a manager?

1. a Competence.
   b Hard work.
2. a Availability of opportunity.
   b Chance of getting a break.
3. a His/her effort.
   b Contacts with proper persons or sources.
4. a Good luck.
   b His/her involvement in the goal.
5. a Favorable opportunities.
   b Basic ability of the person.
6. a Ability to succeed.
   b Good luck.
7. a Technical knowledge.
   b Involvement in the task at hand.
8. a Favourable opportunities.
   b Chance of getting a break.
9. a His/her effort.
   b Favourable opportunities.
10. a Sudden favourable conditions like inheritance of money.
    b Hard work.
11. a Special government schemes.
    b His/her competence.
12 a Ability to take advantage or an opportunity.
   b Chance of getting a break.

b. In your opinion, which of the factors in each pair contributes more towards the failure of a person?

13 a. Lack of competence.
   b Lack of effort.
14. a Lack of proper contacts.
    b Unfortunate circumstances.

15. a Lack of Involvement in the goal.
    b Lack of available resources.
16. a Bad luck..
    b Neglecting the task.
17. a Unfavourable conditions.
    b Lack of ability.
18. a Lack of ability to calculate and act.
    b Not getting a break.
19. a Lack of technical knowledge.
    b Not giving enough time to the task.
20. a Unfavourable conditions.
    b Bad luck.
21. a Lack of effort.
    b Lack of proper contacts.
22. a Not getting a break.
    b Lack of effort.
23. a Lack of availability of resources.
    b Lack of ability to calculate and act.
24. a lack of competence.
    b Bad luck.

	Internal			*External*		
Stable	1a	11b	18a	2a	9b	17a
	5b	12a	19a	3b	11a	20a
	6a	13a	23b	5a	14a	21b
	7a	17b	24a	8a	15b	23a
Variable	1b	9a	16b	2b	10a	18b
	3a	10b	19b	4a	12b	20b
	4b	13b	21a	6b	14b	22a
	7b	15a	22b	8b	16a	24b

2. Brain Dominance Inventory

Objective

To test as to which part of an individual's brain is most dominant and active (right / left).

Introduction

We all have 2 hemispheres in our brain. in most human brains, the left hemisphere is specialized in what we consider linear, or logical, thinking. The right side is our non- logical, pattern making brain.

Most children are born right hemisphere dominant. This right side dominance is more useful as they shape events into patterns during their discovery of the world. Children at their earliest learning stages respond to familiar shapes, smells and sound- all strong right pattern associating behaviors. As they grow and the connection between the 2 hemispheres develops, they begin to demonstrate stronger cognitive skills as right hemisphere functions move to the left. During this period of transference and development, specific functions localize themselves within geographic areas. Children have much greater mental elasticity for movement between hemispheres if need be than do adults. As we age, our mental functions tend to become more localized into specific areas and re-locating them becomes increasingly difficult, if not impossible.

The right hemisphere is the source of our intuition, insight, metaphor, imagination and perhaps collective memory. Right mental processes are sensory involving more feelings as part of the processing. Its instantaneous processing does not allow time for separating distinctions. Right side experiences occur all at once, in complete detail, and do not seem to be bound by time and space.

This hemisphere is heavily involved in the creative process. The right brain provides us pattern-generating and shaping activity and searches for new or richer meaning. It must be stimulated in the first stages of the creative process.

Playfulness is a characteristic of the right brain. it is also a characteristic we identified with highly creative people which described the elements of creativity. Playing stimulates the right side and enables the mind to see new patterns in the familiar, or new opportunities where before none existed. Original thoughts and ideas are formed when the mind of creative discovery and imagination is so engaged.

Rather than wasted time, play and even idleness is often very beneficial behavior. Nearly, everyone has experienced those moments when a calm, relaxed, unfocused mind seems to effortlessly solve problems, generate ideas, or deal with complex situation. Once we have experienced this right hemisphere's creative flowing, we are strongly interested in discovered ways to recreate the event.

Left hemisphere processes are much slower. Left thinking is often seemingly devoid of emotion and is associated with more dissociated or objective process. Left sided thinking is more rational. Here also, is the source of operations that deals with language, sequence, and organization. The left side also perceives the temporal distinctions of past and future. It can create abstractions and is deeply involved in the process of finding the facts.

The left side often relies heavily on the process of intelligence. Consider intellect as directly in contrast with creativity. Whereas intellect reduces to the specific, creative process expand into larger referential contexts. It is this isolating nature of intellect that results in its not always functioning in the best interest of the whole.

Over reliance on the left side thinking can actually produce physical and mental discomfort, because it is failing to acknowledge the value of other sensory data in disagreement with the analytical left. Balancing right hemisphere creative thinking into the process promotes a sense of greater well being through its acknowledgement of broader considerations and long-term emphasis.

Research on the processes of bicameral functioning has revealed that 2 hemispheres actually have 2 different experiences of the same events. Both sides use complex processes for thinking and problem solving. The verbal left demonstrates reductionistic, analytical, critical thinking and the spatial right makes use of metaphorical, generative, big picture thinking. It is the nature of these 2 hemispheres to work in contradictory ways, resulting in the thinker being of 2 minds on an issue.

Women, who tend to synthesize their thinking across a broad range of the brain, often utilize both brain sides when thinking and participating in activities. Men, conversely, tend to isolate functions and activities into smaller areas of the individual hemispheres. Women's brains are more compartmentalized. It is these different mental processes that, in part, explain why the sexes think and perceive differently.

When both sides of the mind become constructively engaged in the thinking, we refer to the process as the whole brain thinking. It is not a subject most of us have much experience in practicing.

Maximizing our creativity comes from the ability to move from left to right dominance when the need arises. This ability is not normally a routine practice of most people, and success requires specific cross-training skills and some practice. Initially, these techniques may seem difficult or unusual but with experience and time you will discover that your thinking approach is beginning to change and you are finding more creative ideas, faster and with greater predictability.

Description of the Test

BDI is a broad guideline test.

Materials and Apparatus

1. BDI questionnaire
2. BDI answer sheet
3. BDI scoring sheet
4. Stationery

Sample

2 Employees.

Employee 1

AGE: 25yrs.

SEX: Male.

DESIGNATION: field executive of a Pharma Company.

Employee 2

AGE: 29 yrs

SEX: Male

DESIGNATION: Field Executive of a Pharma Company.

Instructions

"For each of the items below, circle the letter of the alternative that sounds most like you. These are "forced- choice" questions: you must choose one of them in order for the inventory to be meaningful to you, even if it's a matter of choosing the one that is least unlike you. Complete the inventory quickly- your first response is likely to be the truest of you as you are, not as you would like to be".

Procedure

The administrator arranged all the required materials and then called the employee 1 inside. Rapport was build to make the person feel comfortable. Explaining importance of the test reduced any kinds of fears. Then instructions were delivered. After assuring that the employee had understood the instructions, the test sheet and the answer sheet were given and the signal to start the test was given. After the employee finished responding to all the items, the test questionnaire was taken away, even the answer sheet and the test taker was thanked and asked to leave. Permission to get some time for scoring the test was taken, so that a detailed interpretation could be made available.

The same procedure was repeated for the second employee too.

Scoring

There is a scoring key for the inventory. Each response, either comes under right or left hemisphere. The total for each side should be added up.

If the total for either one of the sides is 15 or more, then that side would be dominant.

If the score for both side ranges from 11 – 15, then it is described as a balanced brain.

Interpretation

Two employees were tested on the BDI Inventory. BDI is a broad guideline test, which basically tests as to which hemisphere (right/ left) of a person's brain is dominant.

The first employee scored 13 in left hemisphere, whereas 12 in the right hemisphere. What the scores suggest is that this person has a balanced brain, which basically meant that both of his hemispheres are equally active and dominant.

He makes use of both the parts of his brain in a more or less equal proportion.

When both sides of a person's brain are equally active, it is called whole brain functioning, which is not found with many people. People falling in this category are thus called "special ones".

The second employee scored 15 for left hemisphere and 10 for right hemisphere; this shows that he is a person who uses the left side of his brain more often.

He is a more practical and logical person who is good at technical work but not so flexible when it comes to languages or creativity

Thus, we can conclude by saying that, basically, one of the employee falls in the special category. The first employee scored 12 in left and 13 in right. Whereas, the second employee scored 15 in left and 10 in right. Thus one has whole brain functioning and the other is left-brain dominant

BDI

Directions: For each of the items below; circle the letter of the alternative that sounds most like you. These arc "forced- choice" questions; you must choose one of them in order for the inventory to be meaningful to you, even if it's a matter of choosing the one that's least unlike you. Complete the inventory quickly, your first response is likely to be the truest of you as you are, not as you would like to be.

I. (a) I tend to worry about getting things right. I feel tense and nervous more often than most people.

(b) I'm relaxed and easygoing. I give it my best shot and then let the chips fall where they may. I tend to roll with the punches.

2. (a) My mood swings fairly enough-sometimes I'm up, sometimes I'm down- and I can really feel the difference.

(b) I'm fairly even-tempered; rarely do I feel any really intense emotion. I'm on an even keel just about all the time.

3. (a) In listening to music, I find that the melody itself, the time, is what catches my attention.

(b) When I listen to music, I find myself responding immediately to the beat.

4. (a) When I am learning something that's new to me, I first want to research the topic, usually by doing some reading and / or hearing an authority lecture on it.

(b) When Im faced with learning something new, I try some way to plunge right into it, like a field trip workshop or apprenticeship.

5. (a) If I were a math major, I would excel in geometry.

(b) Algebra would be my forte, if I were a math major.

6. (a) In high school(or college) science, I most enjoyed chemistry.

(b) I enjoyed Physics best, out of all my high school (college) science courses.

7 (a) I would rather play scrabble.

(b) I'd rather play checkers.

8. (a) I buy things on impulse, even when I know i shouldn't. If I see something that's "me" or if it speaks to me, I usually have to have it..

(b) I'm a deliberate shopper. I decide what I want before ! go looking for it—I don't just shop for the sake of shopping. Sometimes I deliberate for so long that what I want is gone by the time I go to buy it. I often talk myself out of things I might have an impulse to buy.

9. (a) I am often sure of my choice and use of words.

(b) I rarely feel awkward about my grammar and sentence construction.

10. (a) When I learn something new, I flounder around until suddenly a light goes off and I "get it ". Understanding floods in all at once, as though a door had been opened, or a curtain lifted.

(b) When I learn something new, I begin at the beginning and do my best to 'proceed sequentially from task to task. Understanding dawns slowly and methodically until I feel I have mastered the new procedure or concept.

11. (a) If I had a choice, I would be more entertained by a crossword puzzle than by a jigsaw puzzle..

(b) I would enjoy myself more if I were working on a jigsaw puzzle, as opposed to a crossword puzzle.

12. (a) I frequently have hunches.

(b) I think through things methodically

13. (a) I'd prefer to read a book to seeing a movie.

(b) I would choose to see a movie, rather than to read a book.

14. (a) I often have trouble putting my feelings and opinions into words; it's difficult sometimes to say what I really mean.

(b) I am relatively adept at expressing my feeîings and opinions; rarely do I have trouble saying exactly what I mean.

15. (a) When I have to parallel park. I usually get it right the first time.

(b) I usually have to pull out at least once and try it again when I try to parallel park.

16. (a) When I'm planning a trip and someone is giving me directions I prefer to have them written out listing the route numbers and street names, the left and right turnoffs and various landmarks in order.

    (b) I prefer to have a map drawn for me, or to be shown the route on a map when I'm figuring out how to get to where I want to go.

17. (a) When I'm faced with a problem situation, my mind tends to skip around a lot, free associating, remembering and imagining a lot of "what-ifs" until I suddenly have an "aha.".

    (b) I rarely have hunches.

18. (a) I select fabrics with a lot of texture to them, like silk, coudroy, woolen tweeds and linens when I choose clothing.

    (b) I choose relatively understated fabrics, such as simple cottons and wool gabardines.

19. (a) I think mostly about what's appropriate to the environment when I choose clothing.

    (b) I choose clothing, which expresses my identity, and then feel comfortable wearing it just about anywhere.

20. (a) I remember faces very well.

    (b) I don't remember faces well-a lot of people look vaguely familiar to me but if I've only seen someone once or twice, I won't remember them exactly.

21. (a) I'm terrible on names—I recognize faces easily but can't recall the names that go with them.

    (b) I remember people's names well.

22. (a) I believe that there arc events, which have occurred, and phenomena, which exist in our world which none of the sciences, will ever explain.

    (b) I believe that there is a natural law, which governs every event or phenomenon. and that science will therefore eventually be able to explain those things, which now appear to be mysterious.

23. (a) If I were a graduate student, I would succeed better in a traditional MBA program.

    (b) If I were a graduate student, I would succeed better in an MS in Human Resources Development program.

24. (a) I prefer to read biographies and histories, books about people who actually existed and events that actually occurred.

    (b) I prefer reading fantasy and science fiction, novels and short stories.

25. (a) I am or have been at some point in my life, a better-than-average athlete in some sport or activity.

    (b) I've always been less than competent in sports and athletics. BDI Answer sheet

Of the two answers to each question, one is more likely to be chosen by a person whose left-brain functioning is dominant, and the other by a person whose right brain functioning is dominant. Check your answers against the BDI Answer key and then add up your total number of L and R responses (check BDI Manual).

3. Sentence Completion Test

Objective

To check the ACHIEVEMENT MOTIVATION of individuals through SENTENCE COMPLETION TEST.

Introduction

Achievement motivation, extraversion- introversion and neuroticism are now accepted as some of the important dimensions of Personality. Assessment of these personality dimensions for theoretical and practical purposes will be more meaningful if the relationships among them are known.

Although Murray postulated the concept of achievement motivation, Mc Clelland and Atkinson studied it extensively using projective measures similar to TAT. Achievement motivation, usually termed as n-Ach, implies working with zeal in competitive situations with a view to do something constructive and of greater significance. It shows itself in a wide variety of behaviour. Extraversion and neuroticism have been regarded as important aspects of personality since long. Eysenck differs from Freudians and most of the American psychologists and considers extraversion-introversion and neuroticism as two different and independent factors in personality. He regards extraversion and introversion as objective and subjective directions respectively of an individual's attitude and neuroticism as marked by lack of adjustment, with one's environment.

Raphelson and Kausler and Trapp found a significant negative correlation between n-Ach based on fantasy measures and Taylor's Manifest Anxiety Scale (M A S). Since the latter correlates highly with the neuroticism scale of Maudsley Personality Inventory B (M P I) as shown by Bendig, it was inferred that achievement motivation correlates negatively with neuroticism. A similar indication came from the study of Mukherjee and Sinha with Indian sample using Mukherjee's Forced Choice Test verbalized achievement motivation.

The inferences regarding relationships between achievement motivation and neuroticism in the studies cited above were indirect. However, they lead the present authors to hypothesize that verbalized need for achievement (v Ach) as measured by Mukherjee's Sentence Completion Test (S C T) correlates negatively with neuroticism as measured by Shanta Kumari. She found no correlation between v Ach and extraversion and neuroticism. However, her results could not be taken as final as she used the short form of MPI consisting of only 12 items. This study, which was intended to test the above hypothesis, used the original version of MPI and preferred the forced-choice measure of verbalized achievement motivation (v Ach) to the projective measures used by Mc Clelland. Atkinson and others for the simple reason that the need for achievement must be measured by projective method alone which is somewhat subjective and difficult to interpret, since a person is quite conscious of the need for achievement, if he has any.

Reliability and Validity

The test has a Kuder Richardson and test-retest reliability of.71 and.75 respectively. The validity studies of SCT have obtained quite promsing results.

Materials and Apparatus

1. B.N.Mukherjee's forced-choice test of achievement motivation known as Sentence Completion Test (SCT).

2. Stationery
3. Answer sheet
4. Scoring key

Sample

2 employees.

Employee 1

SEX: Female
AGE: 28 Yrs

Employee 2

SEX: Female
AGE: 22

Instructions

"On the following pages are a number of partly completed sentences. Each can be completed meaningfully if you link it up with any of the alternatives offered. Each of the three answers is equally good to make the incomplete sentences meaningful and complete. As this is neither a test of your intelligence nor your proficiency in the use of English, there is no question of a right or wrong answer. You are to select only two answers, one of which should correspond most and the other correspond least with your present likings and attitudes. Look at the example:

I like to———————— A. keep things neat and orderly
B. do things for my friends
C. undertake tasks requiring skill

Which of these answers is more characteristic of what you like? If you like " keeping things neat and orderly" more than the other two activities, then you should put a circle around the letter A on the answer sheet.

The sentences on the following pages are similar to the example given above. On the answer sheet are numbers corresponding to the numbers of the different sentences. Each number is followed by the letters A, B, C. Draw a circle around the letter on the answer sheet which indicates the answer that corresponds most with your characteristics. Put a cross for an answer that is least characteristic of you.

Please note that your answers should be in terms of what you actually like or feel at the present time and not in terms of what you think you should feel.

You are required to answer all the items. Do not skip any thing. Answer as quickly as you can. Please don't put any mark on the test booklet.

Procedure

The test administrator arranged all the required materials and then asked the first employee to walk in.The first part of the session started with rapport building, wherein the employee was made to feel comfortable and relaxed. She was made to understand that this test would help them to know their achievement motivation level. Then the employee1 was given the required material, and then the instructions were delivered. Then this individual was told to start on with the test.When she finished with the test the answer sheet was taken away and after some moments the results were conveyed to her after the administrator had scored them.

The same procedure was repeated for the second employee.

Scoring

For every correct response, the score is 1.It is to match with the scoring key.

Total score is equal to the number of correct alternatives chosen as per the scoring key.

Interpretation

This test basically tested an individual's achievement motivation level. Two employees were tested on this scale.The results obtained were as follows.

Employee1 was a female, aged 28 years. She was a medical representative and is one of the best so she was really enthustiatic about the test. Her overall score came to about 27, which simply shows that she has a very strong drive or motivation for achievement. When reviewing her responses on the test book let individually, one of the observations that was made is that she mostly likes difficult tasks, wants to accomplish all by herself, wants to be famous by doing something that is very significant. At the same time, she even tends to care about those who are in any kind of trouble. Thus we can say that she is highly achievement motivated.

The n-ach person is 'achievement motivated' and therefore seeks achievement, attainment of realistic but challenging goals, and advancement in the job. There is a strong need for feedback as to achievement and progress, and a need for a sense of accomplishment.

The second employee was a female, aged 22 years, who possessed a bachelor's degree in commerce. Her score was 10, which simply means that she is not so strongly motivated to be achievement oriented. While reviewing her responses, individually from her test booklet, what was observed basically was that she lacks too much of achievement motivation, but anyways, she shows a strong desire to earn a lot. She seems to be having high aims and desires but at the same time, she is down to earth. She has his own limits set, which is basically stopping him from being a high achiever. She is at times very bold, wants to do difficult tasks, but at other times, she is very scared, doesn't really want to fall into unwanted troubles.

Conclusion

Thus, we can see that one of the employees has scored 27, whereas the other scored 10, so we can say that one has a strong drive for achievement, and the other a less drive.

4. Motivation Questionnaire

Objective

The objective is to measure motivation (achievement, affiliation, power) using M Questionnaire.

Introduction

American David Clarence McClelland (1917-98) achieved his doctorate in psychology at Yale in 1941 and became professor at Wesleyan University. He then taught and lectured, including a spell at Harvard from 1956, where with colleagues for twenty years he studied particularly motivation and the achievement need. He began his McBer consultancy in 1963, helping industry assess and train staff, and later taught at Boston University, from 1987 until his death. McClelland is chiefly known for his work on achievement motivation, but his research interests extended to personality and consciousness. David McClelland pioneered workplace motivational thinking, developing achievement-based motivational theory and models, and promoted improvements in employee assessment methods, advocating competency-based assessments and tests, arguing them to be better than traditional IQ and personality-based tests. His ideas have since been widely adopted in many organisations, and relate closely to the theory of Frederick Herzberg.

David McClelland is most noted for describing three types of motivational need, which he identified in his 1988 book, Human Motivation:

- Achievement motivation (n-ach)
- Authority/power motivation (n-pow)
- Affiliation motivation (n-affil)

David Mcclelland's Needs-based Motivational Model

These needs are found to varying degrees in all workers and managers, and this mix of motivational needs characterizes a person's or manager's style and behaviour, both in terms of being motivated, and in the management and motivation of others.

Need for Achievement (n-ach)

The n-ach person is 'achievement motivated' and therefore seeks achievement, attainment of realistic but challenging goals, and advancement in the job. There is a strong need for achievement and progress, and a need for a sense of accomplishment.

Need for Authority and Power (n-pow)

The n-pow person is 'authority motivated'. This driver produces a need to be influential, effective and to make an impact. There is a strong need to lead and for their ideas to prevail. There is also motivation and need towards increasing personal status and prestige.

Need for Affiliation (n-affil)

The n-affil person is 'affiliation motivated', and has a need for friendly relationships and is motivated towards interaction with other people. The affiliation driver produces motivation and need to be liked and held in popular regard. These people are team players.

McClelland said that most people possess and exhibit a combination of these characteristics. Some people exhibit a strong bias to a particular motivational need, and this motivational or needs 'mix' consequently affects their behaviour and working/managing style. Mcclelland suggested that a strong n-affil 'affiliation-motivation' undermines a manager's objectivity, because of their need to be liked, and that this affects a manager's decision-making capability. A strong n-pow 'authority-motivation' will produce a determined work ethic and commitment to the organisation, and while n-pow people are attracted to the leadership role, they may not possess the required flexibility and people-centred skills. McClelland argues that n-ach people with strong 'achievement motivation' make the best leaders, although there can be a tendency to demand too much of their staff in the belief that they are all similarly and *highly* achievement-focused and results driven, which of course most people are not.

McClelland's particular fascination was for achievement motivation, and this laboratory experiment illustrates one aspect of his theory about the effect of achievement on people's motivation. McClelland asserted via this experiment that while most people do not possess a strong achievement-based motivation, those who do, display a consistent behaviour in setting goals:

Volunteers were asked to throw rings over pegs rather like the fairground game; no distance was stipulated, and most people seemed to throw from arbitrary, random distances, sometimes close, sometimes farther away. However a small group of volunteers, whom McClelland suggested were:

strongly achievement-motivated, took some care to measure and test distances to produce an ideal challenge - not too easy, and not impossible. Interestingly a parallel exists in biology, known as the 'overload principle', which is commonly applied to fitness and exercising, ie., in order to develop fitness and/or strength, the exercise must be sufficiently demanding to increase existing levels, but not so demanding as to cause damage or strain. McClelland identified the same need for a 'balanced challenge' in the approach of achievement-motivated people.

McClelland contrasted achievement-motivated people with gamblers, and dispelled a common pre-conception that n-ach 'achievement-motivated' people are big risk takers. On the contrary - typically, achievement-motivated individuals set goals which they can influence with their effort and ability, and as such the goal is considered to be achievable. This determined results-driven approach is almost invariably present in the character make-up of all successful business people and entrepreneurs.

McClelland suggested other characteristics and attitudes of achievement-motivated people:

- Achievement is more important than material or financial reward.
- Achieving the aim or task gives greater personal satisfaction than receiving praise or recognition.
- Financial reward is regarded as a measurement of success, not an end in itself.
- Security is not prime motivator, nor is status.
- Feedback is essential, because it enables measurement of succcss, not for reasons of praise or recognition (the implication here is that feedback must be reliable, quantifiable and factual).
- Achievement-motivated people constantly seek improvements and ways of doing things better.
- Achievement-motivated people will logically favour jobs and responsibilities that naturally satisfy their needs, offer flexibility and opportunity to set and achieve goals, eg., sales and business management, and entrepreneurial roles.

McClelland firmly believed that achievement-motivated people are generally the ones who make things happen and get results, and that this extends to getting results through the organisation of other people and resources, although as stated earlier, they often demand too much of their staff because they prioritise achieving the goal above the many varied interests and needs of their people.

Interesting comparisons and relationships can be drawn between McClelland's motivation types, and the characteristics defined in other behavioural models:

Materials and Apparatus

1. Motivation questionnaire
2. Motivation scoring key
3. Stationery

Sample

2 employees.

AGE: 30 YRS

SEX: FEMALE

DESIGNATION: HR Manager at a Pharmaceuticals.

AGE: 22 YRS.

SEX: FEMALE.

DESIGNATION: Intern.

Instructions

"Based on the work of David McClelland, this exercise helps you to find out what are the drives in your motivation. It is important to give honest answers to the questions, if you want an honest assessment."

Procedure

The test administrator arranged all the required materials and then called the second test taker, cause the first test taker was the test administrator herself. First, rapport was established and then instructions for the test were delivered. After assuring that the instructions were clearly understood, the questionnaire was given to the employee, and she was signaled to start responding to the test. After the completion of the test, the questionnaire was taken away and the employee was thanked and escorted. The administrator asked for some time so that the test could be scored and thus interpretation could be made ready.

Scoring

1. The points given by the individual for the statement in each group A, B, C, D, E, F, G, H are to be considered.
2. Classify the statements into 3 motives.
3. Points for the statements for each of these motives are to be added, that is the total score for that motive.
4. Draw a bar diagram for 3 scores, x- axis will show motive and y axis will represent the score.
5. Achievement score should be more, which shows achievement motivation. In executives, power score is generally more as

compared to supervisors. Supervisors or middle level managers have a high score on affiliation.

Interpretation

Two subjects were tested on this motivation inventory. It basically checked 3 kinds of motivation drives (achievement, affiliation and power).

The first subject scored 28 in achievement motivation; 22 in affiliation motivation and 17 in power. The interpretation that follows is obvious, as it can be seen from the scores itself. This person has a strong drive for achievement, secondly for affiliation and thirdly for power. For power the drive is low.

The n-ach person is 'achievement motivated' and therefore seeks achievement, attainment of realistic but challenging goals, and advancement in the job. There is a strong need for feedback as to achievement and progress, and a need for a sense of accomplishment.

The second subject scored 36 in achievement motivation; 15 in affiliation motivation and 14 in power. The interpretation that follows is obvious, as it can be seen from the scores itself. This person has an extremely strong drive for achievement, secondly for affiliation which is quite low and thirdly for power which is lowest. For power the drive is very weak.

The n-affil person is 'affiliation motivated', and has a need for friendly relationships and is motivated towards interaction with other people. The affiliation driver produces motivation and need to be liked and held in popular regard. These people are team players.

The n-pow person is 'authority motivated'. This driver produces a need to be influential, effective and to make an impact. There is a strong need to lead and for their ideas to prevail. There is also motivation and need towards increasing personal status and prestige.

Conculsion

It can be seen that employee-1 is on the right track with regards to her career and need for achievement, affiliation and power. Employee-2 however is a little to the extreme, having a very high need for achievement and extremely low for achievement and power. This could be because she is at the beginning of her career and has a strong desire to achieve. She should try to work on her relationship with others as without the help of others achieving becomes more difficult.

M Questionnaire

Based on the work of David McClelland, this exercise helps you to find out what the drives in your motivation are. It is important to give honest answers to the questions if you want an honest assessment.

Directions

This questionnaire is designed to discover the kind of work you enjoy, in terms of demands and pressures on you, and these affect your performance and satisfaction.

Answer these questions in terms of what you actually do or feel. Please be as frank as you can.This questionnaire will be of little or no value unless you provide a truly accurate description of yourself.

Below are given 8 groups of 4 statements. For each group of statements you are asked to distribute 10 points among 4 possible responses, giving most points to the response most characteristic of you and the least points to the response least characteristic. If a response is not at all characteristic of you, you may give it no points.

A

1. I enjoy practicing and improving my skills.
2. I really enjoy helping other people.
3. An important aspect of any job is the status involved.
4. I like it when one can see a job from its inception through its completion.

B

5. In my work I like to have to interact with a lot of other people.
6. I like to get a real sense of pride from my work.
7. I like to supervise a large number of people.
8. I like jobs that keep one working every minute.

C

9. I enjoy taking the time to talk, and joke with other people.
10. I enjoy jobs which offer a lot of opportunity for creativity and innovation.

11. I like spending time telling people what has to be done.
12. I don't mind jobs where; there is a heavy volume of work.

D.

13. I like to spend most of my time sitting in one place.
14. I like jobs which require a good deal of co-operation from others.
15. I like to make sure that things run smoothly.
16. I like jobs where the quality of output is essential, where it has to be excellent.

E.

17. I like other people to come to me for decisions.
18. I enjoy meeting often with my boss.
19. I enjoy jobs which give a person a chance to really achieve something.
20. One of the most important aspects of my life is to keep other people happy.

F

21. In my work I like to set my standards pretty high.
22. I enjoy jobs(assignments) where you get to know other people really well.
23. I enjoy work where mistakes can be extremely costly.
24. I enjoy spending most of my time managing people.

G.

25. I enjoy meeting often with my subordinates.
26. I enjoy working almost exclusively by myself.
27. I like to sympathize with other people's problems.
28. I am interested in jobs which are a big help in furthering my career.

H.

29. I like to see the end results of my work.
30. I enjoy jobs which are clear cut and well defined.
31. I enjoy being frequently in contact with other people.
32. I enjoy jobs where I have to use my ability to influence others.

5. General Aptitude Test Battery (GATB)

Introduction

GATB was developed by the United States 1970, Employment Service, has been used primarily for employment counselling in government employment offices and for vocational rehabilitation counselling. GATB has come to be recognized as the best validated multiple test battery in existence for use in vocational guidance. There are two forms of this test A&B, different answer sheets, scoring stencil and aptitude score conversion tables have been developed for each form. The nine aptitude measured by GATB are as follows:

1. Aptitude G: Intelligence

It is the general learning ability, the ability to catch on or understand instructions and underline principles, the ability to reason and make judgements; closely related to doing well in school. Parts 3,4,6 measure it. i.e. space, vocabulary and arithmetic reasoning.

2. Aptitude V: Verbal Aptitude

It is the ability to understand meaning of words and to use them effectively. The ability to comprehend languages to understand meaning of whole sentences and paragraphs, measured by part 4-vocabulary.

3. Numerical Aptitude

It is the ability to perform arithmetic operations quickly and accurately measured by parts 2 & 6, computation & arithmetic reasoning.

4. Aptitude S: Spatial Aptitude

It is the ability to think visually of geometric forms and to comprehend the 2 dimensional representations of 3 dimensional objects. It is the ability to recognize the relationships resulting from the movement of objects in space, measured by part 3.3 dimensional space reasoning.

5. Aptitude P: Form Perception

It is the ability to perceive parturient detail in objects or in pictorial or graphic material. It is the ability to make visual perception, comparison and discrimination & see slight differences in shapes and shadings of figures widths and lengths of lines, measured by part 5 & 7, tool matching & form matching.

6. Aptitude Q: Clerical Perception

It is the ability to perceive pertinent details in verbal or tabular material. It is also the ability to observe differences in copy, to read words and numbers & to avoid perceptual errors in arithmetic computation. It is measured by part 1, name comparison.

7. Aptitude K: Motor Coordination

It is the ability to co-ordinate eyes and hands or fingers rapidly and accurately in making precise movements with speed. Ability to make movement response accurately & swiftly, measured by part 8, mark making.

8. Aptitude F: Finger Dexterity

It is the ability to move the fingers, rapidly or accurately, measured by part 11 & 12, assembly & disassembles.

9. Aptitude M: Manual Dexterity

It is the ability to move hands easily & skillfully. Ability to work with the hands in pairing and turning motions, measured by parts 9 & 10, place & turn.

Description

Part 1: Name Comparison

This test consists of 2 columns of names. The subject inspects each pair of names, one in each column, and indicates whether the names are the same or different. It measures clerical perception.

Part 2: Computation

This sub-test consists of arithmetic exercises, requiring the addition, subtraction, multiplication or division. It measures numerical aptitude.

Part 3: Three Dimensional Space

It consists of a series of exercises containing a stimulus figure and four drawings of a 3 dimensional object. The stimulus figure is pictured as a flat piece of metal, which is to be either bent or rolled, or both. Lines indicate where it is to be bent or rolled. The examinee has to indicate which one of the 4 drawings can be made of the stimulus figure. This test measures intelligence & spatial aptitude.

Part 4: Vocabulary

It consists of a set of 4 words. The examinee indicates which 2 words have the same or opposite meaning. It measures intelligence & verbal aptitude.

Part 5: Tool Making

It consists of a series of exercises containing a stimulus drawing and 4 black & white drawings of simple shop tools. The examinee indicates which of the 4 drawings is the same as the stimulus drawing. It measures form perception.

Part 6: Arithmetic Reasoning

It consists of arithmetic problems expressed verbally. It measures intelligence & numerical aptitude.

Part 7: Form Matching

It consists of 2 groups of drawings of variously shaped lines. Examinee indicates which figure in the second group is exactly the same size & shape as each figure in the stimulus group. It measures form perception.

Part 8: Mark Making

It consists of a series of squares in which the examinee is to make 3 pencil marks, working as rapidly as possible. The marks to be made are short lines, 2nd vertical & 3rd horizontal, beneath them. It measures motor co-ordinatio

Part 9: Place

The equipment used for this test consists of a rectangular pegboard divided into 2 sections, each section containing 48 holes. The upper section contains 48 cylindrical pegs. The examinee removes the pegs from the holes in the upper part of the board and inserts them in the corresponding holes in the lower part of the board. This performance is done 3 times. It measures manual dexterity.

Part 10: Turn

The equipment used in test 9 is also used here. The examinee removes the wooden peg from a hole, turns the peg area, so that the opposite end is up & returns the peg to the same hole. 3 trials are given for this performance. It also measures manual dexterity.

Part 11: Assembly

The equipment consists of a small rectangle board containing 56 holes and small metal rivets & washers. Examinee takes the small metal rivet from a hole in the upper part of the board with his/her preformed hand and at the same time removes a small metal washer from a vertical rod with the other Land; he/she puts the washer on the rivets & inserts the assembled piece into the corresponding hole in the lower part of the board using only his performed Land. It measures finger dexterity.

Part 12: Disassemble

Same equipment is used in which the examinee removes the small metal rivet of the assembly from a hole in the lower part of the board, slides the washer on the rod with one hand & rivet into the corresponding hole in the upper part of the board with the other hand. It also measures finger dexterity.

Norms

All parts of GATB had been administered to the 4,000 people, used in final sample of 8,000. The mean age of the standard sample was 30.4 years; only workers of 18 to 54 years of age were considered when the occupational composition of the base population was determined.

The fact that, men tend to score higher on spatial aptitude & lower on clerical perception compared to women, makes it necessary to give attention to the women, makes it necessary to give attention to the problem of stratification of the population on the basis of sex difference.

Conversion norms are provided for a total sample of 585 high school & junior college students tested in 3 different states.

Reliability

Studies were conducted with samples of high school, college 4 adult population; the test-retest reliability with the intervals ranging from one day to 3 years, coefficients found for most of the aptitudes were in the range of 80 to 90.

Validity

In the test development studies, the data collection yield measures predictive of GATB. Research is conducted on a decentralized basis with colleges, schools etc.

Scoring

For each of the 7 parts there are separate scoring keys. Test can be machine scored or hand scored. For every right answer, score of one is given. These scores are then converted according to the table, which is appropriate according to the form.

There are 7 aptitudes measured: -

- Clerical perception (Aptitude Q) (Part I)
- General Intelligence (Aptitude G) (Part II, III, VI)
- Spatial Intelligence (Aptitude S) (Part III)
- Verbal Intelligence (Aptitude V) (Part IV)
- Numerical Intelligence (Aptitude N) with part II, (Part VI)
- Form perception (Aptitude P) part VII & V.
- Motor Co-ordination, part VIII.

Interpretation

The scores on each aptitude are converted using tables (check manual).

The best combination found in manual for professions was – General (125), Spatial (115), Numerical (115), leaving the options of – Electrical, Mechanical, Civil, Automotive, Chemical Engineer, Surgeon, General Practitioner, System Analyst, Public – Health Service Officer etc.

References and Further Reading

1. Aronson, E., Wilson, T.D. and Akert, R.M. (2003). Social Psychology, Upper Saddle River, NJ: Prentice Hall.
2. Aswathappa K. (2002). Human Resource and Personnel Management (3n:1 ed), New Delhi: Tata McGraw-Hill Publishing Company Limited, 32-33.
3. Brain Dominance Inventory (BDI) Manual.
4. Davis K; Newstrom, J.W.(1998). Organizational Behavior. Human Behavior at Work (10th ed). New Delhi: Tata McGraw-Hill Edition,101-103,430-434, 442.
5. Jones, E. E., D. E. Kannouse, H. H. Kelley, R E. Nisbett, S. Valins, and B. Weiner, Eds. (1972). Attribution: Perceiving the Causes of Behavior. Morristown, NJ: General Learning Press.
6. Luthans F.(2002). Organizational Behavior (9th ed). NewDelhi: Mc Graw-Hill International Edition, 122-124,397-399,411-414.

7. Mamoria C.B; Gankar S.V. (2001). Personnel Management. Mumbai: Himalaya Publishing House, 316-347.
8. Pareek, Udai (1997). Training instruments for HRD. New Delhi: Tata McGraw Hill Publication. 123-129.
9. Robbins S.P. (2003). Organisational Behavior. New Delhi: Prentice Hall Inc.,524-525, 582-586.
10. Schuler, H. / Thornton, G.C. / Frintrup, A. / Mueller-Hanson, R,,Test manuals,2002,US
11. Weiner, B. (1986). An attributional theory of motivation and emotion. New York: Sprinper-Verlag.]

25

Organizational Tests

1. Job Design Survey
2. Lead
3. Motivational Analysis Of Behaviour
4. Learning Style
5. Organizational Role Stress
6. Prabhu's Stress Profile
7. Role Efficacy
8. Team Building
9. Conflict Management
10. Counseling Style Inventory
11. Behaviorally Anchored Rating Scale

1. Job Design Survey

Introduction

Most people who work for a living spend a significant amount of their waking hours at the workplace executing the requirements, duties and functions of their job. Their satisfactions and dissatisfactions at work are usually carried over to the home as well (Near, Rice and Hunt, 1980; Sekaran, 1986). Our satisfactions at work thus contribute significantly to the overall quality of our experienced lives. How people react to work is a function of the "fit" or match among: (1) one's own personality predispositions and individual characteristics such as need patterns, tolerance for ambiguity, locus of control, work ethic values, abilities and skills; (2) characteristic of the job, such as, the amount of challenge it offers, the extent of autonomy one has in doing the job, the extent of skills used in performing the job, and the like; and (3) characteristics of the facilitating structures at the workplace such as appropriate work layout, reward systems, the extent to which training facilities are offered, and to what extent innovative risk-taking efforts of employees are encouraged and rewarded. If there is a good fit among these three sets of variables, favorable outcomes can be expected to accrue to the employees as well as to the organization. The employees will experience high levels of job involvement (as contrasted to job alienation), sense of competence (feeling of confidence in one's own competence), and job satisfaction (positive feelings towards the job), and as a result the organization will find itself having low absenteeism and turnover rates, and higher levels of productivity and performance. When we say that the Quality of Work Life (QWL) in an organization is high, what we mean is that the benefits mentioned above accrue to the individuals and to the organization.

Individuals derive both intrinsic and extrinsic rewards and satisfaction in their jobs. Herzberg was one of the first researchers to identify two sets of factors in the job that offer two different types of satisfaction at the workplace-he called them job content factors which are motivators, and job context factors which are satisfiers. We will look at the different ways in which jobs can be designed as to their content and then examine the concept of QWL from the job design perspective. Obviously, if people differ in their needs, personality characteristics, and expectations at the workplace, there cannot be only one way of designing jobs that will offer a high QWL to all employees. This is where the fit between the individual and the job comes in. We will first examine the different kinds of jobs that can be designed and then examine the job-person fit.

Approaches to Job Design

Job design can be described as a deliberate attempt made to structure the technical and social aspects of work. Thus, job design encompasses both organizing the components of the tasks to be done, and the interaction patterns among the work group members in order to get the job done.

Jobs can be designed to range from highly simple to highly complex tasks in terms of the use of the worker's skills. The various job design techniques include job simplification, where jobs are broken down into very small parts as in the assembly line operations where fragmented task is repeatedly done over and over again by the same individual; job enlargement, where two or more simple tasks are combined and the individual does the combined task, as in the case of a clerk who receives applications, distributes them, and ultimately files them; job rotation, where the employee is periodically rotated from one job to another within the work setting; and job enrichment, which offers a greater challenge to the workers because it requires the use of a variety of skills possessed by them. Each of these job design strategies has its advantages and disadvantages as described below. All the four techniques relate more to the technical aspects of the job, the socio-technical approach to job designing, takes into consideration both the technical aspects of the job as well as social system in which the job is accomplished. The Autonomous Work Group approach to job designing stems from the socio-technical school of thought which is aimed at improving the quality of life at work.

Job Simplification

Any assembly line job is a good example of job simplification. The speed of the worker is usually expected to be high because the worker is doing the same simple task over and over again and gains proficiency and deftness in doing the repetitive task. Thus, the productivity of the employee could become very high; because of this the company could earn higher profits. The training costs of the workers for simplified jobs is virtually nil and the jobs can be staffed with employees with very low skill levels. In addition, this would mean that they would not have to be paid much. Thus, job simplification could be very beneficial to the company. However, because the task is so very repetitious, the worker is likely to get bored quickly and easily and would hence tend to remain absent frequently. The quality and quantity of the output may also suffer because of the frustration and boredom that might be experienced by the worker. Also, to attract workers to stay on the job, company may have to offer higher wages or more incentives. Thus, the company may not always reap the benefits of task specialization due to work simplification.

Job Enlargement

Job enlargement simply adds more task to the job so that the worker has a variety of simple tasks to perform rather than doing just one task repetitively. The advantage of this is that it adds a little more variety. Also, some workers may enjoy doing a few simple tasks rather than one piece of repetitive work all the time or engaging in very complex tasks. The problem with job enlargement is that even it could become boring to some after a time and employees may still be dissatisfied.

Job Rotation

Job rotation which involves moving employees among different tasks over a period of time has an advantage over job enlargement. Management does not have to bother with combining tasks, but at the same time, the worker does not get bored with doing one simple task over several years. The worker will now be engaged in doing different types of work during the space of a few weeks or months as the individual is rotated from one job to another. Thus, the company has the advantages of specialization of labour and a workforce which is trained in a variety of tasks, while at the same time, the workers – especially they not so highly skilled ones – continue doing different types of tasks over time which reduces their monotony at work to a considerable extent. The disadvantage is that workers who are looking for more challenging assignments may still feel frustrated performing different kinds of simple jobs.

Job Enrichment

Job enrichment involves building in motivating factors into the job, giving the worker more responsibility and control over work, and offering learning opportunities for the individual on the job. It is in this context that Herzberg made a distinction between job context (environment factors) and job content (built-in characteristics of the job). Enriched jobs are expected to offer more intrinsic rewards to the worker than any of the other job design strategies.

The Job Diagnostic Survey

Hackman, Lawler and their associates have been researching characteristics of jobs which would offer some kind of intrinsic rewards to workers. Hackman and Oldham (1975) developed the Job Diagnostic Survey (JDS) which provides measures for tapping several job-related variables. The job design theory formulated by them states that there are certain core characteristic in the job which will tap into certain critical psychological states of some types of workers which will then result in certain positive outcomes for the individuals and the organization. Their model is explained in detail below.

Job Design Model of Hackman and Oldham

Core Job Characteristics

There are five job characteristics which are central to providing potential motivation to workers. These are: skill variety, task identity, task significance, autonomy, and feedback from the job itself. Each of these factors are described below.

Skill Variety: denotes the extent to which any particular job utilizes a range of skills, abilities, and talents of the employees. Obviously, if a number of different skills are used by the employee on the job, the job is going to provide challenge and growth experience to the worker.

Task Identity: indicates the extent to which the job involves a "whole" and identifiable piece of work. In the job involves beginning an assignment and completing it then the individual can identify with the ultimate creation turned out by him or her and derive pride and satisfaction from having done a good job. If, however, the worker has handled only a tiny part of the whole job, and seldom gets to see the completed product to which he has minimally contributed, (as in the case of an employee in an automobile assembly plant who just paints a piece of metal), it is not going to "turn him on".

Task Significance: refers to the meaningfulness or significance of the impact that a job has on the lives of others – both inside and outside the organization. If what one does has an impact on the well being of other (such as a doctor's or volunteer's work), the job becomes psychologically rewarding to the person who performs it.

Autonomy: reflects the extent to which the job provides an employee the freedom, independence, and discretion to schedule work and make decisions, and formulate the procedures to get the job done without interference from others. The greater the degree of autonomy, the more the person doing the job feels "in control". Since the worker has more freedom to perform the job, this autonomy will provide the worker with both the motivation to do the satisfaction from doing it.

Feedback from the job itself: indicates the extent to which the persons who are working on the job can assess whether they are doing things right or wrong even as they are performing the job. That is, the job itself (and not another individual) provides them feedback on how well they are performing. For instance, as we put the parts of a clock back together, or write an exam answer, or work on a problem, we often mutter to ourselves, "This doesn't seem right!" We are then getting feedback from the job itself that something is wrong (or right) with what we are doing.

Experienced Psychological States

Hackman and Oldham theorize that if the job has the five core characteristics, then, those engaged in performing the job are likely to experience the three critical psychological states of experienced meaningfulness, experienced responsibility, and experienced knowledge of results, which will lead to good outcomes for the individual and the organization. The experienced psychological states are explained below.

Experienced Meaningfulness: denotes the psychological satisfaction experienced by the worker who knows that the work he or she is doing is important, valuable, and worthwhile. That is, the individual feels he or she is engaged in doing something meaningful. This experienced meaningfulness results from using a number of different skills (skill variety in the job), doing an identifiable piece of work (task identity) and engaging in work that has a significant impact on others (task significance).

Experienced Responsibility: the feeling of "being in control" and "being responsible for outcomes" results from the extent of job autonomy that the individual has while working.

Experienced knowledge of Results: the satisfaction of knowing how well one is performing on the job is derived from the fact that the job provides feedback even as the individual is working on it. In other words, an outsider does not have to provide feedback to the employee on how well he or she is performing the job; the employee knows the results of work performance experientially – that is, by one's own self.

As can be seen, all three experienced psychological states emanate from the intrinsic work rewards experienced by the employee, which then, according to Hackman and Oldham, will result in high intrinsic motivation, high quality of work performance, high levels of job satisfaction, high job involvement, and low absenteeism and turnover.

Hackman and Oldham however, qualify their statement that the core job dimensions will lead to experienced psychological states, which in turn, will eventually result in intrinsic motivation, performance, and involvement, by suggesting that these relationships will hold true only for such employees who have a high "growth need strength". Growth need strength refers to the need people have to learn, develop, and grow on the job. Not everybody has a high growth need. Some feel content to stay where they are and have no desire to develop and grow, or learn and advance in the organization. Hackman and Oldham state that only those who have a high growth need strength will experience the critical psychological states when the five core job characteristics are embedded in their work and then experience the positive outcomes.

To put it differently, we can consider the five core job characteristics to be independent variables, the three psychological states as the intervening variables – that is, variables that surface as a function of the independent variables and occur at some point in time before the occurrence of the final outcomes. The outcomes or the dependent variables in this case, are intrinsic motivation, work performance, job satisfaction, job involvement, and low turnover and absenteeism. Growth need strength is the moderator variable which moderates the relationships among the independent, intervening, and dependent variable.

Motivating Potential Score

Hackman and Oldham (1975) also came up with a formula for determining the motivating potential score (MPS) in each job. That is, the propensity of each job to be motivating can be assessed by using the formula:

$$\text{MPS} = \left(\frac{\text{Skill Variety} + \text{Task Identity} + \text{Task Significance}}{3} \right) \text{x Autonomy x Feedback}$$

It has to be noted that because of multiplicative effects of the model, if either autonomy or feedback happens to be totally absent in the job, then the job will have no motivating potential at all.

Problems with the Model

While the model is intuitively appending, researches have found that the theory and the JDS have some flaws. For one thing, the measures developed in the JDS do not empirically establish five distinct core dimensions as theorized by Hackman and Oldham. Not only is this problematic in the United States where the measures have been originally developed (Dunham, 1976), but the same has been found to be true for data collected from bank employees in India as well (Sekaran and Trafton, 1978). Also growth need strength has not always been found to be a moderator. Because of these concerns, Hackman and Oldham's theory that growth need strength is a moderator and hence job enrichment will appeal only to workers with high growth need strength in the worksetting is a moot point. Current research, however, does indicate that job enrichment is significantly related to motivation, satisfaction, and sense of competence in both the American and Indian cultures (Sekaran, 1981, 1985; Sekaran and Martin, 1982; Sekaran and Wagner, 1980).

Socio-Technical System Design and the Quality of Work Life

In all the job design strategies discussed so far, it is the technical aspects of the job that that have been considered. The tasks can be organized in terms of vertical loading or job enlargement, and horizontal loading or job enrichment. These techniques do not pay any attention to the social side of the work system. The social aspects of work include such factors as individual and group influences, organizational culture, leadership and supervision, and other social factors in the work system. The socio-technical approach subscribes to the notion that in any work system, there is a social system operating in conjunction with a technical system – both of which have to be considered if the quality of worklife is to be enhanced. The technical system encompasses factors like technology, type of production processes, workflow systems, physical work setting, and complexity involved in performing the job. The advocates of the socio-technical system argue that technological determinism compromises quality of work life since it neglects the human aspects. Hence, they advocate that both the social and technical aspects of the job have to be simultaneously considered and jointly optimized while job design strategies are pursued.

Job Design and Quality of Work Life

The term "quality of work life" encompasses aspects of good experiences and advantages for employees, the organization, and the society at large. Among the various indices of the Quality of Work Life, are such factors as job involvement, job satisfaction, sense of competence, job performance, productivity, organizational vitality, clean air with minimal pollution, and product safety. Let us briefly examine some of these which are directly related to the employees, and see how they are related to job design.

Job Involvement: indicates the extent of people's identification with or ego investment in the job is to the individual's life, the more he or she gets involved in it, and therefore the individual spends more time and energy on the job. Job involved people are interested in turning out high quality work and are motivated to put forth their best efforts on the job. Research has shown that challenging jobs which have skill variety, influence employees to get involved with their jobs, (Sekaran, 1981).

Job Satisfaction: indicates the positive and affective responses of employees to their job environment. More specifically, job satisfaction indicates employee's satisfaction with 1. The nature of the work they do; 2. The quality of supervision they receive; 3. Co-workers; 4. Pay; and 5. Promotional opportunities. Job satisfaction is correlated to job characteristics (skill variety, autonomy, etc.), and to job involvement. That is, when people are involved in their jobs, they are satisfied with their jobs, and when they experience more job satisfaction, they also get more job involved (Sekaran, 1977). Job stress decreases their job satisfaction (Sekaran, 1981), and job stress could result from role ambiguity, role conflict, role overload, or role difficulty.

Sense of competence: sense of competence denotes the feelings of confidence that one has in one's own competence. By engaging in work that calls for a variety of skills, abilities, and talents, individuals gain mastery over their work environment. As workers engage themselves more and more in work activities, they acquire a greater sense of competence and experience higher levels of job involvement, because the more competent they feel, the more motivated they are to interact with the job and hence become more involved in it. The greater the involvement, the greater also is their sense of competence. Thus, job involvement and a sense of competence mutually reinforce each other. When both, sense of competence and involvement are high, naturally employees' level of job satisfaction increases as well.

Job Performance: would also continue to improve as people's levels of involvement, competence, and satisfaction increase. In essence, all the four factors are significantly correlated. Though it may be controversial as to whether performance causes satisfaction, or satisfaction causes better performance, one can safely say that when job involvement, sense of competence, and job satisfaction, are all present, job performance is likely to follow as natural corollary.

Productivity: is to be expected when there is a fit among the predispositions of workers and the type of jobs they are assigned to do. Since job involvement, motivation, sense of competence, and job satisfaction ensue due to the congruence between the worker and the job, a high level of job performance results: both in terms of quality and quantity. When the same number of workers turn a larger quantum of outputs in the same amount of time, productivity increases for the organization as well. When high quality, safe products and services are the outcomes, society itself benefits.

We thus see that good job designing results in a high quality of work life for individuals, the organization, and the society. It is hence important that managers pay attention to job design. If the skills, abilities, experience, training, and personality dimensions such as tolerance for ambiguity, need patterns, and work ethic values match the types of jobs may appeal to the more achievement oriented individuals, repetitive jobs might appeal to individuals who have low levels of skills and training but have a high work ethic orientation. So, it may not always be beneficial to enrich all kinds of jobs. Moreover, certain kinds of routine, repetitive jobs which do not lend themselves to enrichment, have also got to be done in organizations. While robotics may be a way to get around manning dull jobs, some individuals might actually prefer to do routine jobs and earn some money. Thus, it is wise to take a contingency approach to job design taking into consideration the predispositions of the workers, the characteristics of the job, and the contextual factors. In a country such as India where labour is plentiful in supply, job design adds a particularly challenging dimension to the manager's job.

The purpose/objectives of conducting this job design survey was

- To experience firsthand the job characteristics approach to job design, in this case through Hackman- Oldham Job Diagnostic Survey. (JDS).

- To get personal feedback on the motivating potential of your present or past job and to identify and compare its critical characteristics.

Operational Definition

MPS: (Motivating Potential Score)

Hackman and Oldham (1975) came up with a formula for determining the motivating potential score (MPS) in each job.

That is, the propensity of each job to be motivating can be assessed by using the formula

MPS

Skill Variety: denotes the extent to which any particular job utilizes a range of skills, abilities and talents of the employees.

Task Identity: indicates the extent to which the job involves a "whole" and identifiable piece of work.

Task Significance: refers to the meaningfulness or significance of the impact that a job has on the lines of others- both inside and outside the organization.

Autonomy: reflects the extent to which the job provides an employee the freedom, independence, and discretion to schedule work and make decisions, and formulate the procedures to get the job done without interference from others.

Feedback: indicates the extent to which the persons who are working on the job can assess whether they are doing things right or wrong even as they are performing the job.

Controls

Noise and distractions are kept at the bare minimum.

Made sure that the employee has understood properly.

Instructions are given properly.

Methodology

Sample: - S^1 - Ms. Monica (Receptionist)

S^2 - Mr. Anand (Sr. Project Manager)

Materials used

A sheet of Job Design Survey (JDS).

There are 5 items (statements). Each statement having a 7-point rating scale. Points 1,2,3 indicating a low level. Point 4 indicates a moderate level. Points 5,6,7 indicating high level.

One has to read each statement carefully and describe his/her present job (or a job he/she has held in the past) as objectively as he/ she can by encircling one number that best reflects the job.

Instructions: "This is a very simple questionnaire. There are five statements. Please describe your present job (or a job you have held in the past) as objectively as you can. Circle the number that best reflects the job. Have you understood? Do you have any doubts?"

Procedure

The Ss were made comfortable and then the above instructions were given. After conforming that the S had followed the instructions the 'ready' signal was given.

Discussion

The JDS was conducted on Mrs. Monica who is a Receptionist at Rediffusion Ad Agency, a private section enterprise.

The JDS has five questions, which shows an individual's score on 5 core job characteristics i.e. Skill variety, Task identity, Task significance, Autonomy and feed back. It has a 7 paint rating scale where 1 means – very little, 4 means moderate and 7 means very much. Thus this implies that 1 is low and 7 is high.

The overall motivating potential score (MPS) of a job ranges from 1 – 343. The JDS has been used extensively in research and projects over the last few years, and data from many of these projects is compiled by Oldham, Hackman and Stepiha (1979).

Average JDS scores across 876 different jobs in 56 organizations are mentioned in the manual. The subject shows a very positive attitude towards her job and her life in general. She has 2 years of experience.

Her score on skill variety was 4; the average nominal score is 4-7. Thus she rates the job as having low skill variety. She mentioned that it was true because she just had to receive and forward calls, which did not bring in any kind of skill variety in her job.

Her score on Task identity was 6, whereas the average to high score is 4-7. Thus her job is relatively high on this variable. This is so because she is working all the while on behalf of all the employees / for the organization.

The average on Task significance is 5 and the Ss score is 6. She justifies it by saying that her presentation, mannerism, communication skills reflect here organization image, which plays a very significant role for all the others.

Her score on autonomy is 5, which is higher than the average score of 4-9.

Her feedback score is 7 and the average score is 5. This is so, because she sits at the reception table where the employees of the organization as well as the visitors coming to the organization give their feedback.

Her overcall motivational potential score is 186.67, which against the average of 128 being fulfilling and satisfying.

The second subject on whom JDS was conducted was Mr. Anand, working for Vishan Projects Pvt. Ltd., as a Sr. Project Manager. He shows total satisfaction towards his job. This can be seen very clearly from the obtained data. He had ranked 7 on skill variety that is much higher than the job characteristics norm 4-7.

He also ranks himself 7 each on task identity and task significance also higher than the job characteristic norm.

He ranks himself 5 each on autonomy and feedback that again is equal to the job characteristic norm. The results show that Anand enjoys doing his job because he is able to use all the 5 job characteristics that enhance his working conditions and the end product. His MPS score obtained was 175, which is again much higher than the average of 128.

He attributes his satisfaction towards his work because he is able to do many things at a time without losing track of his ultimate goal.

2. LEAD

Introduction

Emphasis is on helping leaders to develop people to their fullest potential. This involves shifting their leadership style forward and backward (according to Situational Leadership) and thus utilizing various degrees of direction and support as followers increase or decrease in maturity or development levels. This continual shifting of leadership style seems to require leaders to be flexible, i.e. to be able to use a variety of leadership style depending on the situation. That raises two questions: (1) Are most leaders able to be flexible or do they tend to be limited only to one or two leadership styles? (2) If leader continually change their leadership styles, how will that effect their follower's perception of their intentions?

The first question is something that has been examined at the Center for Leadership Studies for more than a decade through the use of Leader Effectiveness and Adaptability Description (LEAD) instruments. Answering the second question was an important impetus in the development of the Contracting for Leadership Style process developed by Hersey and Blanchard to increase the effectiveness of management by objectives (MBO), a widely used formal superior-subordinates negotiation system.

The LEAD instrument developed by Hersey and Blanchard was designed to measure three aspects of leader behavior: (l) style. (2) Style range, and (3) style adaptability. The leadership style of an individual is the behavior pattern that person exhibits when attempting to influence the activities of others as perceived by those others. This may be very different from the Leader's perception of his own behavior, which we will define as self-perception rather than style. Comparing one's self-perception of leadership style with the perceptions of others can be very useful, particularly since one's self-perceptions may or may not reflect actual leadership style depending on how close a person's perception are to the perceptions of others. For this reason, two LEAD instruments were developed; LEAD-Self and LEAD-Other. The LEAD-Self measures self-perception of how an individual behaves as a leader; the LEAD-Other reflects the perceptions of a leader's subordinates, superiors, and peers or associates.

Leadership Style

Research at the Center for Leadership Studies has discovered that most leaders have a primary leadership style and a secondary leadership style. A leader's primary style is defined as the behavior pattern used most often when attempting to influence the activities of others. In other words, most leaders tend to have a favorite leadership style. A leader's supporting style(s) is a leadership style that person tends to use on occasions. It is important to note that all leaders have a primary leadership style, that is, they tend to use one of the four basic leadership styles described in Situational Leadership more often than not in leadership situations. However, they may not have any secondary leadership style. Therefore, a leader could have no secondary styles or up to three secondary styles, but a leader would always have at least one primary style.

Style Range or Flexibility

An individual's style range is the extent to which that person is able to vary his or her leadership style. Leaders differ in their ability to vary their style in different situations. Some leaders seem to be limited to one basic style: these rigid people tend to be effective only in situations in which their styles are compatible with environment. Other leaders are able to modify their behavior to fit any of the four basic styles; still others can utilize two or three styles. Flexible leaders have the potential to be effective in a number of situations. The style range of a leader can be illustrated in terms of task and relationship behavior.

Style Adaptability

Style range indicates the extent to which leaders are able to vary their styles; style adaptability is the degree to which they are able to vary their style appropriately to the demands of a given situation according to Situational Leadership. People who have a narrow style range can be effective over a long period of time if they remain in situations in which their style has a high probability of success. Conversely, people who have a wide range of styles may be ineffective if these behaviors are not consistent with the demands of the situation. Thus, style range is not as relevant to effectiveness as style adaptability; a wide style range will not guarantee effectiveness.

Flexibility: A Question of Willingness

The importance of a leader's diagnostic ability cannot be overemphasized. It is the key to adaptability. However, most leaders are more concerned about flexibility than when to use which leadership style. That gets us back to one of the questions raised. Are most leaders able to be that flexible or do they tend to be limited to only one or two leadership styles?

It has been an experience at the Center for Leadership studies that there are few, if any, leader who cannot learn to use all four basic leadership styles. In fact, people use those behaviors almost every day. At least once a day don't you tell somebody what to do and watch them closely (Style S1), explain what you want somebody to do and permit them to ask clarifying questions (Style S2), share ideas with people and support their efforts (Style S3), and turn over responsibility to someone to "run with the ball" (Style S4)?

Learning to use the four basic styles is not the issue; the question is one of willingness, anyone has the ability, but if the person does not want to learn, then there is not much that you can do.

When people are willing to learn to use all the leadership styles, we have found an interesting phenomenon. When people learn to use the leadership style that previously was not even considered a secondary style, these compensating styles often become their most effective styles. While these styles may never become comfortable, they can become the most effective, in many cases, because they've been learned. Therefore, such leaders know a lot more about these styles because they have practiced them consciously. People often use their comfortable or primary leadership styles by the "seat of their pants." This is true not only in terms of leadership styles but also in many other areas of their lives. Your primary style is often one that you do not have to think about using. But once you learn other styles through conscientious study, these compensating styles can be your most effective. Thus, we find willingness-not ability – is the main issue in terms of style flexibility.

Use of LEAD Instrumentation

When staff members at the Center for Leadership Studies diagnose an organization, part of that diagnosis often involves of the LEAD instruments. The process consists of having managers throughout the organization complete the LEAD-Self instrument (how they perceive their own leadership style). At the same time each of these manager's subordinates, superior and several associates or peers fill out the LEAD-Other instrument.

Once the data have been analyzed, a LEAD-Profile is prepared for each individual manager. On that profile the managers are given an opportunity to see if there is any significant difference between how they perceive their own leadership style and how others in the environment perceive their style.

The purpose of distributing and analyzing the LEAD-Self and LEAD-Other data is to determine if there is any discrepancy between self-perception and the perception of others. In analyzing that data and feeding it back to participating managers, a useful framework developed by Joseph Luft and Harry Ingham is used.

Johari Window

The framework developed by Luft and Ingham is called the Johari window (taken from the first names of its authors). The Johari window is used by Hersey and Blanchard to depict leadership personality, not overall personality as it is sometime used. The difference between leadership personality and leadership style in this context is that leadership personality includes self-perception and the perception of others; leadership style consists only of an individual's leader behaviour as perceived by others, that is, superior, subordinates(s), associates, and so on. Thus, leadership personality equals self-perception plus other perception (style).

According to this framework, there are some attitudes or behaviour engaged in by leaders that they know about themselves. This known to self area includes their knowledge of the way they are coming across, the impact they are leader's personality is unknown to self; that is, in some areas leaders are unaware of how they are coming across to others. It may be that their followers have not given them feedback or it may be that a leader has not been alert enough to pick up some of the verbal or nonverbal feedback that actually exists within the environment.

We can also look at leadership personality including behaviors and attitudes that the known to others in a leader's organizational setting, as well as areas unknown to others. In terms of what is known and unknown to self and known and unknown to others, we can create four areas that comprise the total window, as depicted in figure:

	Known to Self	Unknown to Self
Known to Others	PUBLIC	BLIND
Unknown to Others	PRIVATE	UNKNOWN

The Johari Window

The arena that is known to self and also known to others in any specific organizational setting is called the public arena – it is known to all (the leader and others, that is, superior, subordinates(s), and peers) within that organizational setting.

The arena that is unknown to self (the leader) but is known to others is referred to as the blind arena. It's unknown to the leader either because followers have been unwilling to share feedback with or communication ("level") to that leader on how he or she is coming across; or it may be that the data are there in terms of verbal and non-verbal behavior, but the leader is not able or does not care to "see" them. The arena that is known to self but unknown to others is referred to as the private arena since it is only known to the leader. Again, it may be private because the leader has been unwilling to share or disclose this to others in the organizational setting; or it may be private because the others in the system are not picking up the nonverbal and verbal responses that are available from the leader in the system.

The last arena, unknown to self and unknown to others, is called the unknown. In Freudian psychology, this would be referred to as the subconscious or unconscious.

There is a certain portion of a leader's personality that is above the surface–that is, it is very graphic. Anyone who looks in that direction can hardly help but see the basic size, consistency, makeup, and configuration. But much of this iceberg exists beneath the surface and unless we make conscious efforts to probe and understand, we will really never have any insight into its consistency. And yet much of that part of a leader's personality referred to as unknown may be having a relevant impact in terms of the kinds of behaviors is which a leader engages when he or she is trying to influence the behavior of others.

Feedback

There are two processes that affect the shape of the Johari window (the configuration of the four arenas). The first, which operates in the direction illustrated in figure is called feedback. This is the extent to which others in the organizational setting are willing to share with the leader on how he or she is coming across. It is the willingness of others to be open and to give relevant feedback to the leader. But again you have to look at it from both perspectives. It is also the extent to which the leader is attempting to perceive the verbal and nonverbal feedback that exists in the system.

Feedback		
	Known toSelf	Unknown toSelf
Known to Others	PUBLIC	BLIND
Unknown to Others	PRIVATE	UNKNOWN

Effect of feedback on the Johari window

Many managers cut off and eventually stifle feedback from their people by arguing with them about their feelings and perceptions.

Another suggestion can give managers an additional clue to how they can encourage their people to share their feelings and perceptions with them.

Treating staff members with respect will lead to a relationship in which they feel free to share and talk. As can be seen in figure the more relative feedback that takes place within an organization, the more the public arena of a leader begins to extend into and displace the blind arena and thus the smaller blind arena that leader has.

Disclosure

The other process that affects the shape of the Johari window is disclosure. This is the extent to which leaders are willing to share with others in their organizational setting data about themselves. The way we use the term disclosure is different from the way others in the field often use it. First, the most relevant disclosure is not what people say about themselves but rather their behavior. It is not words that mean, it is people that mean. And if you want to understand people better, you really have to look at the behavior those people engage in to gain relevant insights into their values and what this behavior represents.

Second, we think disclosure is appropriate in organizations only when such disclosure is organizationally relevant. This is a different way of viewing disclosure than urged by some people in the sensitivity training and personal growth field, who feel all disclosure is appropriate. In the process of disclosure, the more and organizationally relevant information that leaders disclose about the way they think or behave, the more the public arena opens into the private arena and the smaller and smaller that arena becomes, as shown in figure. An interesting phenomenon occurs in settings where there is simultaneous feedback and disclosure between leaders and the people with whom they work. Not only does the public arena of these leaders begin to extend itself into the blind and the private arenas, but there is also a high probability that some of what was previously unknown (not known to either the leaders or other people in the organization) will begin to surface into the public arena.

Feedback

	Known toSelf	Unknown toSelf
Known to Others	PUBLIC	BLIND
Unknown to Others	PRIVATE	UNKNOWN

Effect of feedback and disclosure on the Johari Window

'Situational Leadership' by Paul Hersey and Kenneth H. Blanchard

Situational Leadership is based on an interplay among (1) the amount of guidance and direction (task behavior) a leader gives; (2) the amount of socio-emotional support (relationship behavior) a leader provides; and (3) the readiness ("maturity") level that followers exhibit in performing a specific task, function or objective. This concept was developed to help people attempting leadership, regardless of their role, to be more effective in their daily interactions with others. It provides leaders with some understanding of the relationship between an effective style of leadership and the level of maturity of their followers.

Thus, while all the situational variables (leader, follower(s), superior(s), associates, organization, job demands, and time) are important, the emphasis in Situational Leadership will be on the behavior of a leader in relation of followers.

Maturity of the followers or Group

Maturity is defined in Situational Leadership as the ability and willingness of people to take responsibility for directing their own behavior. These variables of maturity should be considered only in relation to a specific task to be performed. That is to say, an individual or a group is not mature or immature in any total sense. All persons tend to be more or less mature in relation to a specific task, function, or objective that a leader is attempting to accomplish through their efforts.

In addition to assessing the level of maturity of individuals within a group, a leader may have to assess the maturity level of the group as a group, particularly if the group interacts frequently together in the same work area.

So leader have to understand that they may have to behave differently one-on-one with members of their group from the way they do with the group as a whole.

Basic Concept of Situational Leadership

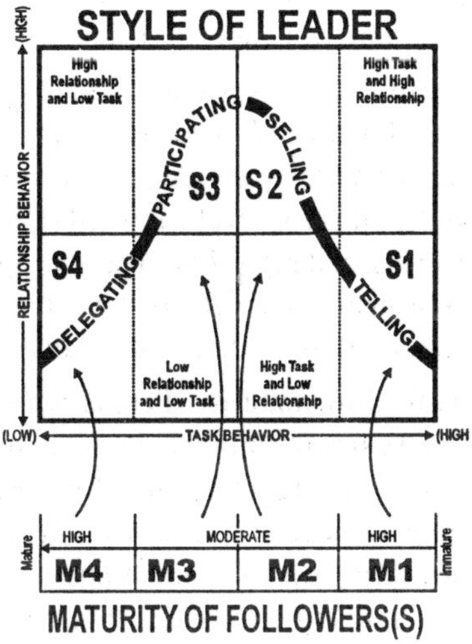

Figure: Situation leadership

According to Situational Leadership, there is no one best way to influence people. Which leadership style a person should use with individuals or groups depends on the maturity level of the people the leader is attempting to influence as illustrated in figure.

The attempt in figure is to portray the relationship between task-relevant maturity and the appropriate leadership styles to be used as followers move from immaturity to maturity. As indicated, the reader should keep in mind that the figure represents two different phenomena.

The appropriate leadership style (style of leader) for given levels of followers maturity is portrayed by the prescriptive curve going through the four leadership quadrants. This bell-shaped curve is called a prescriptive curve because it shows the appropriate leadership style directly above the corresponding level of maturity.

Each of the four leadership styles – "telling," "selling," "participating," and "delegating" – identified in figure, is a combination of task and relationship behavior. Task behavior is the extent to which a leader provides direction for people, telling them what to do, when to do it, where to do it, and how to do it. It means setting goals for them and defining their roles.

Relationship behavior is the extent to which a leader engages in two-way communication with people: providing support, encouragement, "psychological strokes," and facilitating behaviors. It means actively listening to people and supporting their efforts.

The maturity of followers is a question of degree. As can be seen in figure, some bench marks of maturity are provided for determining appropriate leadership style by dividing the maturity continuum below the leadership model into four levels: low (M1), low to moderate (M2), moderate to high (M3), and high (M4).The appropriate leadership style for each of the four maturity levels includes the right combination of task behavior (direction) and relationship behavior (support).

"Telling" is for low maturity. People who are both unable and unwilling (M1) to take responsibility to do something are not competent or confident. In many cases, their unwillingness is a result of their insecurity regarding the necessary task. Thus, a directive "telling" style (S1) that provides clear, specific directions and supervision has the highest probability of being effective with individuals at this maturity level. This style is called "telling" because it is characterized by the leader's defining roles and telling people what, how, when, and where to do various tasks. It emphasizes directive behavior. Too much supportive behavior with people at this maturity level may be seen as permissive, easy and, most importantly, as rewarding of poor performance. This style involves high task behavior and low relationship behavior.

"Selling" is for low to moderate maturity: People who are unable but willing (M2) to take responsibility are confident but lack skills at this time. Thus, a "selling" style (S2) that provides directive behavior, because of their lack of ability, but also supportive behavior to reinforce their willingness and enthusiasm appears to be most appropriate with individual at this maturity level. This style is called "selling" because most of the direction is still provided by the leader. Yet, through two-way communication and explanation, the leader tries to get the followers psychologically "into" desired behaviors. Followers at this maturity level will usually go along with a decision if they understand the reason for the decision and if their leader also offers some help and direction. This style involves high task behavior and high relationship behavior.

"Participating" is for moderate to high maturity: People at this maturity level are able but unwilling (M3) to do what the leader wants. Their unwillingness is often a function of their lack of confidence or insecurity. If, however, they are competent but unwilling, their reluctance to perform is more of a motivational problem than a security problem. In either case, the leader needs to open the door (two-way communication and active listening) to support the follower's efforts to use the ability he already has. Thus, a supportive, nondirective, "participating" style (S3) has the highest probability of being effective with individuals at this maturity level. This style is called "participating" because the leader and follower share in decision making, with the main role of the leader being facilitating and communicating. This style involves high relationship behavior and low task behavior.

"Delegating" is for high maturity: People at this maturity level are both able and willing, or confident, to take responsibility. Thus, a low-profile "delegating" style (S4), which provides little direction or support, has the highest probability of being effective with individuals at this maturity level. Even though the leader may still identify the problem, the responsibility for carrying out plans is given to these mature followers. They are permitted to run the show and decide on the how, when, and where. At the same time, they are psychologically mature and therefore do not need above average amounts of two-ways communication or supportive behavior. This style involves low relationship behavior and low task behavior. It should be clear that the appropriate leadership style for all four of the maturity designations – low maturity (M1), low to moderate maturity (M2), moderate to high maturity (M3), and high maturity (M4) – correspond to the following leadership style designations: telling (S1), selling (S2), participating (S3), and delegating (S4). That is, low maturity needs a telling style, low to moderate needs a selling style, and so on.

The purpose or the objective of conducting the LEAD Test is to measure the self-perception of how an individual behaves as a leader and the dominant leadership style.

Operational Definitions

Telling

Style that provides clear, specific directions and supervision has the highest probability of being effective with individuals at low maturity level. This style is called "telling" because it is characterized by the leader's defining roles and telling people what, how, when, and where to do various tasks. It emphasizes directive behavior.

Selling

This style provides directive behavior, because of their lack of ability, but also supportive behavior to reinforce their willingness and enthusiasm appears to be most appropriate with individual at low to moderate maturity level. This style is called "selling" because most of the direction is still provided by the leader. Yet, through two-way communication and explanation, the leader tries to get the followers psychologically "into" desired behaviors.

Participating

In this style the leader needs to open the door (two-way communication and active listening) to support the follower's efforts to use the ability he already has. Thus, a supportive, nondirective, "participating" style has the highest probability of being effective with individuals at moderate to high maturity level. This style is called "participating" because the leader and follower share in decision making, with the main role of the leader being facilitating and communicating. This style involves high relationship behavior and low task behavior.

Delegating

This style provides little direction or support, has the highest probability of being effective with individuals at high maturity level. Even though the leader may still identify the problem, the responsibility for carrying out plans is given to these mature followers. They are permitted to run the show and decide on the how, when, and where.

At the same time, they are psychologically mature and therefore do not need above average amounts of two-ways communication or supportive behavior. This style involves low relationship behavior and low task behavior

Controls

1. Noise and distractions are kept at bare minimum level.
2. Instructions are given properly.
3. Made sure that the employees have understood the instructions well.

Methodology

Sample: - S1 - Ms. Disha Parab

Exec. HR Manager, Rediffusion Ad Agency

S2 - Mr. Anand Nair

Sr. Project Manager, Vishan Projects Pvt. Ltd.

Materials Used

The LEAD (self) questionnaire consists of 12 situations with four options for each situation. Each alternative corresponds to a specific leadership style. The respondent has to choose one alternative out of the four, which would help to identify the primary and the secondary leadership styles that the respondent uses.

Instructions

"Assume YOU are involved in each of the following twelve situations, Read each item carefully. Think about what YOU would do in each circumstance. Then circle the letter of the alternative action choice that YOU think would most closely describes your behaviour in the situation presented. Circle only one choice.

Do not respond to the item as of they were parts of a test or in terms of what you think a leader or manager ought to do. Respond to the items in terms of the way you think you have behaved in the past when you were faced with situations similar to those described or in terms of the way you think you would behave if you were faced with each of the situations described.

Respond to the items sequentially; that is, so item 1 before you do item 2, and so on. Do not spend too much time; respond to each item as if you were responding to a real life situation. Do not go back over each; stay with your original response."

Procedure

The Ss were made comfortable and then the above-mentioned instructions were given to them. Conforming that they had followed the instructions a 'ready' was given to start with the test.

Discussion

The LEAD questionnaire was given to a HR Manager of Rediffusion Ad Agency, Mrs. Disha Parab. The scale gives two types of scores, the first one being a single score which ranges from + 24 to – 24. This reflects the flexibility that a leader shows vis-a-vis the follower's maturity level. A higher positive score indicates greater awareness of follower's maturity level.

At the same time a lower negative score shows that the leader is not aware of the follower's maturity level and thus is not flexible in his/her leadership approach. The 2nd type of score is a set of 4 scores which show which style is preferred by the leader.

This score shows out of 12 situations, in how many situations the leader uses a telling style or a selling, participative and delegating style. It shows the frequency of each style in the leader's behavior.

The score on the flexibility dimension of the S is which inspite of being low is positive. This indicates that the S is moderately flexible in situation specific behavior and on the 2nd dimension the S scored equally on the Telling and Selling Style acquiring a score of 4 on both them. Her score on the participative and delegating style was 3 & 1 respectively. Thus the employee insists on using a highly task focused style of leadership. This style of leadership will work very well with followers who are at lower level of maturity.

But in terms of followers who are mature these styles of leadership will seem to be highly intrusive.

The 2nd S was Mr. Anand Nair, Sr. Project Manager, Vishan Projects Pvt. Ltd. His score on the 1st dimension of flexibility was – 1, again indicating a moderate level of flexibility in leadership approach. And on the 2nd dimension of style, his score on telling was 3, on selling it was 5 and on participating 4, he did not use the delegating style even once.

Thus he preferred using high relationship oriented behavior, but his focus on task is also not low as reflected by very similar scores on the 3 dimensions. But a behavior low on both task and relationship was something he was not comfortable with.

Thus his behavior is appropriate for low to moderate level of maturity but at higher levels of maturity where the followers do not need much intervention from leaders. This behavior may be termed intrusive.

2. Leadership: Its Nature and Impact In Organizations

Introduction: It's Basic Nature

When two or more people come together and interact with each other, a group is formed. Groups can be various types. Family, school, societies, organization, are various types of groups. No group can function effectively without a person who can guide it. Such a person is its leader. A leader designs, co-ordinates, executes and controls various functions of the group. He is indispensable for the effective functioning of a group. Without a leader there will be confusion and chaos in the group.

One must not confuse leadership with management. Leadership is a part of management, not all of it. Management may plan and organize things but leaders have to persuade people to follow. A manager should ideally be a leader though a leader may not be a manager. A strong leader could be a poor manager and vice versa. There are several differences between leaders and managers. They are as follows:

Leaders have followers but managers do not have any followers. Subordinates may obey a manager out of fear rather than due to his leadership qualities. All leaders are not managers nor are all managers, leaders. Though leaders have followers they may not possess formal authority and power.

Leaders fulfill the needs of their followers. People follow those in whom they see a means of satisfying their personal goals. Although leaders influence subordinates in achieving organizational goals they give more emphasis on helping them in meeting their personal needs. But the main aim of a manager is to meet the goals of his organization.

Leaders have an emotional appeal. They appeal to the emotions of their followers. Managers on the other hand, are expected to be rational and make decisions based on an analysis of reality.

One interesting thing that must be remembered is that leaders are not the only ones to influence their followers. The followers also have their impact on their leaders. The age, sex, personal background and personal responsibilities of the followers have an effect on the leader.

The term leader comes from the word lead which means to excel, to guide, govern and command others. A leader is a person who leads a group of followers. Therefore, unless he has an edge over his followers in managerial, technical, professional or other skills he will not be able to command respect and faith of others. However, more superiority over others in various skills is not sufficient. He must have the competence and ability to govern and guide people's actions.

Different people define leadership differently. However, they all agree on certain points. On that basis, leadership may be defined as "the ability of an individual to influence others to achieve goals without the use of force."

The following are some of the definitions of leadership given by different persons:

Livingstone: "Leadership is the ability to awaken in others the desire to follow common objectives."

Koontz and O' Donnell: "Leadership is the ability to exert interpersonal influence by means of communication towards the achievement of goals."

Keith Davis and J. W. Newstron: "Leadership is the process of encouraging and helping others to work enthusiastically towards objective."

The Michigan Studies

A group of researchers from the Michigan University Survey Research Center divided leader behaviors into two types – employee-centered and production-centered leader behaviors. Employee-centered leaders are those who are greatly concerned about the welfare and satisfaction of their subordinates while the production-centered leaders placed a stronger emphasis on how well the job gets done, rather than on the subordinates' concerns. Results of the Michigan Study indicated that supervisors who were more employee-centered and exercised loose supervision had employees who were high performing, compared to employees of supervisors who were more production-oriented and supervised their subordinates more closely.

The Ohio State Leadership Studies

The Ohio State University researchers who conducted similar types of investigation looked at two dimensions of leader behaviour-consideration and initiating structure. A leader who is high in consideration is sensitive to employees' needs and feelings while a leader who is high in initiating structure is primarily concerned about giving workers the necessary task instructions and clarifying the work requirements and agenda.

Other Approaches to Leadership

Despite the popular contingency approaches to leadership and management styles, some researchers and management consultants still believe in certain universalistic approaches to effective leadership. We will discuss two of these models here – Likert's (1967), System Four and Blake and Mouton's (1969) Managerial Grid.

Likert's System Four

Rensis Likert suggests that managers operate under four different systems. In system 1, the manager behaves in a very authoritarian manner and actually exploits the subordinates. In system 2, the manager takes a paternalistic approach while still being autocratic. Behaving as a benevolent autocrat, the leader maintains strict control over the subordinates albeit in a paternalistic manner. In system 3, the manager uses a consultative approach, that is, though the leader consults the subordinates, here she still maintains the right to make the final decision. Finally, in system 4, the manager uses a democratic style. Likert feels that the best way for all organizations to manage employee is to move toward system 4. Proponents of the contingency models, however, question this assumption.

The Managerial Grid

The five basic approaches to management identified by Blake and Mouton (1969) are based on the two dimensions of "concern for people" and "concern for production" that are associated with leaders. These dimensions are presented in a framework called the Managerial Grid.They put "concern for production" and "concern for people" on the x and the y-axis respectively, in the Managerial Grid. Each axis is divided into 9 points. As the leader advances from 1 to 9 on the x-axis, his concern for people becomes maximum when he reaches point 9.

The 2 dimensions combine in different degrees and result in 5 basic managerial leadership styles as shown below.

There are many possible combinations, but we will discuss the 5 most important.

9-1: This style represents maximum concern for production and minimum concern for people. Such managers are often referred to as autocratic taskmasters. They use authority to ensure obedience from their subordinates.

1-9: This style stands for maximum concern for people and minimum concern for production. Attention is concentrated primarily on meeting the needs of subordinates and creating a comfortable and friendly atmosphere in the organization. This pattern corresponds to the laissez faire style of leader behavior.

1-1: this style is characterized by minimum concern for both production and people. Such leaders expect minimum work from the subordinates just to keep the organization working.

5-5: here the leader tries to get along well with people and also gets the work done.

9-9: this is the best style of leadership. Here, managers have the highest possible concern for both people as well as production. Production activity is at its maximum level.

On the basis of this Managerial Grid, Blake and Mounton have developed a training programme. This program has been extensively used in America and also used in India and other Eastern countries. This program helps managers to analyze their existing managerial style and tries to adapt the 5-5 to 9-9 style.

Transactional and Transformational Leadership

Bass (1985) had made a distinction between transactional and transformational leadership. Transactional leaders take an exchange perspective to their relationship with subordinates and exchange rewards for the efforts of employees. Bass argues that if leaders are to obtain performance from the subordinates far beyond the normal limits, they should practice transformational and not transactional leadership.

Transformational leadership is exercised when the leader intellectually stimulates the subordinates, excites, arouses, and inspires them to perform far beyond what they would have thought themselves capable of. By providing a new vision, the transformational leader transforms the followers into people who self-actualize. Charismatic leadership is central to transformational leadership.

Leadership in the Indian Culture

Leadership in Indian organizations had generally been found to be, at best of the benevolent authoritarian type (Bass, 1981; Haire, Porter and Ghiselli, 1966). Hofstede (1980), empirically established, that compared to most other countries, India has a high Power Distance Index, Power Distance denotes a society's acce|tance of the way in which power is distributed in organizations. In cultures with a high power distance, power is distributed unequally, with a powerful group at the top of the hierarchy making decisions that are highly centralized. Such systems usually function well because those at the lower levels of the hierarchy have a need to feel dependent on others for guidance and administration. It is also possible that in some cases, subordinates could go to the other extreme and engage in counter dependent behaviors in high power distance situations (Hofstede, 1980).

With this changing composition of the workforce, a different leadership style is perhaps called for to better utilize the skills and expertise of the younger generation. The authoritarian style of leadership. Sinha (1976) found that employees in Indian organizations often prefer authoritative leadership. Such leadership depicts a strong task orientation and a strong personal involvement and effort by the leader. While this may have been true in the past, a question that we should ask ourselves if whether such a leadership style will be functional in the future. The changing demographics of the workforce, at least in the urban cities in India, have to be taken into consideration as we examine the concept of effective leadership styles. Those working in urban organizations in India are younger, more educated, and technically better. Authoritative leadership is obviously not the best suited to tap the full potential of today's well-trained, and relatively less dependent employees. One reason why many technocrats and scientists have so far been migrating or are now desirous of immigrating to western countries could be because of the outlet they find for their creativity in other countries. Especially in the west, creativity and innovation are encouraged and allowed to blossom and flourish under more egalitarian organizational relationships. In effect the need for dependence on others that had hitherto been a characteristic of the older generation in India, may be yielding place to a need for autonomy and participative experiences desired by the younger, more educated generation of new employees. If such is indeed the case, a more situational approach to leadership taking the abilities and aspirations of the employees into consideration, would appear to be more appropriate for the India of today.

The objective of the leadership questionnaire was to identify the leadership style of a leader.

Operational Definitions

Transactional Leadership

Bass (1985) had made a distinction between transactional and transformational leadership. Transactional leaders take an exchange perspective to their relationship with subordinates and exchange rewards for the efforts of employees. Bass argues that if leaders are to obtain performance from the subordinates far beyond the normal limits, they should practice transformational and not transactional leadership.

Transformational Leadership

Transformational leadership is exercised when the leader intellectually stimulates the subordinates, excites, arouses, and inspires them to perform far beyond what they would have thought themselves capable of. By providing a new vision, the transformational leader transforms the followers into people who self-actualize. Charismatic leadership is central to transformational leadership.

Controls

1. Noise and distractions are kept at the bare minimum level.
2. Instructions are given properly.
3. Made sure that the employee has understood the instructions well.

Methodology

Sample: - S1 - Ms. Disha Parab

HR Manager, Rediffusion Ad Agency

S^2 - Mr. Anand Nair

Sr. Project Manager, Vishan Projects Pvt. Ltd.

Materials used

A 2-sheet questionnaire consisting of 20 items. Each item has 2 statements A and B. one has to divide 5 points between the two according to one's beliefs, perceptions of oneself or according to which of the two statements characterizes oneself better. The five points may be divided between A and B statements in any one of the following ways.

5A, 0B. 4A, 1B. 3A, 2B. 1A, 4B.0A, 5B, but not equally i.e. 2 1/2 between the two.

Instructions

"For each of the following twenty pairs of statements, divide 5 points between the two according to your beliefs, perceptions of yourself or according to which of the two statements characterizes you better. The five points may be divided between A and B statements in any of the following ways – 5A, OB; 4A, 1B; 3A, 2B; 1A, 4B, 0-A, 5B – but not equally (2½) between the two. Weigh your choices between the two according to which one characterizes you or your beliefs better".

Discussion

The leadership questionnaire helps in identifying the leadership style of the respondent. Both the respondents were from Rediffusion DY&R. The first respondent was Ms Disha Parab who is the HR Executive. She takes care of all the HR functions. The Second respondent was Mr. Anand Nair who is the Sr. Project manager for Vishan Projects Pvt. Ltd.

One can see that both have got a higher score on transformational leadership as compared to Transactional leadership. Disha has got a score of 54, and Anand has got a score of 53 on transformational leadership style. Disha has got a score of 22, and Anand 48 on transactional leadership style. One can see that the difference in the scores of Disha is much higher than the difference between the scores obtained by Anand. Both have an ideal leadership operating style. Transactional leaders are those who exchange rewards for good behavior, efforts, and inputs from people. They will also intervene if standards are not met. Transformational leaders are those who take group beyond expectations, will raise the follower's level of consciousness about the value and importance of designated outcomes and also ways of reaching them. These leaders will transcend the self-interest for the sake of team, organization, society and the nation. They will expand/alter the need levels on Maslow's hierarchy. Such leaders also provide vision, sense of mission, instill pride, gains, respect and trust. He will communicate higher expectations from the followers; will also provide mental stimulation from time to time. He will have individual level of concentration, and personal attention will treat each employee with personalized touch, these people identify themselves as the change agents. These leaders are value driven, are life long learners, have the ability to deal with complexity, ambiguity, and uncertainty.

As Anand has all these traits he can lead the group members to exceptional levels of performance. In today's business and organizations one has to modify the way they deal with people, handle issues and problems. One has to take into consideration various perspective. Everyone today realizes that the most important asset of any organization is the people who need to be valued. If one thinks about this deeply he/she will realize that transformational leadership is all about treating humans as humans. So one has to take a very human approach, which will definitely increase effectiveness and efficiency.

Being a part of the HR department even Disha gives a lot of importance to this approach. According to her she has to be more of a people's person, which her scores validate.

3. Motivational Analysis of Behaviour

Introduction

Some kind of motivation is implicit directly or indirectly in any human endeavor. Motivation is an art of incentive and appeal through which an individual is stimulated to do a certain thing. In each phase of human life, motivation is very important. In a way, a man does nothing without any motivation, which may pertain either to his family, personal, social or national affair. If one has no motivation for a particular work, either he will not start it or will leave it in the middle after starting it. Motivation is a tendency towards activity for achieving some immediate or remote goal. A motivation rises within an individual and it may be recognized by the work in which he appears to be actively engaged. Motivation arises in different ways in various persons according to their intentions and goals in life; the desire for doing a work or not doing, it arises from one's inner motivation. There is always some purpose behind what one does. This purpose may be material, social or spiritual; but it is there. For achieving a goal, there is an inner restlessness, which activates an individual. This inner restlessness may be regarded as a motivation. Need, drive and incentive are necessary factors for feeling a motivation. For understanding the nature of motivation, these factors must be understood.

Needs

Man has some natural needs. Most of his behaviors are always controlled by such needs. There are two types of needs - primary and secondary. One cannot survive if these primary needs are not fulfilled. Secondary needs arise due to experience. Various persons have different experiences, many of the secondary needs arise from our force of habits. A person loses his balance if his primary needs are not fulfilled. Need is such a phenomenon within an individual which develops a tension in him. This tension leads him to organize his environment in such a manner that he may achieve his goal. Each need requires certain objects or activities. When they are obtained, the tension in the individual is released.

Drive: For meeting the mentioned needs, a person becomes restless and harbors a tension until the same is met. The feeling of this restlessness is known as drive. A drive is a center-force, which propels an individual in a particular direction for meeting a certain need.

Incentive: Normally, it is seen that unless there is an incentive in view, one does not exert him much. That is why in industries, we find the practice of promotion, bonus, rewards and other facilities for the workers who appear to be quite spectacular in their performance, incentive activates one's drive for fulfilling some of his needs. An incentive may be either positive or negative.

Motivation Propelling Towards Work: We find that persons appointed in the same scale of pay in an industry or at any other place have different types of motivations. Some have the motivation to support their families in a more decent manner. Some may have the objective to amass as much wealth as possible in order that he/may become a big person for controlling certain things in the society. Some may have the motivation to reach the Parliament and ultimately control the affairs of the state. Thus, we find that various types of inequalities existing in our society stimulate different persons with varying-motivations. Directly or indirectly, these motivations energize us in a constructive manner for achieving something really good or in an aggressive manner to harm someone in order to go ahead by fair or foul means.

Extrinsic versus Intrinsic Motivation

In recent years industry has increased the proposition of earnings paid to workers as wages and at the same time has increased the number of fringe benefits. Retirement plans, Life and health insurance, rest pauses, and vacations with pay have been added to wages as rewards for workers. Each of these incentives is intended to influence satisfaction with working for a particular company rather than to increase the satisfaction of work itself. When the satisfaction lies outside the work activity itself, we may speak of the motivation as extensive in nature. This kind of motivation may cause a person to choose an unpleasant job that offers attractive rewards and forget that he will have to spend most of his time in work activity that he dislikes. Furthermore, he cannot enjoy those incentives unless he stops working.

In contrast, play activity has no such extrinsic attractions. As a matter of fact, play usually costs money and earnings may be reduced if the employee takes time off. As such, the extrinsic motivation is one of driving a person away from play, yet play activity can compete with work activity for an individual's time. If this is true there must be more to the picture than the extrinsic incentives, those overlooked incentives are within the field of activity. Work and play satisfaction can come from the activity itself, as well as from fulfillment of social and personal needs. The motivational values associated with the activity are called intrinsic because the satisfaction occurs during the activity.

Finding ways to incorporate more intrinsic motivation into the work situation is a matter of innovation. Non-financial incentives and methods for increasing job interest are forms of intrinsic motivation.

Complexity of Behaviour

The Complexity of Motivation: One thing that psychologists know is that an individual rarely if-ever behaves or responds in a situation as a result of a single motive. They clearly recognize the complexity of human behaviour and understand that a person often does not know the true reason for his behaviour. Because of this complex behaviour, an individual is, in many instances, unpredictable.

A major error in the industry has been the oversimplification of the concept of motivation. Since along time it has been often assumed that the primary reason that people work is to earn money. This is absurd as well as unquestionably false. Man has many motives, and unless we recognize the part played by each, one cannot possibly begin to understand his behaviour.

When a psychologist talks about motivation, he is concerned with studying the individual with respect to ever-changing physiological conditions and a multitude of previous experiences. Because of these two factors, physiological changes and previous experiences, it must be recognized that motivation may stem from within an individual or from factors acting on him from the outside. Further more, these two categories are not mutually independent; on the contrary, they are interwoven all the time.

The simpler motives originating from physiological imbalances within a species are generally known as hunger, thirst, oxygen need, the need for rest and sleep, curiosity, and sex. A good many motives act on the individual as a result of the multitude of his experiences, these are in a large part determined by the social pressures of the society in which he lives. Although these social motives are sometimes given only vague and indirect expressions, they nevertheless must be recognized as just as important as the so-called simpler motives if we are to be successful in understanding why man behaves the way he does. Gregariousness, self-assertiveness, acquisitiveness, the desire for prestige, and the desire to conform are only a few of the many social motives that act on man. Motivation is truly complex. Different forms of behaviour are sometimes similarly motivated. A desire to be outstanding or to acquire prestige may cause one person by entering matrimony and still another by remaining single. The next person may decide to fulfil this desire by acquiring wealth. All these different forms of behaviour may lead to the same amount of success by achieving the same end. The converse is also true. Different motives may sometimes result in one form of behaviour. Thus a person may write a book because he wants to acquire wealth or gain prestige or have an opportunity for self-expression or creativeness. It would help if we amplify the performance = (ability X motivation) function a bit.

Performance can be regarded as almost any behaviour, which is directed towards a task or goal accomplishment. It may involve the production of a certain number of pieces, resolving a conflict with a co-worker, getting a project done by a certain date, or being seen as a satisfactory performer by one's boss. It is intended to illustrate some obvious points. Performance is not synonymous with effort, ability, or a combination of the two. The choice to work on the task, the understanding of what is to be done, the choice to persist, and the environmental constraints all play an important role. It seems most meaningful to view motivation as a label for the determinants of (a) the choice to initiate efforts on a certain task, (b) the choice to expend a certain amount of effort, and (c) the choice to persist in expending effort over a period of time. That is, motivation has to do with a set of independent/dependent variable relationships that explains the direction, amplitude, and persistence of an individual's behaviour, holding constant the effects of aptitude, skill, and understanding of the task, and the constraints operating in the environment.

Motivation and Work: People work for various reasons, sometimes for a combination of reasons and sometimes for different reasons at different times. In India, the vast majority of people work for money for livelihood and maintenance of the family. Those who get beyond the stage of "making the two ends meet", may work for gaining good social status or position, to further professional attainment, freedom, challenge and a variety in jobs and even for the interest in the job itself. The reasons for work at various stages of working life may also change. A young graduate may enter a job initially for his livelihood and independence, then for improving on social position and recognition and so on.

Conflicts In Motivations

When a person confronts two kinds, of motivations, he gets into a fix and is not able to decide as to which course to follow. Suppose there is a worker who is confirmed and permanent in his service and the company allows all his regular benefits in addition to bonus and other facilities and he feels quite satisfied with his existing position. But another company offers him an identical job on double the salary that he is already enjoying but on a temporary basis for a year with the condition that he will be made permanent after a year and then he will get all other benefits, which other workers of the company enjoy.

Now the worker will be naturally in a fix. He would not easily decide whether to remain in his previous position or leave it for the temporary service on a double salary. Thus, there arises a motivational conflict in his mind. In an industry, there are generally three types of such conflicts:

Negative or Unpleasant Incentive: Sometimes a worker has to face two types of negative or unpleasant incentives. In this situation, there arises a conflict in his mind. For example, a worker wants to leave the factory because of the lack of guarantee of service there. At the same time, he has an offer on a lower salary in another factory but with the guarantee of permanence. It is generally seen that in this type of conflict, the worker will like to remain in his former service, as he considers that as less unpleasant and hopes for getting himself permanently instituted.

Negative and positive Incentive: Sometimes, a worker faces' strange situation, which is mixed with pleasant and unpleasant (or positive and negative) incentives. This situation creates a conflict in his mind. For example, a worker at the place of work enjoys a handsome salary, but there is always a risk to his health because of the particular nature (environment) of the factory. He has in view an offer from another factory on a lower salary, with no risk to his health. Now there arises a conflict in the mind of the worker. He takes time to decide his course of action. In such a situation, it is generally seen that the worker chooses to remain in his present job, because of the higher salary, which he is already enjoying.

Positive Incentives: It also happens sometimes that a worker faces two types of positive incentives. For example, a worker has to choose between two types of positive incentives. One is that of monthly increment of twenty rupees to his salary and the other is of yearly bonus in lieu of the same. Under this situation, he cannot take a decision easily. He deliberates over the matter and thinks over all the pros and cons implied in the issue.

Limitations to Motivation

Certain limitations must be observed in the use of techniques of motivation for raising production. There are some persons who are habituated to exert themselves to the maximum extent. Such persons add greatly to production. Some other persons are very slow in their work and with some motivation; their speed of work may be accelerated. Both these types of persons have their limitations. So the levels of motivation should not be carried too far, otherwise it will bring undue fatigue in both the cases. Some motivation may be used in either case, just for enforcing the will to work in a pleasant mood. When any motivation is carried to an unpleasant extent, then its effect is harmful to production. It may be kept in mind that the purpose of motivation may also be there just to encourage the workers to sharpen their abilities further, which they may do by employing a more effective method of work. Motivation is the backbone of industrial development. Therefore, its application is very necessary.

Precautions in the Use of Motivation

Simplicity of Motivation: Any motivation to be given should be easily understandable by the persons for whom it is intended and also by the observers. For example, if a worker is to be praised for his good work, the cause of praise should be explained to the concerned worker and also to other workers in the industry. If it is done, the other workers will not regard it as a nepotism and partiality and will not express their resentment through their behaviour against the worker concerned and the manager who has given the praise.

Adequacy of Motivation: The motivation should be adequate enough to be effective immediately or at the earliest. A worker generally likes that motivation which stimulates him immediately. A worker is naturally interested in strengthening his financial position. If a motivation immediately adds to its strengthening, its effect is immediate and the implied purpose towards speeding up production is also served.

Interests and Attitudes: The motivation to be given should be according to the interests and attitudes of the workers concerned. If this is not done, it will not have its desired effect. If a worker's financial condition is poor, he may be more interested in having some money in reward and not an empty praise. The motivation should be such as to bring about a favorable change in his attitude towards productive work. The manager of the industry should also see that the implied motivation satisfies the workers concerned.

Effective Motivation: The given incentive should be effective enough for motivating the worker immediately. If an incentive fulfils some immediate need of the worker, but it does not motivate him for putting his best in the work, then the same will be useless. The given incentive should have a permanent effect otherwise the workers will consider it merely an eyewash.

Some Ways of Giving Motivations to Workers

Emulation: In industries, the technique of emulation for accelerating production has been successfully used. Emulation may be of two types. In one type, the worker is encouraged to break his own previous record and the other is that of breaking the production record of another worker. Emulation may be either between individuals or between teams. But in this technique, it is necessary that the previous record of production of the individual or of the team, as the case may be, should be placed. In placing the previous record for emulation, it is necessary to devise some means of production measurement and the individual or the team must be made aware of its previous record in terms of this measurement. Then the individual or the team will try to surpass this record. Emulation may be either in relation to surpassing one's own previous record or that of another.

Praise as a Motivation: Praise is a very good technique of motivation for all types of workers in any field of human endeavor. So whenever a worker does some good work, he must be praised. Praise satisfies his ego and he is automatically encouraged to do his best. It is generally seen that supervisors or managers rebuke workers on errors or on poor production, but on recording good production they keep silence. This attitude on their part discourages workers. Even when a worker's production is not upto mark, he may be politely and affectionately encouraged to try further and on good production, they must praise the workers. Praise may be as strong a motivating force as increment in salary or some other reward in cash or kind. However, if it appears necessary to rebuke some worker for his poor performance, it should not be done in the presence of others.

Group Co-operation: When in an endeavor the entire group is involved, then it is better if the group itself determines its production target. Then this target will be considered as self-imposed and everyone involved will try his best to meet it. In all types of industries, this technique has proved quite helpful in speeding up production both qualitatively and quantitatively.

Ascertaining Worker's Desires: Ascertaining the workers' own desire from their jobs is a difficult task in the sense that variations will be quite natural in the viewpoints of various individuals and it will be also difficult to make their desire pertaining to their jobs as the basis for motivations to them. Various psychological studies have revealed that some workers have given preference to their pay and some have expressed greater desire for favorable conditions of work. In comparison to male-workers, female-workers have expressed preference to good conditions of work and not so much on Chances of promotion on high salaries. Some attach greater importance to security and safety. Thus, there is no unanimity regarding the desires of various workers. However, in the interest of growth of industry, it is very necessary to meet, as far as possible, the worker's desires in relation to their jobs. Then, there will be satisfaction in them and fewer instances of strikes and slowdowns.

The objective of conducting this motivation analysis of behavior is to identify the amount of importance attached to different types of motivations.

Operational Definitions

Achievement: This motive is characterized by concern for excellence, competition with the standards of excellence set by others or by self. The setting of challenging goals for oneself, awareness of the hurdles in the way of achieving those goals and persistence in paths to reach one's goals.

Affiliation: This motive is characterized by a concern for establishing and monitoring close personal relationship by value on friendship and the tendency to express one's emotions.

Influence: This motive is characterized by concern to make an impact on others. A desire to make people do what one thinks is right, and urge to change matters and develop people.

Control: This motive is characterized by concern for orderliness, a desire to remain informed and an urge to monitor and take corrective action when needed.

Extension: This motive is characterized by concern for others, interests in subordinate goals and an urge to be relevant and useful to larger groups including society.

Dependence: This motive is characterized by desire for help from others in one's own self development, checking significant others, submitting ideas or proposals for approval having an urge to maintain an "approach" relationship.

Controls

Noise and distractions are kept to a bare minimum level.

Instructions are properly given.

Made sure that the employees have understood the instructions well.

Methodology

Sample: - S^1 - Mr. Anand Nair (Sr. Project Manager)

S^2 - Ms. Disha Parab (Executive, HR Manager)

Materials used: The questionnaire consists of 60 items, with 6 dimensions to be tested. There are 5 items on each dimension. There are approach and avoidance scores of the respondents on each motivational drive. The total score can range from 5- 20. This questionnaire will provide a profile of motivational aspects of role behavior.

Instructions

"Read each statement given in the enclosed instrument – and identifying how true it is about you – indicate this by writing 1, 2, 3 or 4 against the number of the item on the answer sheet. Do not write anything else on the instrument itself. Use the following key to give your answers:

If you hardly show this behaviour.

If you show this behaviour sometime.

If you often show this behaviour.

If you behave this way most of the time."

Discussion

Motivational Analysis Organization Behavior (MAOB) was developed to study manager and employee behavior in organizations. The MAO-B contains 60 items, 5 for each dimension (approach and avoidance) of each of the 6 motives. During administration the participants should be told that it would provide them with a profile of motivational aspects of role behavior.

They should also be told that there are no right or wrong responses. The scoring is quite easy. These totals give scores for 6 motives. The total score of each dimension of the 6 motives can range from 5 to 20. The respondents operating effectiveness quotient (OEQ) for each of the 6 motives – specific aspects of behavior defined by the net score of approach dimensions can be obtained by using the formula.

$$OEQ = \frac{P - S}{P + V - 10} X 100$$

Total scores for approach and avoidance dimensions respectively of a motive–specific behavior for Disha Parab, HR Manager, Rediffusion Ad Agency, scores around all the 6 motives are very similar. She scores 17 on achievement, 15 on influence, 18 on control, 15 on dependency and application and 19 on extension.

Her need for any of the other needs is very different from the highest need. There is almost a difference of 3 points. This shows that she is relatively equal in her need for all the 6 motives.

But her tendency to influence by expertise is lower than the other needs. This was also reflected on the way she carried herself. She was the utmost vulnerable person and was very co-operative.

The 2nd S was Mr. Anand Nair, Sr. Project Manager, Vishan Projects Pvt. Ltd., His scores for achievement was 21, influence – 24, control – 17, dependency – 21, extension – 16 and affiliation – 15. Thus the most important needs for the individual are that of achievement, and influence. Thus he tries to reach standards of excellence and challenging goals. He has a high concern for proving himself. This is also reflected by the fact that his need for dependency is high.

Hence, his motivation seems to be centered on winning his own as well as other's approval. He also has a high need for extension and is happy that the work that he does is helpful to the society. His need for influence by expertise and control as well as his need for affiliation are relatively low.

In fact, his avoidant behavior for each of the motives is exceptionally high for all the 4 motives expect for Achievement and Dependency wherein his approach and avoidance tendencies are equal.

4. Learning Style

Introduction

To learn in an organizational context is to gain knowledge and skills, accompanied by a desirable change in behaviour.

Learning is, of course, indispensable to survival and growth. It is true that people with limited learning ability can survive– sometime even thrive – so long as the environment is relatively stable. However, once there is turbulence, complexity, or hostility they find it difficult to cope and then experience decline.

Organizational learning, too, can be shallow or profound, an incapacity to learn and adapt, can land an organization in trouble as soon as the environment turns turbulent, complex, or hostile.

Organizational learning can be said to be taking place when members of the organization collectively learn and alter their organizational behaviour. As Chris Argyris and Don Schon put it, "Organizational learning occurs when members of the organization act as learning agents for the organization; responding to changes in the internal and external environments of the organization by detecting and correcting errors in organizational theory-in-use, and embedding the results of their inquiry in private images and shared maps of the organization".

Mechanisms that increase the participation of members in learning, collective sense –making of information, and the ability and freedom of members to try ideas out and learn from the results, should enhance such organizational learning.

Models of Learning

There are many different models of learning. Instruction and books of absorbing the information dish out one model commonly employed in schools and colleges. A radically different model, widely used in apprenticeship situations, is one of learning from experience without much formal training and education. A third model is one of action learning – learning from feedback on one's proactive, entrepreneurial actions, there are also dialectical models of learning exemplified by the common debate, in which a thesis is countered by an antithesis and eventually some form of synthesis generally emerges.

Gestalt psychologists have emphasized the role of anomalies and apparent contradictions in triggering insights – a form of learning through radically altered perception.

Behaviorists have thought of learning as behaviour modification, achieved through appropriate rewards and punishments.

Freudians have developed cleansing models of learning – in which resistance to acceptance of reality, rooted in repressed childhood traumas, is broken down by 'catharsis', or re-living of these traumas.

Sociologists have pointed to the power of situational demands and the roles one has to play in learning or molding of behaviour.

Organizational psychologists have emphasized the importance of experiencing observation, reflection, conceptualization, and active experimentation in learning. They have also emphasized making contact with whatever one is opposed to; giving voice to the under-represented, dominated, or denied; responding constructively to the unpleasant rather than suppressing or denying it. These alternative but often complementary ways of learning offer of rich pool of ideas for viewing organizational learning and for developing practical ways of enhancing it in organizations. Besides textbook learning and apprenticeship, there are rich, relatively under-tapped options in organizational learning through debates, contradictions, rewards and punishment, catharsis, role changes, exposure, reflection, experimentation, voicing the unvoiced, brainstorming, etc.

A Model of Organizational Learning

Organizational learning is an exciting, new approach to organization development. Udai Pareek has suggested that organizational learning is the process by which the organization acquires, retains, and uses inputs for its development, and that this development is characterized by an enhanced capacity for continued self-learning and self-renewal. Organizational learning, he has argued, is driven by several factors; experimentation and flexibility; teamwork, mutual support and collaboration; contingency planning (planning that takes into account alternative future scenarios); building on existing strengths ('incremental'); use of ad hoc or temporary systems such as task forces for attaining sharply focused, limited objectives; and competency building (as through training). Udai Pareek has developed an instrument for assessing the extent to which organizations utilize various mechanisms related to these dimensions.

Usage of Learning Mechanisms in Indian Organizations

The most commonly used learning mechanism were: staff being sent to external training programs and conferences, use of skilled staff for implementing changes, modification of plans based on project implementation experience, use of innovative experts for briefing staff, and periodic staff meetings to share the results of experiments. It may be noted that 3 out of these 5 most commonly used mechanisms were for aiding innovation and experimentation. This suggests an inadequate use of mechanisms related to implementation and stabilization of innovations and new projects. The least used mechanisms were task force for institutionalizing (that is, stabilizing and consolidating) changes and innovations, sharing of learning with other organizations, task force based evaluation of implemented innovations, task force based empirical evaluation of innovations, and staff seminars on new developments. With the exception of item (task forces for implementing new projects), thc use of task forces as learning devices seems to be relativity less frequently used.

On the whole the organizational studies used the learning mechanisms only moderately. If the study sample is representative of the more progressive among Indian corporate organizations, there is clearly much scope to increase the use of learning mechanisms in Indian organization.

In an age of complexity, turbulence, and competition, organizational learning ability may well provide the edge that ensures survival and prosperity. For choosing management styles, therefore, one important consideration may be how 'learning-friendly' they are:

The altruistic, participative, bureaucratic, and entrepreneurial styles are especially learning-friendly, followed at some distance by the professional and organic styles. Defective intuitive (pathological distrust of any formal expertise), defective conservative (pathological aversion to anything new), and defective authoritarian (brute force and arbitrary management) are especially inimical to organizational learning. Three learning mechanisms seem to be especially strategic, for they may catalyze the use of many other learning mechanisms as well as superior organizational performance. These are: the widespread use of task forces to evaluate changes and innovations on the basis of evidence (rather than on a priori or subjective grounds), the use of skilled persons for implementing changes and innovations (rather than the favorites of related to the business of the organization for the staff. None of these are difficult or expensive mechanisms, but their use may catalyze corporate management revolutions in Third World conditions.

The objective of conducting this test is to identify the person's learning preferences so that the person is in a better position to select learning experiences that suit his/her style.

Operational Definitions

Activists

Activists involve themselves fully and without bias in new experiences. They enjoy the here and now and are happy to be dominated by immediate experiences. They are open- minded, not skeptical and this tends to make them enthusiastic about- anything new. Their philosophy is "I'll try anything once". They dash in where angels fear to tread. They tend to throw the caution to the wind. Their days are filled with activity. They tackle problems by brainstorming. As soon as the excitement from one activity has died down they are busy looking for the next. They tend to thrive on the challenge of new experiences but are bored with implementation and longer-term consolidation. They are gregarious people constantly involving themselves with others, but in doing so they hog the limelight. They are the life and soul of the party and seek to center all activities around themselves.

Reflectors

Reflectors like to stand back and ponder experiences and observe them from many different perspectives. They collect data, both first hand and from others and prefer to chew it over thoroughly before coming to any conclusion. The thorough collection and analysis of data about experiences and events is what counts so they tend to postpone reaching definitive conclusions for as long as possible. Their philosophy is to be cautious, to leave no stone unturned. Look before you leap, sleep on it. They are thoughtful people who like to consider all possible angles and implications before making a move. They prefer to take a back seat in meetings and discussions. They enjoy observing other people in action. They listen to others and get the drift of the discussion before making their own points. They tend to adopt a low profile and have a slightly distant, tolerant, unruffled air about them.

When they act it is as part of a wide picture which includes the past as well as the present and others observations as well as their own.

Theorists

Theorists adapt and integrate observations into complex but logically sound theories. They think problems through in a vertical step-by-step logical way. They assimilate disparate fact into coherent theories. They tend to be perfectionists who don't rest easy until things are tidy and fit into their rational scheme. They like to analyze and synthesize. They are keen on basic assumptions, principles, theories, models and systems thinking. Their philosophy prizes rationality and logic. If it's logical it's good. Questions they frequently ask are, does it make sense? How does this fit with that? What are the basic assumptions? They tend to be detached, analytical and dedicated to rational objectivity rather than anything subjective or ambiguous. Their approach to problems is consistently logical. This is their mental set and they rigidly reject anything that does not fit with it. They prefer to maximize certainly and feel uncomfortable with subjective judgements, lateral thinking and anything flippant.

Pragmatists

Pragmatists are keen on trying out ideas, theories and techniques to see if they work in practice. They positively search out new ideas and take the first opportunity to experiment with applications. They are the sort of people who return from management courses brimming with new ideas and they want to try out in practice. They like to get on with things and act quickly and confidently on ideas that attract them. They don't like beating around the bush and tend to be impatient with ruminating and open ended discussions. They are essentially practical, down to earth people who like making practical decisions and solving problems. They respond to problems and opportunities as a challenge. Their philosophy is, there is always a better way.

Controls

1. Noise and distractions are kept at the bare minimum level.
2. Instructions are given properly.
3. Made sure that the employees have understood the instructions properly.

Methodology

Sample: - S[1] - Ms. Disha Parab

HR Manager, Rediffusion Ad Agency

S2 - Mr. Anand Nair

Sr. Project Manager, Vishan Projects Pvt. Ltd.

Materials used

Peter Honey and Alan Mumford develop the Learning Style Questionnaire (LSQ). This questionnaire helps the individual to pinpoint his/her learning preferences so that he/she is in a better position to select learning experiences that suit his/her style.

Honey and Mumford have described four learning styles. The individual after taking this test could be labeled as an Activist or Reflector or Theorist or Pragmatist depending on his score.

Instructions

Take each set of four words separately and place a 4 by the word which best describes the way you learn, a 3 by the next best 2 by the next best and a 1 by the least best. (Do not give any two words in one set the same score).

Discussion

The (LSI) Learning Style Inventory measures your relative emphasis on the 4 learning modes by asking you to rank a series of 4 words that describe different abilities. Combination of scores indicates the extent to which you emphasize abstractness over concreteness (AC-CE). Similarly with any other pair of scores. The LSI describes how one can learn; the way one can find out about and deal with ideas and situations in one's life. Different people learn best in different ways. This scale just tries to identity that style.

The first S was Mrs. Disha Parab, Executive HR Manager, Rediffusion Ad Agency. Her scores on the LSI were; CE 11, OR 14, IE 23 and AE 17. Thus the Ss highest score with the IE and the second highest score was for AE. Thus the S is predominantly pragmatic. Thus she is keen on trying out ideas, theories and techniques to see if they work in practice. They positively search out new ideas and take the first opportunity to experiment with applications. They strive to get on with things and act quickly and fast. She would be a practical, down to earth and realistic person.

But the negative points are that they lend to reject anything without an obvious application, they are not interested in theory or basic principles. Also tends to take the first solution available on hand. Such a person is more task oriented rather than person oriented.

Her score on CE and OR is average, this reflects that she is not very open to new experiences and that she does not reflect much in the beginning, rather reflects in the end. Thus, she needs to work on increasing her awareness, reflection and observation and also on her openness to experience.

The results of S2 Mr. Anand Nair, Sr. Project Manager, Vishan Projects Pvt. Ltd., show the same results as S1. Even his scores are high on IE and AE showing his orientation of a pragmatic person.

He too needs to work on increasing his awareness, reflection and observation and also on openness to experience.

5. Organizational Role Stress

Introduction

In any social system, such as family, club, religious community, work organization, etc., individuals have certain obligations towards the system, which in turn gives each one of them a defined place in the society. This system of mutual obligations can be called a role and the individual's place, a position or an office. For example when one joins a new club, one is admitted as a member. One also agrees to abide by certain rules, carry out certain activities when required volunteer for certain work. The other members of the club expect all this from the individual, and one also expects to do the needful. All these expectations, together with one's response to them compromise the role.

Role is the position one occupies in a social system, as defined by the functions, one performs in response to the expectations of the 'significant' members of a social system, and one's own expectations from that position or office.

A role is not defined without the expectations of the role senders, including the role occupant. The position of a personnel manager may be created in an organization, but his role will be defined by the expectations (stated or unstated) that different persons have from the personnel manager, and the expectations that he in turn, has from the role. In this sense, the role senders, including the role occupant, define the role in each system.

How A Person Takes A Role?

When a person becomes a member of a social system, he 'receives' certain expectations from other members, and he responds to these, at the same time projecting his own expectations from the role. Either one of them (responding to others' expectations or projecting one's own expectations from one's role) may dominate the other. One may react very positively and with great satisfaction to other's expectations, and fulfill them to best of one's abilities. Such a 'reactive' (responsive) approach will help the individual take the role effectively. In contrast, another individual may use the expectations he has from his role (what Kahn and Quinn call reflexive role expectations) and develop a role behaviour influenced by these expectations. This is a 'proactive' approach to role performance. Some authors have contrasted these two approaches, calling the first, 'role taking' and the second, 'role making', the main difference being the use of one's own expectations in defining a role and determining one's own role behavior.

Two Role Systems

An organization can be defined as a system of roles. However, a role itself is a system. From the individual's point of view there are two role systems: the system of various roles, which the individual carries and performs, and the system of various roles of which his role is a part. The first, we will call role space and the second, a role set. Each individual occupies and plays several roles. A person X is a daughter, a mother, a member of a club, a member of a voluntary organization. All these roles constitute the role spacc of X. at the center of thc role space is the self. As the concept of role is central to that of an organization, so also the concept of self is central to the several roles of a person.

A person performs various roles, which are centered on the self. These relationships define the role space. Role space is then a dynamic interrelationship between the self and the various roles an individual occupies, and also amongst these roles.

The distance between a role and the self indicates the extent to which the role is integrated with the self. When we do not enjoy a particular role or do not get involved in it, there is distance between the self and the role. We shall use the term self-role distance to denote this.

Need for Role Interventions

Various types of interventions have been developed, focusing on the different dimensions of the organizations. The oldest of such interventions relate to working with individuals and bringing about some change in their attitudes, skills, and general orientation. Basic psychological theories have helped in designing such interventions. Advances in psychotherapy, a new understanding of the individual and his psychodynamics, and an increased interest in the individual, have all helped in developing a variety of effective interventions, as far as the change in the individual is concerned. The more recent interventions focus on change in groups, mainly smaller groups. Greater interest has recently been shown in the interventions focused on the technology of work and jobs in the organization.

One dimension of an organization, which has remained, comparatively neglected is that of a role. Only two interventions, with role as the main focus, have so far been reported in literature: 1) role analysis technique (RAT) by Dayal and Thomas and 2) Role Negotiation by Harrison. RAT is primarily used to analyze and define a role, and has limited scope. Role negotiation is a much more dynamic intervention.

Role is an important dimension in understanding an organization and planning its effectiveness. It is through role that an individual gets linked with the system (of which he is a member). This linkage is a vital 'entity', which may help increase organizational effectiveness by integrating the individual with the organization. In this sense, role becomes an important dimension for planning the effectiveness of both the person and the organization.

The main problem for an individual is how to continue to live autonomously as a person and at the same time maximize the effectiveness of various roles, thereby integrating the self with the roles.

Characteristics of Role Focused Interventions

The interventions primarily focus on organizational roles. Although some of them can be used in dealing with the problems related to an individual's non-work roles, the primary focus is on the work roles and an increase in their effectiveness.

The main purpose behind these interventions is to increase the mutuality of roles in an organization. Organizational effectiveness to a large extent depends on such mutuality. Mutuality ensures that the problems, which an organization faces, are solved by teams of people who use their expertise in looking at various aspects of the problems, and collaborate in ensuring speedy, efficient and effective solutions.

These interventions should not be seen only as techniques; they represent an approach and a philosophy of working in an organization. The issues that are particularly relevant in role interventions are mentioned.

1. **Mutuality versus Exclusiveness:** Role interventions attempt to build mutuality amongst the roles. Help giving and receiving is possible only in a relationship of mutuality. Mutuality is a function of trust, and a perception of the importance and power of the other role as well as one's own. If a role occupant perceives his own role, or the other role to lack power, other kinds of relationship may develop between the two roles.
2. **Creativity versus Conformity:** Role interventions attempt to stimulate persons in an organization to search new solutions to the problems they face in working together. The emphasis is on attempting alternative ways of solving a problem. Role-interventions tone down the use of traditional methods of problem solving, if these methods have not proved to be efficacious. Creativity can be achieved by looking at the problem from different angles, and IRE (inter-role expectation) stresses this. Creativity is related to internal locus of control.
3. **Confrontation versus Avoidance:** The main philosophy underlying role intervention is that problems can be solved if they are brought to the surface and a conscious attempt made to search out a solution. Instead, of avoiding the problems either by not looking at them or by working on non- issues, these interventions attempt to help the various role occupants confront their problems in order to find a solution. According to this approach,

confrontation of a problem is necessary to reach a lasting solution.

4. **Exploration Versus Expectation of Readymade Solutions:** Role interventions attempt to help people evolve a solution rather than expect any such solution from experts or from other persons in the organization. The usual tendency is to look for a readymade solution, which may relieve tension, especially if it is suggested and prescribed by an authority figure like an expert or the top management. The underlying philosophy of role focused OD is that such a solution may not be effective in solving a problem. Effective solutions can come about only through exploration rather than through acceptance of an ideal solution. Exploration would mean a joint effort at understanding the problem and weighing the alternate solutions.

Role interventions use a structured approach along with process orientation. Although the various steps involved in these interventions are aimed at generating data, using structured exercises, the work on the data involves group work, and the solutions can only be achieved through process-oriented work on the problems brought to the surface by the structured exercises. By using the structured exercises, the usual threat which process work produces is reduced. Confrontation of the problems and issues of inter-role relationships are brought up during the discussion in which process interventions by a consultant become important.

To sum up, the main purpose of role-focused interventions is to increase creativity and the coping ability of individual employees, and also promote mutuality amongst the organizational roles.

Life Stress

Stress is produced by several happenings in life. In general, every transition or change produces stress. People in newer states experience a higher stress of transition. Young people between 20 and 30 yrs of age have been found to report twice as much stress when, compared to older people. Stress disorders have been found more frequently amongst the urban population than the rural, and are greater in the higher educational categories.

Role Stress

Role can be defined as a set of functions, which an individual performs in response to the expectations of the significant members of a social system, and his own expectations about the position that he occupies in it. There are two role systems: role space and role set.

Role Space Conflicts

Role space (the dynamic relationship amongst the various roles an individual occupies and his self has three main variables: self the role under question, and the other roles he occupies. Any conflicts amongst these are referred to as role space conflicts or stress.

1. **Self-Role Distance:** This stress arises out of the conflict between the self-concept and the expectations from the role, as perceived by the role occupant. If a person occupies a role, which he may subsequently find as conflicting with the self-concept, he feels stressed. For example, an introvert who is fond of studying and writing, may develop as self-role distance if he accepts the role of a salesman in an organization, and comes to realize that the expectations from the role would include his meeting people and being social. Such conflicts are fairly common, although they may not be so severe.

2. **Intra-Role Conflict:** Since an individual learns to develop expectations as a result; of his socialization and identification with significant' others, it is quite likely that he sees certain incompatibility between the expectations (functions) of his role.

3. **Role Stagnation:** As the individual grows older, he also grows in the role that he occupies in an organization. With the advancement of the individual the role changes, and with this change in role, the need for taking up a new role becomes crucial. This problem of role growth becomes acute especially when an individual who has occupied a role for a long time enters another role demands that an individual outgrow the previous one and take charge of the new role effectively. This is bound to produce some stress. In organizations which are fast expanding, and which do not have any systematic of manpower development, managers are likely to experience this stress of role stagnation when they are promoted.

4. **Inter-Role Distance:** Where an individual occupies more than one role there is bound to be conflicts between the different roles that he occupies. For example, a lady executive often faces the conflict between her organizational role as an executive and her familial

role as a wife and a mother. The demands of her husband and children for sharing her time may be incompatible with the organizational demands. Such inter-role conflicts are quite frequent in a modern society, where an individual is increasingly occupying multiple roles in various organizations and groups.

Role Set Conflicts

The conflicts, which arise, as a result of incompatibility amongst these expectations by the 'significant' others (and by the individual himself) are referred to as role set conflicts.

1. **Role Ambiguity:** When the individual is not clear about the various expectations that people have from his role, the conflict that he faces is called role ambiguity. Role ambiguity may be due to lack of information available to the role occupant, or due to lack of understanding of the 'cues' available to him. Role ambiguity may be in relation to the activities, responsibilities, priorities, norms, or general expectations. Generally role ambiguity may be experience by persons occupying roles which are newly created in the organization, roles in organizations which are undergoing change, or process roles (with less clear and concrete activities).
2. **Role Expectation Conflict:** When there are conflicting expectations or demands by different role senders (persons having expectations from the role), the role occupant may experience this stress. There may be conflicting expectations from the boss, subordinates, peers or clients.
3. **Role Overload:** When the role occupant feels that there are too many expectations from the 'significant' others in his role set, he experiences role overload. Role overload has been measured by asking questions about people's feelings on whether they could possibly finish work given to them during a modified workday and whether they felt that the amount of work they do might interfere with how well it was done. Most of the executive role occupants experience role overload. Role overload is more likely to occur where there are large variations in the expected output, and when delegation or assistance cannot procure more time.
4. **Role Erosion:** A role occupant may feel that the functions, which he would like to perform, are being performed by some other role.

The stress felt may be called role erosion. Role erosion is the subjective feeling of an individual that some important role expectations he has from the role are shared by other roles within the role set. Role erosion is likely to be experienced in an organization, which is redefining its role and creating new roles. Studies indicate that in several organizations, which were redefining their structure, the stress of role erosion was inevitably felt. In an organization, a particular role was abolished and in its place two roles were created to cater to the executive and planning needs. This led to a great erosion, and a feeling that the new roles were less important as compared to the previous role.

5. **Resource inadequacy:** resource inadequacy stress is experienced when the resources required by the role occupant for performing the role effectively are not available; these may be information, people, material, finance, or facilities.

6. **Personal Inadequacy:** When a role occupant feels that he is not prepared to undertake the role effectively, he may experience stress. The role occupant may feel that he does not have enough knowledge, skills, or training, or he/she has not had time to prepare for the assigned role. Persons who are assigned new roles without enough preparation or orientation are likely to experience this type of stress.

7. **Role Isolation:** In a role set, the role occupant may feel that certain roles are psychologically closer to him, while others are at much greater distance. The main criterion of distance is the frequency and ease of interaction. When linkages are strong, the role isolation will be low and in the absence of strong linkages, the role isolation will be high. Role isolation can therefore be measured in terms of the existing and the desired linkages. The gap between the desired and the existing linkages will indicate the amount of role isolation..

To sum up, in relation to organizational roles, the following ten stresses are worth considering:

Self-Role Distance (SRD)

Inter-Role Distance (IRD)

Role Stagnation (RS)

Role Isolation (RI)

Role Ambiguity (RA)

Role Expectation Conflict (REC)

Role Overload (RO)

Role Erosion (RE)

Resource Inadequacy (Rin)

Personal Inadequacy (Pin)

The Organizational Role Stress Scale (ORS Scale) can be used to measure these role stresses.

Coping With Stress

When individuals experience stress, they adopt ways of dealing with it as they cannot remain in a continual state of tension. We will call this coping. The word coping has been used mainly with two meanings – ways of dealing with stress, and the effort to 'master' conditions of harm, treat or challenge. We will use the term coping in as in the first meaning (ways of dealing with stress), and distinguish between effective and ineffective coping.

Generally, effective coping strategies are 'approach' strategies, which confront the problem of stress as a challenge, and increase the capability of dealing with it. Ineffective strategies are 'escape' or 'avoidance' strategies, which reduce the feeling of stress, for example, by denying the reality of stress, or through the use of alcohol, drugs or other aids to escapism.

Research has shown that social and emotional support available to the person helps him to effectively cope with stress. Persons maintaining close interpersonal relationships with friends and family are able to use more approach strategies. Social support includes both material support (providing resources), and emotional support (listening to the person and encouraging him). However studies have also shown that unsolicited support may have negative consequences.

Approach or effective strategies of coping include efforts to increase physical and mental preparedness for coping (through physical exercise, yoga and meditation, diet management), creative diversions for emotional enrichment (music, art, theatre, etc). Strategies to deal with the basic problems that cause stress; and the collaborative work to solve such problems. The various coping strategies or styles used in role stress have been studied, and the findings show that approach styles have a strong relationship with internality, optimism; role efficacy, job satisfaction and effective role behaviour in organizations. Two contrasting strategies (avoidance or dysfunctional and approach or functional) for some role stresses are explained below.

Let us take self-role distance. Many individual who find a conflict between their self-concept and the role they occupy in an organization, may play that role in a routine way to earn their living. They take no interest in their role, and this is indicative of self-role distance i.e. they have rejected the role. On the other hand, some other individuals may seriously occupy their roles and in due course of time, completely forget their self-concept and play that role effectively, but reject their self. Both these approaches are avoidance approaches and are dysfunctional. If an individual rejects the role he is likely to be ineffective in the organization. However, if he rejects the self, he is likely to lose his effectiveness as an individual, which in turn will adversely affect his mental health.

An approach or functional strategy of dealing with this stress is to attempt role integration. The individual may analyze the various aspects of the roles, which cause self-role distance, and may begin to acquire skills, which help him to bridge this gap, or carry his own self into the role by defining some aspects of the role according to his own strengths. In other words, an attempt both to grow into the role and make the role grow to use the special capabilities of the person would result in role integration, where the individual gets the satisfaction of occupying a role, which is nearer to his self-concept. Such integration is not easy to achieve, but with systematic effort, it is also not very difficult to attain.

Similar is the case with role expectation conflict. When the various expectations from the role one occupy conflict with one another, role stress may develop. One way to deal with this stress is to eliminate these conflicting expectations from the role. This process called role shrinkage prunes the role in such a way that some expectations can be given up. Role shrinkage may help in avoiding the problem, but it is a dysfunctional approach since the advantage of a larger role is lost. Instead of role shrinkage, if role linkages are established with other roles, and the problem solved by devising some new ways of compromising the conflicting expectations, the individual can experience both the processes of growth as well as satisfaction. For example, if a professor who experiences conflict between the three expectations from his role – those of teaching students, doing research and consulting organizations, finds that the stress is essentially one of personal inadequacy, not having enough skills, he may take recourse to role shrinkage. However, one way to deal with this problem is to develop role linkages with other colleagues who are good at research, and work out an arrangement whereby research is not neglected. A better way of resolving the problem could be to find ways of doing things in a more nontraditional and productive manner.

Role stagnation is a common stress within organization. Individuals who acquire new roles as a result of promotion or taking over of more challenging roles may feel apprehensive because the role is new and requires skills which the role occupant may not have. In such a situation, the usual response is to continue as in the previous role about which the individual is sure, and which he had been doing successfully. In many cases this is the tragedy of the organizations - even after advancement people at the top continue to play the role of lower level managers. A foreman, for example, in due course of time may become a General Manager, but he may still continue to play the role of a foreman. This as a consequence frustrates the new foreman and others who expect the GM to devote his time to the more productive aspects in one organization, after several self-search sessions, it became clear to many senior management level personnel that their tendency towards close supervision was really a tendency to continue playing their old roles. This is especially so if the individual role requires many new skills which have to be developed. For example, planning roles and the roles of scanning the environment require altogether new skills. In the absence of such skills, the usual tendency is to fall back on the old tried out roles. This is called role fixation, and is an avoidance strategy.

It is necessary for an individual to grow out of his role as a boy into that of an adolescent, and out of adolescence into adulthood. Similarly, it is important for people to grow out of their old roles into new ones and face up to the new challenges. An approach or a functional strategy to resolve this conflict is that of role transition. Role transition is the process whereby a previous role however successful and satisfying it may have been is given up to take a new and a more developed role. Various processes, including anticipatory socialization, role clarity, substitute gratification and the transition procedure, help role transition. In order to make role transition more effective it is necessary to have anticipatory socialization that is preparatory to the taking up of the new role. This would also include delegation of responsibility and functions to people in subordinate roles, so that a person can be free to experiment, and get help in such experimentation from others, such a process of role transition mav be very useful.

In inter-role distance an individual may experience stress due to conflict between the roles he occupies, and which conflict in expectations. The usual approach to deal with this problem is to either partition the roles clearly, so that a person is a husband or a father when he is at home, and an executive when he is in his office. The other alternative is role elimination, which is accepting one role at the cost of the other. In such a case, the individual takes recourse to rationalization. Take for example; an executive who neglects his family at home and in this process eliminates his role as a father and a husband. He rationalizes this process by thinking that he makes a unique contribution to the company and can therefore afford to neglect his family, or that he earns enough for his family, which in turn, should pay the price of losing him as a husband and a father. Such rationalizations are a part of the process of role elimination. These are avoidance strategies.

A more functional approach to the problem is role negotiation, which is the process of establishing the mutuality of roles and getting necessary help to play the roles more effectively. For example, an executive who is unable to find time for his family may sit down and negotiate with his wife and children on how best he can spend time with them within the given constraints. One executive in the largest nationalized bank in India solved the problem by working out an arrangement with his family whereby he would give his Sundays to them and would not normally accept invitations to dine out unless both he and his wife were invited. This proved to be highly satisfying because neither of the roles had to be sacrificed or eliminated.

For role ambiguity the usual approach is to make the roles clear by putting the various aspects on paper. This called role prescription in which various expectations are defined clearly. As an alternative, the individual may remove ambiguity by fitting into the role as described in some of the expectations. This process is called role taking.

Both are avoidance strategies. An approach strategy may be to seek clarification from various sources and to define the role in the light of such clarifications. A more creative option is to define the role according to one's own strengths and take steps in making the role more challenging. This is the process of role making.

To deal with the stress of role overload i.e., a feeling of too many expectations from several sources, the role occupant usually prepares a list of all functions giving top priority to those, which are important. This kind of prioritization may help put things in the order of importance. However, a problem that might arise is that the functions with which a person is less familiar and comfortable may tend to be pushed lower down the priority list, and remain neglected. Those functions, which a person is able to perform without any effort, would get top priority. From this point of view the approach is dysfunctional. This is an avoidance strategy. A more functional approach may be to redefine the role and see each of its aspects may be delegated to others. This in turn may help the other individuals grow. This approach is called role slimming. The role does not lose its vitality in the process of delegating some functions; in fact the vitality increases with decrease in obesity.

In role isolation (when there is tension and distance between two roles in an organization) the usual tendency is for each role occupant to play the role most efficiently and avoid interactions. In other words the role occupant confines himself to his own role. This may be called role boundness. He voluntarily agrees to be bounded by the role. This strategy aims at avoiding possible conflict. We find that individual executives and managers who are highly efficient in their own roles but whose linkages with other roles are very weak do not take on corporate responsibility. The individual withdraws into a kind of isolated efficiency. He derives satisfaction out of playing the individual role effectively and efficiently, but does not contribute as much as he could have towards the overall responsibility to the organization. This is likely to be dysfunctional, as it does not help the individual play his role in the larger interest of the organization. A better method (and an approach strategy) is role negotiation.

In role erosion an individual feels that some important functions, which he would prefer to perform, are being taken care of by some other roles. The usual reaction in such as situation is to fight for the rights of the role and to insist on the clarification of roles.

Though a solution is sought in making structural clarifications, this is not likely to be functional and helpful since it skirts the basic conflict, which continues. An approach strategy may be that of role enrichment. Like job enrichment, role enrichment can be achieved by analyzing the role systematically, and helping the individual see the various strengths and challenges in the role, which might not have been apparent earlier. Significant role set members can also help make the role more challenging and satisfying to the role occupant.

Coping Strategies for Role Stress

Role Stresses	*Dysfunctional Strategies*	*Functional Strategies*
1. Self-role distance	: Role rejection, self rejection	: Role integration
2. Inter-role distance	: Role partition, role elimination	: Role negotiation
3. Role stagnation	: Role fixation	: Role transition
4. Role isolation	: Role boundness	: Role linkage
5. Role ambiguity	: Role prescription	: Role clarification
6. Role expectation conflict	: Role taking	: Role making
7. Role overload	: Role reduction	: Role slimming
8. Role erosion	: Role visibility	: Role development / enrichment
9. Resource inadequacy	: Role atrophy	: Resource generation
10. Personal inadequacy	: Role shrinkage	: Role linkage

To summarize, the effective management of stress involves channelising stress towards productive purposes, preparing role occupants to understand the nature of stress, helping them to understand their strengths and usual styles, and equipping them to develop approach strategies for coping with stress.

The purpose of the organizational Role Stress Scale was to measure the 10 role stresses mentioned above.

Operational Definitions

1. **Inter-Role Distance:** Where an individual occupies more than one role there is bound to be conflicts between the different roles that he occupies. For example, a lady executive often faces the conflict

between her organizational role as an executive and her familial role as a wife and a mother. The demands of her husband and children for sharing her time may be incompatible with the organizational demands. Such inter-role conflicts are quite frequent in a modern society, where an individual is increasingly occupying multiple roles in various organizations and groups.

2. **Role Stagnation:** As the individual grows older, he also grows in the role that he occupies in an organization. With the advancement of the individual the role changes, and with this change in role, the need for taking up a new role becomes crucial. This problem of role growth becomes acute especially when an individual who has occupied a role for a long time enters another role demands that an individual outgrow the previous one and take charge of the new role effectively. This is bound to produce some stress. In organizations which are fast expanding, and which do not have any systematic of manpower development, managers are likely to experience this stress of role stagnation when they are promoted.

3. **Role Expectation Conflict:** When there are conflicting expectations or demands by different role senders (persons having expectations from the role), the role occupant may experience this stress. There may be conflicting expectations from the boss, subordinates, peers or clients.

4. **Role Erosion:** A role occupant may feel that the functions, which he would like to perform, are being performed by some other role. The stress felt may be called role erosion. Role erosion is the subjective feeling of an individual that some important role expectations he has from the role are shared by other roles within the role set. Role erosion is likely to be experienced in an organization, which is redefining its role and creating new roles. Studies indicate that in several organizations, which were redefining their structure, the stress of role erosion was inevitably felt. In an organization, a particular role was abolished and in its place two roles were created to cater to the executive and planning needs. This led to a great erosion, and a feeling that the new roles were less important as compared to the previous role.

5. **Role Overload:** When the role occupant feels that there are too many expectations from the 'significant' others in his role set, he

experiences role overload. Role overload has been measured by asking questions about people's feelings on whether they could possibly finish work given to them during a modified workday and whether they felt that the amount of work they do might interfere with how well it was done. Most of the executive role occupants experience role overload. Role overload is more likely to occur where there are large variations in the expected output, and when delegation or assistance cannot procure more time.

6. **Resource inadequacy:** resource inadequacy stress is experienced when the resources required by the role occupant for performing the role effectively are not available; these may be information, people, material, finance, or facilities.

7. **Personal Inadequacy:** When a role occupant feels that he is not prepared to undertake the role effectively, he may experience stress. The role occupant may feel that he does not have enough knowledge, skills, or training, or he/she has not had time to prepare for the assigned role. Persons who are assigned new roles without enough preparation or orientation are likely to experience this type of stress.

8. **Self-Role Distance:** This stress arises out of the conflict between the self-concept and the expectations from the role, as perceived by the role occupant. If a person occupies a role, which he may subsequently find as conflicting with the self-concept, he feels stressed. For example, an introvert who is fond of studying and writing, may develop as self-role distance if he accepts the role of a salesman in an organization, and comes to realize that the expectations from the role would include his meeting people and being social. Such conflicts are fairly common, although they may not be so severe.

9. **Role Ambiguity:** When the individual is not clear about the various expectations that people have from his role, the conflict that he faces is called role ambiguity. Role ambiguity may be due to lack of information available to the role occupant, or due to lack of understanding of the 'cues' available to him. Role ambiguity may be in relation to the activities, responsibilities, priorities, norms, or general expectations. Generally role ambiguity may be experience by persons occupying roles which are newly created in the organization, roles in organizations which are

undergoing change, or process roles (with less clear and concrete activities).

10. **Role Isolation:** In a role set, the role occupant may feel that certain roles are psychologically closer to him, while others are at much greater distance. The main criterion of distance is the frequency and ease of interaction. When linkages are strong, the role isolation will be low and in the absence of strong linkages, the role isolation will bc high. Role isolation can therefore be measured in terms of the existing and the desired linkages. The gap between the desired and the existing linkages will indicate the amount of role isolation..

Controls

Noise and distractions are kept at bare minimum.

Instructions are properly given

Made sure that the employees have understood the instructions.

Methodology

Sample: - S[1] - Ms. Disha Parab

Exec. HR Manager, Rediffusion Ad Agency

S[2] - Mr. Anand Nair

Sr. Project Manager, Vishan Projects Pvt. Ltd.

Materials Used

The Organizational Role Stress Scale (ORS Scale) can be used to measure these role stresses. The ORS Scale contains 5 items for each role stress (a total of 50 statements), it uses a 5-point scale (from 0-4). Thus the total scores on each role stress range from 0-20. To get the total scores for each role stress, the ratings given should be totaled horizontally (for 5 items) and entered on the space given for this purpose. The ORS Scale has high reliability and validity.

Instructions

"Please do not write on these pages. Responses should be given on a separate answer sheet provided to you. People have different feelings about their roles. Statements describing some such feelings are given below. Use the answer sheet to write your responses. Read each statement and indicate in the space against the corresponding number in the answer sheet, how often you have the feeling expressed in the statement in relation to your role in your organization. Use the numbers given below to indicate our own feelings.

If you find that the category to be used in answering does not adequately indicate your own feelings, use the one, which is closest to the way, you feel. Do not leave any item unanswered. Answer the items in the order given below.

Write

0 if you never or rarely feel this way.

1 if you occasionally (a few times) feel this way.

2 if you sometimes feel this way.

3 if you frequently feel this way.

4 if you very frequently or always feel this way."

Discussions

The first person on which the ORS Scale was conducted was Anand Nair who is Sr. Project Manager at Vishan Projects Pvt Ltd. The minimum score one can obtain is 0., maximum score is 20, and therefore showing that any score between 1-5 is low, scores between 6-15 would be moderately high and between 16-20 would be extremely high. Anand got a score of 13 on IRD. He has scored low on PI, RA and RI, (0,3,4) respectively; indicating that tnese are not very significant stresses contributing to the role stress.

PI refers to Personal Inadequacy meaning that role occupant feels that he is not prepared to occupant undertake the role effectively. In this case he does not feel that he does not have enough knowledge, skills, training. Second and third lowest scores are on RA and RI (3 and 4) respectively. Anand has a very clear understanding about the structure under which he is working and the responsibilities and duties given to him. There is not much of ambiguity he experiences because what is required out of his role is clearly mentioned, and the residual ambiguity is a part of the job. He does not seem to have role isolation as there are strong linkages and a lot of ease of interaction. He has got a moderately high score of (6,7,9) on REC, RO, SRD respectively, show that he does experience Role Expectation Conflict, which means there are times when he experiences conflicting expectations from the boss, subordinates, peers or clients. He also experiences Role Overload as he feels that there are too many expectations from the significant others in his role set. One of the stresses is also Self-Role Distance falling under the category of Role Space Conflict. In this a person occupies a role, which he may subsequently find as conflicting with the self-concept, he feels stressed. The other set of stresses that he has scored high on are RS, RE, and IRD (10, 12, 13) respectively. Role stagnation is a common stress within the organization, individuals who acquire new roles as a result of promotion or taking over of more challenging roles may feel apprehensive because the role is new and requires skills which the role occupant may not have, therefore they continue as in the previous role about which the individual is sure, the avoidance strategy applied by the individual is Role Fixation. As he scores high on this stress, lets discuss about the intervention he can use to reduce this stress. It is important for people to grow out of their old roles into new ones. An approach strategy is Role Transition. It is a process whereby a previous role, howsoever successful and satisfying it may have been is given up to take a new and a more developed role.

He also feels that the functions, which he would like to perform, are being performed by some other roles. (RE). An approach strategy may be that of role Enrichment. The last one is IRD, here an individual may experience stress due to conflict between the roles he occupies, and which conflict in expectations. The dysfunctional strategies used are Role Rejection or Self-Rejection. A more functional strategy would be of Role Integration.

Lets discuss the second respondent named Disha Parab aged 30 yrs who is a Sr. HR Executive in Rediffusion DY&R. table 2 shows the scores obtained by Disha on 10 role stresses. The highest score that she obtained was 15 on RI and RIn. Lowest on PI (5). She scored moderately on IRD (6), SRD (8), RA (8), RO (9), REC (10), and RS (10). She scored moderately high on RE, RI, RIn (13,15,15) respectively. Even Disha does not feel that she is not prepared to undertake the role effectively, therefore having the lowest score. The next set of scores to be discussed are IRD, SRD, RA, RO where she has scored (6,8,8,9) showing that she experiences stress due to the conflict between the roles she occupies and which conflict in expectations. The approach that she sometimes takes up is of role elimination. A more functional approach would be Role Negotiation. She also experiences a conflict between her self-concept and the Role she occupies in the organization it means rejecting a role. A more functional strategy is an attempt to Role Integration. She feels less clear about the various expectations that people have from her role that conflict that she faces is called Role Ambiguity. An approach strategy that can be used is Role Clarification. She experiences role Overload, when she experiences many too many expectations from the significant other and an effective intervention would be Role Slimming.

She has scored high on REC and RS. One experiences REC when there are conflicting expectations on demands by different role senders. A more functional strategy could be Role Making. One experiences RS when individuals acquire new roles as a result of promotion or taking over of more challenging roles may feel apprehensive because the role is new and requires skills which the role occupant may not have, so they continue to play the previous role of which they are sure. Role Fixation is the common avoidance strategy that people apply and must be avoided. One must use a more functional strategy of Role Transition.

RE, RI and RIn are the highest scores obtained.

She feels that the functions, which she would like to perform, are being performed by some other roles. A solution to this problem would be Role Development or Role Enrichment. She also experiences stress when there is tension and distance between two roles in an organization and an approach strategy for this problem would be Role Linkage.

RIn stress is experienced when the resources required by the role occupant for performing the role effectively are not available. Functional strategy to deal with the Resource Generation.

6. Prabhu's Stress Profile

Nature of Stress

The present world is a fast changing world. There are a lot of pressures and demands at work. They require the employee to be on his toes all the while. There are deadlines to be met, difficult jobs to be completed, unavoidable delays in job completion, failure of machines and instruments, a difficult boss to be pleased, an envious colleague to be dealt with, job insecurity, job transfers, necessity of updating one's knowledge, adjusting to occupational hazard etc. The list is almost endless.

The term stress is used in two distinct ways. First, it is often applied to conditions in the world around us that induce feelings of discomfort and tension. In this context, the item stress refers to the presence of various stressors.... external sources of pressure. Second, it is also applied to the internal as induced by such stressors...the unpleasant feelings we label as "stress". Both of these perspectives are useful.

Stress can be defined as: a demand placed on our psychological and physical functioning that threatens an individual's adaptation to a given situation.

The type and the degree of the stress experienced depends not only on the situation and events which give rise to it, but also on the individual's perspective, constitutional makeup and the strategies that he has developed to cope with stress.

1. People feel a sense of loss of control of the events in their life. They feel helpless to change what is going on and to successfully intervene in the process.
2. There is an anticipation or occurrence of physical or psychological pain. For example, the individual fears being injured or killed (as in a disaster) or it is threatened with a loss of self-esteem (as in divorce).
3. There is a loss of social or emotional support. In a disaster, friends and relatives may be missing or killed. Less drastic events such as divorce, jobless or marriage may separate individuals from family members and old friends.
4. The event or some aspect of it is perceived as unpleasant or aversive and the individual tries to actively avoid it.

In general, whenever the environment presents a demand that threatens to exceed the person's capabilities and resources for meeting it he experiences stress. Not that there was no stress at work previously, it definitely was there. But it was more a physical stress than mental. Also it used to be of shorter duration and less frequent. Today no person or job is free from stress. The effects of stress can range from mild to lethal. It can sap a person's physical and mental energy and throw him out of gear.

Therefore, today, a lot of attention is being paid to the understanding and prevention of stress. These reactions can be classified into three major types-psychological, physiological and coping behaviors.

(a) **Physiological Reaction:** We often show physiological reactions to stress. At such times there is an increase in our heart rate, blood pressure, respiration, etc. More blood is supplied to the skeletal muscles and body extremities. Hans Selye, the scientist who has done a lot of research on stress thinks that these reactions help to cope with the stress producing threatening or dangerous situation.

(b) **Psychological Reactions:** At times we show psychological reaction to stress like fear, tension and anxiety. We try to analyze the situations and find out how dangerous or threatening it actually is.

(c) **Coping Behaviour:** Coping behaviour is an attempt to deal directly with the source of stress. This category covers a wide range of behavior. It could be an action that makes us feel relaxed and better (e.g., convincing oneself that there is not much reason to worry).

Stress: Its Major Cause

Stress should be accepted as an inevitable part of life. Different situations and circumstances in our personal lives and a job produce stress. We shall divide them into factors related to the organization or job and factors related to the person, which include his experiences and personality traits.

Organizational causes: Many aspects related to the job or organization can cause stress. The most important ones are:

1. **Occupational demands:** Before taking up a job one must consider the level of stress it will involve and one's ability to handle it. Some type of job cause more stress than others. For example, a farmer's or a librarian's or even a clerk's job is much less stressful than that of a production manager, a fire fighter or a traffic controller. In a survey of 130 different occupations, it was found that certain jobs could lead to high stress (e.g., physician, office manager, waitress or waiter). Others (e.g., maid, farm workers, etc.) cause much less stress. Recent research by Shaw and Risking

show aspects of the job related to high or low stress. Regardless of the work involved, the more the number of these characteristics (as below) a job has, the more severe is the stress that it produces.

Making decisions

Monitoring devices or information

Performing complex

Exchanging job-related information with others

Being in a stressful environment

Being in a hazardous job situation

Engaging in general personal contact

Performing unstructured versus structured work

Being alert to changing conditions.

2. **Role conflict:** People play various different roles in their lives. They have to satisfy various different people who hold contrasting expectations about their behaviour. When the individual's own role conflicts with the one that is imposed upon him by others it produces role conflict. Role conflicts can occur at work, at home, etc. For example, a woman who has to stay on the job late in the evening faces conflict due to her roles as an employee as well as mother and wife. Growing family commitments conflict with her job responsibilities can lead to stress.

3. **Role ambiguity:** Role ambiguity is a common source of job related stress. It results from uncertainty that individuals experience with regard to job related role. For example, a person who does not know exactly what is expected from him, his responsibilities, the limits of his authority, specific production requirements, job evaluation criteria used to evaluate him, etc. experiences stress of this type. It is one of the major causes of job related stress. About 35 to 60% employees surveyed in a study report experiencing it to some extent. Fortunately, in most organization, the roles are well defined. In such organizations the individual has no problem in fulfilling his role expectation. But, in organizations where the roles are not well defined an employee experiences job dissatisfaction, tension and depression.

4. **Work Overload:** Overload means of overwork. Overload could be of two types – quantitative overload and qualitative overload.

In quantitative overload there is too much work to be completed in too little time. This happens when seasonal demands increase. For instance, just before rains, in an umbrella-manufacturing unit there is a lot of haste to produce more at fast speed. This type of stress often leads to illness.

In qualitative overload the amount of work may not be much but it could be very complicated and demanding on one's mental capacity. It makes a person feel that he lacks the skill or ability to perform a given job. He may even leave the job if a better alternative is available. If no alternative is available he may remain absent and show increased dissatisfaction and irritability.

5 **Work Underload:** Work underload means too little work. According to research findings, too little work can be as stressful as too much work. It leads to boredom, monotony, and lack of stimulation to do anything. Research has shown that both high and low levels of stress can be equally harmful. Only moderate amount of stress can cause less harm. Therefore, it is necessary that one keep oneself busy to the extent that one's abilities are not overtaxed and one feels capable of dealing with the situation. Work underload can also be qualitative in nature. Qualitative underload means lack of intellectual or mental stimulation. Thus routine and monotonous job can also, often, become stressful.

6 **Responsibility for Others:** In an organization, different persons are responsible for different things. Some are responsible for financial matters like taxes, budgeting, accounting, etc. Others deal with physical matters, procuring supplies, overseeing production, maintaining equipment, marketing, etc. Yet others like supervisors or managers have to deal with people. Individuals who are responsible for others; to motivate, reward or punish them and make decisions about them experience higher tension and anxiety than others. Their task is very much demanding and stressful.

7 **Change:** Minor changes in the work situation are unavoidable. But major changes cause disturbance and stress. One feels secure in familiar surroundings. Changes in supervisor or management, changes in managerial style, changes in work place, transfers, and introduction of new machines and new techniques of production disturb the stability and predictability of the work environment.

In the rapidly changing technological world of today such type of changes survive in the competitive market. However, all are not able to cope up equally well with such changes. It is especially difficult for older employees to change their work habits or adjust to changes in environment.

8. **Lack of Social Support:** Various studies have revealed that people who can count on the support of others when faced with a stressful situation can deal more effectively with stress than others who are less fortunate in this respect. Social support reduces the strain produced by a stressful situation. It acts as a buffer. It also leads to greater job satisfaction. Many individuals seek social support when faced with high stress. It is often said that "misery lbves company.' Knowing that others are facing similar problems as one reduces the stress one experiences.

9. **Lack of Involvement In Decisions:** Lack of employee participation in decisions affecting their jobs has a disturbing effect. Most employees feel that they know a lot about their work. Therefore, when they are not consulted while taking decisions relating to their jobs they experience stress. If employees are permitted to involve themselves in making decisions affecting their jobs they report less role conflict and higher job satisfaction.

10 **Other Sources:** Besides the above-mentioned factors, there are various other sources of stress within the organization. One of it refers to the working conditions like loud noise, over-crowding, repetitive work, extreme temperature, strained relationship with co-workers, piece work system (a pay system in which a worker is paid according to the amount of work or number of units he produces) swing shifts and flexible work hours can cause considerable stress. Changes in company policy, reorganization of internal structure, mergers and major changes in management also lead to stress.

Personal factors: Individuals differ in their ability to deal with stress. Some can adjust to high levels of stress while others break down even under minor stress. An individual's life events, personality etc. have an effect on his ability to withstand stress.

1. **Life Events:** Stressful life events have an effect on a person's health. An individual's adjustment to stressful events in personal life has an effect on his adjustment to job related stress.

Individuals with stress levels between 150 to 300 points have a 5% chance of becoming seriously ill during the next 12 months. Those with stress levels above 300 points have a 70% chance of becoming seriously ill. People who are able to deal effectively with stress have certain distinguishing characteristics. They are people who have a sense of purpose and see meaning in life. They believe that they have a control over their lives and feel that they can influence their own lives. They don't feel threatened by changes and challenges. They view them as opportunities for development.

2. **Tension Discharge Rate:** Though all individuals experience some form of tension or the other on the job, they differ in terms of what they do with it. They differ in their tension discharge rate. It refers to the rate at which individuals dissipate job-related tensions at the end of the day. Some leave their job-related tensions in the work place while others carry them home. The person in the former category experiences less tension and suffers from lesser ill effects of stress. It is very beneficial to learn to leave your worries behind you at the end of the day.

3. **Personality Pattern:** Stress does not affect all in the same way. People differ in their stress tolerance ability. Researchers have come to the conclusion that tolerance to stress depends on the type of personality an individual has. Basically, there are two types of personality patterns – type 'A' and type 'B'.

   People with type 'A' personality pattern are highly competitive, over ambitious, aggressive, with a constant sense of urgency about time. They impose various deadlines on themselves. They run about completing their tasks with a feeling that time is fast running out. They want things to happen immediately and get irritated if there is any delay. They achieve one thing after another. Their life style leads to a lot of stress and strain. They cannot relax or enjoy leisure. They show various physiological reactions under stress. Finally, it could result in a heart attack or some other serious illness. Type 'B' people could also be ambitious but they can work under stressful conditions without suffering from any stresses or strains. They work hard but don't get frustrated or irritated if they are not able to achieve their goals. They are sort of immune to stress.

4. **Locus of Control:** Another factor that affects vulnerability to stress is known as locus of control. It could be either internal or external. According to Rotter, people with an internal locus of control believe that they can control the forces and events, which shape their lives with their own abilities. People with an external locus of control believe that forces and events in their lives are not under their control and so they cannot shape their lives the way they want to.

Rotter developed at test called "Rotter's Sentence Completion Test" to measure an individual's locus of control. This test has shown that people with high internal control are less susceptible to stress than those with external control. They feel confident that they can accomplish things with their own internal resources. It has been found that people who are flexible, adaptable, action oriented and willing to face adverse circumstances as challenges rather than threats are good in problem-solving skills and cope with stress in a better way than those who lack or are low in these qualities.

Effects of Stress

Stress has a very great impact on our health and psychological well being. Moderate stress helps by activating us and enhancing our performance. It affects employees at all hierarchies and ages. High stress is highly unpleasant. Stress has the following effects.

1. **Health:** Han Selye was the first person to reveal the relationship between stress and health. He showed how emotional strains in our life could cause physical problems. According to him stress affects us in three stages. He called it the "General Adaptation Syndrome" (GAS).

   In the first stage known as the stage of alarm reaction the person is shocked by t he stress arousing event. Slowly, his body starts feeling Tired, he gets a headache and feels washed out. When such physiological changes continue for a long time the person starts resisting the effects of stress. This is known as the stage of resistance. During this stage various hormones in the body try to restore the body's internal balance. As a result of this the symptoms slowly disappear.

   However, if the stress persists, the person reaches the third stage known as the stage of exhaustion. In this stage, the person's energy may be exhausted and the symptoms of stress reappear. This stage can lead to a serious illness or even death.

Stressful events increase our blood pressure, heart rate and acceleration of various bodily functions. Extra sugar is released in the blood stream, which provides more energy to the brain and limbs. The individual becomes alert and energetic enough o cope up with the emergency. The GAS research made people aware of the relationship between body and mind. If stress is experienced very frequently the body's reserved energy gets exhausted and the person becomes vulnerable to infections and disorders.

Stress can cause hypertension, heart disease, skin allergies, ulcers and even cancer. A branch of medicine known as psychosomatic medicine studies all this. Psychosomatic disorders refer to physical disorders caused by psychological factors like emotional stress.

2. **Alcoholism and Drug Addiction:** Most people try to avoid stress. When it is unavoidable some people attempt to deal with the problem while others try to withdraw or continue to try to avoid it. People from the latter category, many times take to drugs or alcohol.

Alcoholics and drug addicts are likely to remain absent from work and cause loss of production. They are also more prone to accidents. These two habits spoil their careers and wreck their families.

The managements previously dismissed employees who were found to be drug or alcohol addicts. However, today managements take a different approach towards them. They design special programs to help such employees give up the habit. Such programs are known as "Employee Assistance Programs." They provide employees with counseling and treatment. Sometimes they advice them to approach agencies which specialize in such help. Thus there is a realization among organizations that drug and alcohol addiction are serious problems and need to be dealt with immediately.

Besides drugs and alcohol some people may find an escape route in smoking, heavy eating or sleeping pills. People who are immature and not so well adjusts to life may even take to antisocial or violent behaviour under chronic stress. Some may breakdown psychologically and go insane. A few may even commit suicide.

3. **Burnout:** Burnout is defined as a syndrome of emotional, physical and mental exhaustion resulting from prolonged exposure to intense stress. Although most people do adjust to stresses on the job stress wears out a few. They feel exhausted and show feelings of helplessness. They seem to use all their energy in dealing with day-to-day life and its problems. They have no energy or inclination to take interest in others. They feel unhappy, bored and irritable on the job. Such persons suffer from mental exhaustion. They take a pessimistic attitude towards life and people.

The burnout syndrome is found to be more common in some professions than in others. There are various factors that lead to a burnout. In a study by Gaines and Kermier, the police department was assessed on emotional exhaustion. It was found that women experience greater exhaustion than males. Individuals working on clerical tasks reported less exhaustion than those in the patrol department. Individuals on interesting and motivating job reported less exhaustion. Also individual's who perceived the rules of the organization to be flexible experienced less exhaustion.

Burnout costs heavily to the individual as well as the organization. Burnout victims are likely to drop out or wait their jobs or withdraw from their careers. Their quitting the organization or job is beneficial to the organization. It helps to improve productivity. It is also good for themselves because is helps them to come out of a frustrating and tense situation. However, it is a loss to society in terms of expertise, training and talent.

Some burnouts do remain on the job but wait eagerly towards retirement. They are likely to become "dead wood" – unproductive members of the organization.

However, burnout does not always lead to the end of one's career. If the individual becomes aware of the problem and tries to solve it, it can be reversed. Since prolonged exposure tom stress is the major cause of burnout, the most effective way of reversing the effect of burnout, the most effective way of reversing the effect of burnout is allowing some relief to the person by reducing his stress.

However, some people use their own negative tactics of reducing stress like drinking alcohol, consuming drugs, smoking, absenteeism or having extramarital affairs. Though they help a person to forget his stress for sometime, their future consequence are often worse than the stress they experienced.

Personal tactics of stress management: There are various ways in which a person can shield himself from the negative impact of stress. One way is to increase one's "Stress tolerance" by increasing physical fitness. Persons who exercise regularly and avoid putting on weight have lesser chances of suffering from stress-related illnesses like blood pressure or heart disease. Secondly, a person can participate in coping skills training.

It involves making people realize the stress producing potential of different situations and using various different techniques for dealing with those situations. The most popular technique is known as relaxation training.

Another technique used to achieve relaxation is meditation. Gary Swartz found that meditators report much lower daily anxiety than non-meditators and also suffer from fewer psychosomatic problems like ïolds, headaches, insomnia and asthma. Sometimes, a technique like massage is also used to achieve relaxation.

According to the famous psychologist, Skinner, behaviour that leads to positive consequences tends to be learnt and behaviour that does not lead to positive consequences or when leads to unpleasant consequences or punishment is not likely to be learnt. He thinks that making appropriate use of reward and punishment can modify human behaviour. Many undesirable characteristics of 'A' type of people and those high on external locus of control can be modified through this technique. Though doubts are expressed about the long-term effects of this technique it can at least be used to bring about temporary changes at least in some behaviour. This can give breathing time to the person to realize his harmful ways of thinking and behaviour and modify them.

Besides the above-mentioned tactics there are other ways of reducing stress. Developing a hobby or interest helps to distract the mind from the tension of work. Going on a short vacation or even a weekend trip helps. Introducing changes in the procedure of doing a job or the structure of a job also makes one feel better. All these tactics help individuals to reduce stress through their own personal efforts.

Organizational tactics of stress management: Organizations can also help employees reduce stress. They can do it by changing their own structure or procedures or changing the nature of jobs.

1. **Changes in Organizational Structure and Function:** This strategy of stress reduction involves producing changes in the organizational set up. These changes help employees work in a relativcly stress-free environment.

   Any change requires adjustment. In the beginning the necessity of adjusting to a change produces stress. This type of stress can be avoided by not producing shocking or sudden changes without taking the employees into confidence. Involving workers in decisions regarding changes in the organization proves useful. Or at least the necessity and reason behind changes should be explained.

   Decentralization is one way of making a positive change in the organizational structure. It is a process through which authority is spread more widely throughout an organization. It reduces the helplessness that workers experience and thereby decrease their stress. Performance appraisals and fair distribution of organizational rewards also help. Giving them a change to make decisions affecting them is also advisable. There should be greater communication in the organization and a rapid flow of information from all levels.

2. **Changes in the Nature of Job:** Routine, repetitive, jobs produce boredom and stress. Job enlargement increases the scope of the job and includes different activities in it. Enriching the job by providing more opportunities to the workers for planning and performing their jobs also helps. Reducing travel and unpleasant working conditions is also useful.

   Organization should take care while selecting people. If a job involves higher level of stress tolerance, the person selected to work on such a job must be hardy and with high capacity to tolerate stress. A psychological test can be used to select the right kind of persons for the job.

Stress can also be minimized by clearly defining the role of an individual. Role ambiguity produces stress. Each worker should be clear about his duties, obligations, responsibilities and freedom. Working women often suffer more from role conflict than males when their personal roles like managing homes, looking after children, etc. are affected when the management asks them to work overtime to fulfill the organizational objectives. Women who have family responsibilities should be excluded from such work or at least they should not be forced to do it.

Organization should not overload a worker. Organizations should not expect too much from workers to reduce costs or to earn more profit. The quantity of work expected from a worker should be such that he can cope up with it without feeling tired or stressed. Similarly work underload should also be stressful and therefore must be avoided. It makes a worker feel helpless not knowing how to spend the time on the job.

In spite of all these precautions, organizations will always have some people who are overstressed. These unfortunate employees should be taught the techniques of reducing stress. In progressive organization, stress counselors and psychologists take up such cases and assist the individuals in various ways to cope with stress

Studies of stress reveal the following:

- The annual cost of stress-related absenteeism, lower productivity, rising health insurance costs, and other medical expenses.
- 30 percent of executives believe their work has adversely affected their health.
- 40 percent of workers wonder whether they are going to have a job next year.
- The number of stress-related workers' compensation claims tripled in one decade, jumping from 5 percent to 15 percent of all claims.
- 46 percent of workers have thought seriously about quitting their jobs in the past year as a result of stress.
- 69 percent of workers have thought that health problems related to stress made them less productive.
- 34 percent of American workers expected to burn out on the job soon.

The objective of this test is to identify the personality type and the stress levels of the employees.

Operational Definitions

Type A Personality People:

- Are extremely competitive.

- Act impatiently with the rate at which most events take place.
- More walk and eat rapidly and are always in a hurry.
- Feel strongly about success and social acceptance.
- Explosively accentuate words in ordinary speech, even when there is no need for it.
- Speak rapidly the last words of most sentences.
- Are polyphasic (i.e. try to do two or more things at the same time).
- Set several goals at once and rarely content themselves with working on just one project at a time.
- Find it difficult to refrain from discussing subjects that interest them.
- Get upset easily and become hostile toward those they perceive as competition.
- Feel vaguely guilty when they relax.
- Tend to set unrealistic goals for themselves.
- Experience a chronic sense of time urgency.

Type B Personality People:

- Are generally easy going.
- Are seldom impatient (They are contented by wait for success, for lunch time, for trains etc.).
- Don't suffer from a sense of time urgency and are less concerned with schedules and deadlines.
- Are able to see things in a longer perspective, set long-term goals.
- Are realistic about what they can achieve and their goals reflect this realism.
- They tend to work on only one or two goals at a time.
- Generally live under little or no free-floating hostility and feel little need to display or discuss their achievements.
- Tend to play for play's sake, know how to relax seldom complete.
- Relax without guilt, and do not worry much and not relatively anxious about their future.

Physiological Problems

Would cover symptoms like, headaches, stomachaches or tension in the stomach, backaches, stiffness in the neck and shoulders, increased blood pressure, fatigue. If the total score obtained by the respondent on these items is above 18 then he/she is suffering from a physiological problem.'

Behavioral Problem

Would cover symptoms like crying, forgetfulness, unprovoked shouting, blaming others, bossiness, compulsiveness, anger, agitation, smoking, teeth grinding. If the total score obtained by the respondent is above 33 then he/she is suffering from a behavioral problem.

Emotional Problem

Would cover symptoms like worrying, depression, impatience, frustration, loneliness, powerlessness, and inflexibility. If the total score obtained by the respondent is above 21 then he/she is suffering from an emotional problem.

Controls

1. Noise and distractions are kept at the bare minimum level.
2. Instructions are properly given.
3. Made sure that the employees have understood the instructions properly.

Methodology

Sample: - S[1] - Ms. Disha Parab

Exec. HR Manager, Rediffusion Ad Agency

S[2] - Mr. Anand Nair

Sr. Project Manager, Vishan Projects Pvt. Ltd.

Materials used

A Personality Questionna're, which consists of 10 questions. A second questionnaire divided into 3 categories describing various symptoms related to Physiological, Behavioral, and Emotional Problems.

Instructions

"This is a personality test. Please rate yourself on items (1-10) listed in the questionnaire by circling the answer that is most true for you.

1. Indicates Never.

2. Indicate Rarely.
3. Indicate Average.
4. Indicate Sometimes.
5. Indicate Always."

"This is the second questionnaire. Do you experience any of the following? Circle the Appropriate Number for each item.

1. Indicates Never.
2. Indicate Rarely.
3. Indicate Sometimes.
4. Indicate Often.
5. indicate Always."

Discussion

This test consists of Personality test and the stress profile, which captures the physiological, behavioral and emotional dimension of a person.

The obtained data clearly shows that both the Ss are of A type Personality, showing characteristics outlined by Friedman and Rosenman. They are extremely competitive, act impatiently with the rate at which most events take place. Walk and eat rapidly and are always in hurry, féel strongly about success and social acceptance, explosively accurate words in ordinary speech even when there is no need for it. Speak rapidly the last words of most sentences, are polyphasic, set several goals at once and rarely content themselves with working on just one project at a time. Find it difficult to refrain from discussion subjects that interest them, get upset easily and become hostile toward those they perceive as competition. Feel vaguely guilty when they relax, tend to set unrealistic goals for themselves and experience a chronic sense of time urgency. All the above-mentioned characteristics are observed in both Ss. Their Personalitys hold ideal for the kind of position they hold.

The Stress Profile shows that both the Ss are in general Normal, but both of them suffer from physiological and emotional problems. They do not show any kind of behavioral problems. But they need to consult a physician and a psychologist to work on their physiological and emotional problems.

When the symptoms are compared with the personality type it is seen that both the subjects score is high and both are A type personality and therefore both of them are vulnerable to cardiac attack. Therefore they need to take all possible precautionary measures.

Table 1: Personality Test

	Name of S	*Score*
1.	Mr. Anand Nair	41
2.	Mrs. Disha Parab	40

Table 2: Stress Profile Scores

	Name of S	*Physiological*	*Behavioral*	*Emotional*	*Total*
1.	Mr. Anand Nair	18	24	21	63
2.	Mrs. Disha Parab	21	16	21	58

Table 3: Interpretation

Symptoms

	High	*Low*
A+	Needs	
A	Immediate	Vulnerable
A-	Attention	
B+	Complaining	Carefree
B	Sort	

7. Role Efficacy

Introduction

The Concept of Role Efficacy–It is integration of the two (the person and the role) that ensures a person's effectiveness in the organization. Unless a person has the requisite knowledge, technical competence and the skills required for the role, he couldn't be effective. Equally important is how the role, which he occupies in the organization, is designed. If the role does not allow the person to use his competence, and if he constantly feels frustrated in the role, his effectiveness is likely to be low.

The integration of a person and the role comes about when the role is able to fulfill the needs of the individual, and when the individual in turn is able to contribute to the evolution of the role. The more we move from role taking (responding to the expectations of the other persons) to role making (taking initiative in designing the role more creatively in a way such that the expectations of the others as well as of the role occupant integrated), the more the role is likely to be effective. Effectiveness of a person-in-a-role-in-an-organization will depend on own potential effectiveness, the potential effectiveness of the role and the organizational climate. The potential effectiveness can be called efficacy.

Personal efficacy would mean potential effectiveness of a person in personal and interpersonal situations. Role efficacy would mean the potential effectiveness of an individual occupying a particular role in an organization. Role efficacy can be seen as the psychological factor underlying role effectiveness.

Aspects of Role Efficacy

Role efficacy has several aspects. The more these aspects arc present in a role, the higher the efficacy of that role is likely to be. These aspects can be classified into three groups or dimensions. One dimension of role efficacy is called 'role making' as opposed to role taking. The former is an active attitude towards the role (to define and make the role as one likes), whereas the latter is a passive attitude (mainly responding to the other's expectation).

Dimension 1: Role Making.

1. **Self - Role Integration:** Every person has his strengths experience, technical training, special skills, and some unique contribution that the he may be able to make. The more the role a person occupies provides an opportunity for the use of such special strengths, the higher the efficacy is likely to be. This is called self-role integration. The self or the person and the role get integrated. This self or the person and the role get integrated through the possibility of a person's use of his special strengths in the role. In one organization, a person was promoted to a responsible position. This was seen as a covetable reward and it made the person very happy. However, he soon discovered that in the new position he was not able to use his special skills of training, counseling and organizational diagnosis. In spite of his working very well in the new role, his efficacy was not as high as it was the previous one. Later when the role was redesigned

to enable him to use his rare skills, his efficacy went up. All of us want that our special strengths are used in the roles so that it may be possible for us to demonstrate how effective we can be. As such, integration contributes to high role efficacy. On the other hand, if there is a distance between the self and the role, efficacy is likely to be low.

2. **Proactivity:** A person, who occupies a role, responds to the various expectations that people in the organization have from that role. While this certainly gives him satisfaction it also satisfies others in the organization. However, if he is also expected to take initiative in starting some activity, the efficacy will be higher. Reactive behaviour (responding to the expectations of others) helps a person in being effective to some extent, but proactivity (taking initiative rather than only responding to the others expectations) contributes much more to efficacy. If a person feels that he would like to take initiative but has no opportunity to do so in the role that he occupies in the organization, the efficacy will below.

3. **Creativity:** It is not only initiative which is important for efficacy. An opportunity to try new and unconventional ways of solving problems or an opportunity to be creative is equally important. In one state government department people performing clerical roles met as a part of a reorganization experiment to discuss how each individual could experiment with a system of cutting delays in processing papers. The results were amazing. Not only did the satisfaction of people in that department go up, but also delays were considerably reduced and some innovative systems emerged. Certainly, these were further discussed and modified, but the opportunity people got in being creative and in trying out innovative ideas increased their role efficacy and their performance markedly improved. If a person perceives that he has to perform only routine tasks, it is detrimental towards a high role efficacy. If he feels that the role does not allow any time or opportunity to be creative, the efficacy is bound to be low.

4. **Confrontation:** In general, if people in an organization avoid problems, or shift the problems to the others, their role efficacy will be low. The tendency to confront problems and find relevant solutions contributes to efficacy. When people facing

interpersonal problems sit down. Talk about these problems, and search out solutions, their efficacy is likely to he higher when compared with situations in which they either deny such problems or refer them to their higher officers.

Dimension 2: Role Centering

5. **Centrality:** If a person occupying a particular role in an organization feels that the role he occupies is central in the organization, his role efficacy is likely to be high. Every employee would like to feel that his role is important to the organization. If persons occupying various roles feel that their roles are peripheral i.e. not very important, their potential effectiveness will be low. This is true for all persons and not only for those at the lowest level. In a large hospital, Class IV employees like ward boys and attendants had very high motivation when they joined the hospital. They would bring their friends and relatives from nearby villages to proudly show their place of work. However within a few months they sat gossiping in groups. Tiey were rated as very low in their effectiveness. An investigation of this problem showed that within a few months of their joining the hospital, their perception about the importance of their role changed; they felt that their role was not important at all. In contrast with this, in another hospital, the gatekeeper was trained to screen visitors who wanted to visit outside the visiting hours. He used his discretion in making or not making exceptions and referred a case to the nurses or doctors for only clarification and guidance. Interviews with Class IV employees in this hospital showed that they perceived their roles as quite important. One obvious factor underlying the low motivation of the former and the higher motivation of the latter was the perceived importance of the roles.

6. **Influence:** A related concept is that of influence or power. The more influence a person is able to exercise in the role, the higher the role efficacy is likely to be. One factor, which may make roles in the public sector or civil service more efficacious, is the opportunity to influence a larger section of the society. On the other hand, if a person feels that he has no power in the role he occupies in the organization, the efficacy is likely to be low.

7. **Personal Growth:** One factor, which contributes effectively to role efficacy, is the perception that the role provides the individual

with an opportunity to grow and develop. There are several examples of people leaving one role and becoming very effective in another primarily because they had more opportunity to grow in the latter. A head of a training institute accepted the position, taking a big financial cut in his salary because he felt that he had nothing more to learn in the previous position, and in the new position he had opportunities to grow further. Examples of executives switching over to faculty roles at the management institutes indicate the importance of self-development in role efficacy. If a person feels that he is stagnating in a role without any opportunity to grow he is likely to have a low role efficacy. In many institutes of higher learning the roles of the staff pose problems of low efficacy. The main factor behind this is the lack of opportunity for them to grow systematically in their roles, institutes which are able to plan the growth of such people in the roles will have high efficacy and obtain a great deal of contribution from them.

Dimension 3: Role Linking

8. **Inter-role Linkage:** Linkages of one's role with other roles in the organization increases efficacy. If there is a joint effort in understanding problems, finding solutions, etc., the efficacy of the various roles involved is likely to be high. Of course, the presumption is that people know how to work effectively. Similarly, if a person is a member of a task group set up for a specific purpose, his efficacy, other factors being common, is likely to be high. The feeling of isolation of a role (that a person works without any linkage with other roles) reduces role efficacy.

9. **Helping Relationship:** In addition to inter-role linkage, the opportunity for people to receive and give help also increases role efficacy. If persons performing a particular role feel that they can get help from some source in the organization whenever the need arises, they are likely to have higher role efficacy. On the other hand, if there is a feeling that no help is forthcoming when asked for, or that the respondents are hostile, role efficacy will be low. A helping relationship is of two kinds – feeling free to ask for help and expecting that help would be available when it is needed as well as the willingness to give help and respond to the needs of others.

10. **Super-ordination:** A role may have linkages with systems, groups and entities beyond the organization. When a person performing a particular role feels that what he does is likely to be value to a larger group, his efficacy is likely to be high. The roles, which give opportunities to the role occupants to work for super-ordinate goals, have the highest role efficacy. Super-ordinate goals are goals, which serve large groups, and those, which cannot be achieved without some collaborative effort. One major motivation for people at the top, to move to public sector undertakings is to have an opportunity to work for larger goals, which are likely to help larger sections of the society. Many people have voluntarily (accepted cuts in their salaries to move from the private sector to the public sector at the top level, mainly because the new role would give them an opportunity) to serve a larger interest. Roles in which people feel that, what they are doing is helpful to the organization, in which they work, result in role efficacy. But if a person feels that he does not get an opportunity to be of help to a larger group, the role efficacy is likely to be low.

Aspects of Role Efficacy

Dimension 1: Role Making (contrasted with role taking)

1. Self-role integration (versus role distance); Integration between self-concept and the role demands.
2. **Proactively (versus reacting):** Initiating action
3. **Creativity (versus routine):** Experimenting and trying new idea/ strategies
4. **Confrontation (versus avoidance):** Facing problems to attempt their solution.

Dimension 2: Role centering (contrasted with role entering)

5. **Centrality (versus peripherality):** Feeling important or central in a system.
6. **Influence (versus powerlessness):** Feeling the one's occupying a role can make some impact in the system.
7. **Growth (versus stagnation):** Feeling that the one occupying a role grows and learns in the role.

Dimension 3: Role linking (contrasted with role shrinking)

8. **Inter-role linkage (versus isolation):** Linkage of one's role with the other roles.
9. **Helping relationship (versus hostility):** Giving and receiving help amongst roles.
10. **Superordination (versus deprivation):** Linkage of one's role with a larger entity cause.

Role Efficacy and Effectiveness

Research shows that persons with high role efficacy seem to experience less role stress, anxiety and work-related tension, they rely on their own strengths to cope with problems use more purposeful behaviors, they are active and they interact with people and the environment; persist in solving problems mostly by themselves, and sometimes by taking the help of other people, show growth orientation, attitudinal commitment, positive and approach behaviour, and feel satisfied with life, and with their jobs and roles in the organization. This is a profile of effective managers. Role efficacy should be related to the quality of work life (measured by influence, amenities at the work place, nature of job, and supervisory behaviour). Step-wise multiple regression yielded supervisory behaviour) as the most important dimension in role efficacy. Role efficacy has also been found as related to the type of roles, location of the work place and the length of employment (and age).

Regarding organization aspects, a participative climate in which the employees get a higher job satisfaction, contributes to role efficacy. It seems that a climate promoting concern for excellence, use of expertise and concern for the larger issues also contribute to role efficacy. On the other hand, a climate characterized by control and affiliation seems to lower employees' role efficacy. Innovation fostering climate was found to be a strong predictor of role efficacy.

Role efficacy has also been reported as a strong moderator or a mediating variable, showing the dramatic influence of role efficacy in predicting, or enhancing the effect on organization climate.

Role Efficacy Index

Role Efficacy Index represents the percentages of role effectiveness of respondent in an organization. It ranges from 0 to 100.

A high REI indicates that the respondent perceives that he has a great deal of opportunity to be effective in the role. REI is calculated for different instruments by different formulas.

$$\text{Total Role Efficacy Scale} = \frac{\text{Total Score} + 20}{60} \times 100$$

Satisfactory reliability was found for the Role Efficacy Scale.

Increasing Role Efficacy

Role Efficacy can be used for planning improvement in an organization. When managers have low work commitment, or their motivational level is low, an organization development Programme with role efficacy may be useful. The strategy consists of a diagnostic phase (measuring role efficacy at several levels in an organization), strategy planning to increase role efficacy (which may include decisions about where to begin, and how to proceed), implementation of the strategy, review and follow up evaluation and re-planning. The main focus of such an OD program will be a dose of role efficacy for several parts of the organization.

It has been found useful to apply other diagnostic tools in addition to the role efficacy instruments in generating diagnostic data.

One strategy, which has worked, very well is to start at the middle management level. A series of Role Efficacy Labs can be organized for the middle management level. After most of the middle-level managers have gone through these labs, action may simultaneously be started at the next higher as well as the next lower level.

After the three levels have been covered, the top management group may develop long-range strategies, based on the findings of the groups at the three levels and the data generated in the follow up programs.

In this OD strategy Role Efficacy Lab (REL) has a central place. It may be useful to discuss REL in some detail.

Role Efficacy Lab (REL)

REL is a short process-oriented program to diagnose the level of role efficacy in a group of employees (generally managers) in an organization, and to take steps to raise that level. We have found a 3-day REL useful for this purpose, although the lab can be of a longer duration, if some other aspects are included in it.

Counseling

As it is important to work on role efficacy by redesigning the role, it is similarly so to work on role efficacy from the point of view of a role occupant. Role efficacy may be low because the role occupant may be unable to either perceive those aspects, or to use his own power to build those aspects in the role. The necessary counseling and help in planning action to build these aspects (by the individual), may be useful. For example, if the person perceives that linkages with other roles are weak, it may be useful to work with him on what can be done to build stronger linkages with the other roles. Or, if he feels that a role does not provide opportunities to learn new things and grow, he can be helped to perceive various parts of the role, which may contribute to learning new things and his growth. The purpose of such counseling is to help the individual realize as to what prevents him from being effective and taking the necessary steps without waiting for the role to be redesigned in order to have a higher role efficacy. Such counseling may become a part of performance counseling.

Action Guidelines

Role efficacy can be increased by the joint effort of the role occupants, their senior managers and the organization (the top management). A special intervention can be designed for this purpose.

However, a role occupant and preferably several role occupants in a group can generate ideas for increasing the efficacy of their own roles. Similarly a supervisor can have ideas about increasing the efficacy of the roles that he supervises. The top managers can also take some steps, and ideas for such steps, can be generated by groups of managers at various levels.

Increasing each of its 10 aspects can increase role efficacy.

Role Making

In role taking the role occupant accepts the expectations of others. In contrast, role making involves active participation by the role occupant in defining his role – the priorities in his functions the ways in which he would achieve them, and the ways of becoming effective in the role. Four aspects of role making are discussed here: self-role integration, proactivity, creativity and confrontation.

Self-Role Integration

When the qualities and the background of a person match with the functions of the role (expectations by the significant persons, and those of the role occupant), the role efficacy will be high. Unless the role occupant is able to utilize his background education and special training in the role, he may not feel satisfied and the role may also remain less effective. In addition to formal education and training, each person has special skills and other qualities, which can be effectively utilized for organizational work. One person may be very good in negotiation; another may be good in bringing about compromise.

There are two approaches to self-role integration. The placement approach stresses the need for searching suitable incumbents for the roles. The role is defined and a person matching the role description is searched through a good placement program, reducing the problems of self-role distance.

However, the other approach is more proactive. An attempt is made to see what strengths the individual has, and how these can be utilized in the role.

Two other approaches can also be tried out. An employee can be used in temporary systems, which can benefit from his special strengths and qualities.

Secondly, the role itself can be redesigned in such a way that it utilizes the strengths of the role occupant.

The organization can also take into consideration the new dimensions represented by the role occupant for redesigning the role.

Several approaches to role redesigning have been suggested (job enrichment role or work redesigning, work humanization, etc.

Proactivity

The term 'proact' can be contrasted with the term 'react'. In the latter action is in response to (and in the pattern of) an act from some source, while in the former the action is taken independent of the act from the source. For example, if a person shouts back at his friend's accusations he shows reactive behaviour. However, if he does not use this pattern (of shouting) but responds calmly and suggests that they discuss the problem together, he is showing proactive behaviour. Proactivity gives initiative to the person to start a new process or set a new pattern of behaviour. In reactive behaviour the initiative lies with the source, and the person merely acts according to the pattern set by that source. In other words, the 'usual' responses are reactive. Proactivity involves unusual behaviour. In this sense proactivity means freeing one's self from and taking action beyond the immediate concern.

A person showing proactivity, function at all the three levels – feeling, thinking and action. Some of the implications are discussed here.

At the feeling level the person transcends his role boundary and sees things from the point of view of the other role sender. This is empathy. He appreciates the other point of view (at least understands, even if he if he does not agree), and is able to 'feel' the other person. This also means that he transcends logic and reasoning, and is able to 'reach' the feelings. Then things may acquire new meanings.

At the thinking level the person may transcend his own immediate feelings and emotions and reason to understand a problem, he may transcend time and think of the future. (I terms of the long term implications) he may transcend individual events and see a pattern leading to his own "action theory"

At the action level, proactivity means transcending immediate cause, i.e. taking initiative. There are three ways in which this can be done. Transcending symptoms (i.e. looking for causes of problem), Transcending traditionality and uniformity (i.e. searching several alternative modes of action), and Transcending content (i.e. initiating a new process–for example, the process of joint exploration). In Transactional Analysis proactivity is stressed in terms of transcending circularity (being sucked into a game). Instead of falling into the trap of a 'game' a proactive individual makes a new move, which stops the game and starts a new set of adult-adult transactions. Proactivity thus shows a high level of maturity and both individual employees and the organization can do a lot to promote it.

Creativity

We are so caught up with our daily tasks, that we only use the short cut of traditional and tried out ways of dealing with problems. While these methods save time and energy, they also blind us from perceiving the advantage of new ways of solving a problem. The more we work under pressure, the less is our inclination to try a different approach–the risk seems to be too high. And yet complex problems require new approaches for solutions.

Organizational learning does not imply repetitive action it implies applying past experience to current problems to reach beyond. This can be called creativity. Other terms such as innovations, experiments, new approaches, etc., also convey the same meaning.

There are several aspects of creativity in an organization. It is reflected in new suggestions generated by employees, attempts at improving upon previous ways of working, trying out a new idea to which one has been exposed, innovating new methods, and thinking about a problem while ignoring the so called 'constraints'. The last one is also called lateral thinking i.e. thinking aimed at generating alternatives. There is enough evidence that such thinking contributes towards the development of new products, new methods and new processes.

Creativity can be developed by the joint efforts of individual employees and the management. The suggestions scheme is a good example of a mechanism promoting creativity. However, what is more important is how the suggestions are used.

Criticism of innovative attempts stifle creativity.

Confrontation

The terms confrontation is being used with some reservation and means 'putting a front' contrasted with "putting the back" (escaping) the problem. A better term would be/confrontation-exploration (CE).

Let us use the term confrontation in this sense of confrontation-exploration, i.e. facing a problem and working jointly with others to find a solution to the problem. The following factors should be kept in mind while promoting such a mode of behaviour.

1. **Culture of Confrontation-exploration (CE):** If the C-E culture prevails in an organization/department/section, the employees are more likely to use the C-E mode while dealing with problems and conflicts. CE culture is created when the senior managers themselves us the C-E mode of behaviour with the employees. The more the employees experience such a mode with their supervisors, the more likely they are to internalize it and use it themselves.

2. **Risk of Confrontation not Too High:** Confrontation-Exploration is risky. The individual using C-E mode runs the risk of offending the other person(s), leading to a bad relationship. He also runs the risk of failing to solve the problem, and thereby losing face. (Had tried and failed, compared with not trying and therefore not failing). If an individual sees such risks as too high, he will not use the C-E mode. Managers can minimize these risks by the helping people analyze and learn from the incidents of failure. Punishment (event disapproval is punishment) can make the risks too high, and encouragement can minimize them.
3. **Higher Pay-off of Confrontation:** If the employees perceive that avoidance has more undesirable consequences than confrontation, or that the C-E mode will give them more advantages, they are likely to try and use the C-E mode. Whenever in the review of problems it is revealed that an employee avoided a certain problem the supervisor may show disapproval of such action, and suggest how he could use C-E mode in relation to the problem. Similarly, approval of C-E attempts may help establish its higher pay-off.
4. **Self-confidence:** A person, who has in his ability to deal with a problem and work through a relationship despite difficulties, generally uses the C-E mode. Steps may be taken to create such self-confidence in the employees.
5. **Supervisory Support:** Confrontation requires support from the top. If an employee uses C-E mode, his action needs to be supported by the supervisor and other senior managers. Encouraging employees to use C-E mode and then letting them down if the situation takes an undesirable turn will discourage them from confronting problems in future.
6. Supporting an employee does not mean that the mistakes he makes are overlooked: Far from it. While supporting him, the entire episode may be analyzed with the concerned employee at an appropriate opportunity, to help him learn what was effective, and what was not and how could effectiveness be increased in the future.
7. **Reinforcing Confrontation:** Confrontation needs to be recognized as a desirable behaviour and it needs to be rewarded. If an organization works out a system of identifying outstanding

example of C-E, more employees will be motivated to try such a mode.

Centrality

Centrality is concerned with the perceived importance of a role. The role occupant needs to perceive his role as important and this is only possible when enough importance is given to the role and it is expressed (communicated) as such.

There are primarily three ways in which a role is seen as important. First if the role is linked with a larger cause, it is seen as important. Secondly, a role may be perceived as important if the effectiveness of other roles is seen as dependent on the good performance of this role. Thirdly, a role becomes central when good performance of that role is perceived as contributing to enhancement of the image of the organization (especially by senior manager).

As we have already said, importance (centrality) needs to be perceived as well as communicated. If the importance of a role is not communicated it may not have any effect on the sense of centrality.

Influence

Every member of a group wants to have power or influence. Power or influence is the scope a person has of making impact on the other individuals, matters, things or groups. The impact can vary from a complete control to a kind of indirect impact which can sometimes be far more extensive and deeper than the former. Influence is not a fixed quantity in an organization– it can increase, allowing more people to have a greater influence, or it can diminish.

Influence constitutes one dimension of role efficacy. The higher the sense a person has of having influence in his role, the higher will be the efficacy. It may be useful to understand the dynamics of role influence in an organization. The narrowest scope of influence is one's own role. A person would like to use his power to do something in his own role. The scope of influence becomes larger when one can do something in one's own section, and then in one's own department, and then in one's own organization. The largest scope is when a role occupant can make an impact beyond the organization.

Growth

Self-development or personal growth is an important motivating force contributing to role efficacy. A role occupant has a need to grow to make his role more effective. There is also strong need to grow into the next higher role (advancement or promotion). Any employee is interested in his development in general. Thus there are three dimensions of growth; current role, transition to the next role, and general development. Attention should be paid to all these aspects.

Growth is generally associated with training. Training is certainly one important system. All human resource (personnel) systems have the potential for employee development. Performance appraisal can help the employees learn how to set challenging goals, and how to analyze their own performance. Performance counseling can help them develop new skills and attitudes. Potential appraisal and career development/ career planning systems can help them develop those attributes which will enable them to be effective in higher roles. The reward system can reinforce and develop desirable behaviour. And training is obviously a growth-oriented system in the organization (in-house, on-the-job, external and distance training). Growth potential of all these systems need to be exploited.

Managers can go beyond the formal systems to increase the growth opportunities of the employees; similarly, employees can themselves do a lot in this regard. Special facilities can contribute to the efforts of self-development-e.g. a good library; reimbursement of membership fee of a professional society, or of subscription to a professional journal; special seminars or periodical meetings to share new developments; spending organizational time for the on-going educational efforts of an employee; rewarding people who successfully complete some required educational/training courses; rewarding outstanding performance of employees in training/educational courses; voluntary help by employees/unions to those who want to pursue further education/training etc. If organizations are seriously interested in employee development, a large number of action suggestions can be worked out for implementation.

Encouragement contributes a great deal to growth.

Inter-role Linkage

An organization is a system of roles, which are linked with one another. One factor influencing the potential effectiveness (efficacy) of a role is the amount of interlinkages existing between a role and the other roles. The role occupant measures the existing amount against the desired amount. We may consider three dimensions of such inter-role linkages-the levels, the basis, and the types of interlinkages.

A role occupant desires to have linkages with other roles at all the levels in his role set – the higher level, lower level (with the employees working under him) and the horizontal level (with peers in his own and in the other departments). Several conditions promote such interlinkages, of which at least four seem to be important: common goals, interdependence, empathy, and crisis management.

Interlinkages may be built when two or more role occupants work for a common goal. Most of the interdepartmental linkages are built around common goals. Secondly, two roles may develop linkages if they have an interdependent relationship and such interdependence is perceived. Thirdly, interlinkages may be built when one role occupant understands the problem of the other role occupant. Linkages are built when a role occupant empathizes with and respond to the others' need. Then sharing between the two becomes easier. An employee usually has such a relationship with his boss or his subordinate.

And finally, in dealing with a crisis situation some role occupants may come together and they may be required to interact in order to meet the crisis. These are temporary groups created for a purpose.

Inter-role linkages are either task linkages (interactions around a task or a goal) or emotional linkages (having closeness and accessibility to another role). Both are important. The availability of another role occupant and his eagerness both to respond to the linkage needs and to take initiative in building linkages, contribute to a satisfactory amount of inter-role linkages.

Individual role occupants can do as mush as an organization in promoting such linkages. An instrument is available to diagnose the areas of role isolation (weak linkages) which can then be dealt with through several action suggestions.

Helping

A helping relationship goes beyond work-related linkages. Helping can be personal or role-related. In either case at least three processes are involved in helping: empathy, support and sacrifice. The beginnings of a helping relationship lie in empathy. Unless a person a role occupant has empathy for the other person or role occupant, there can be no help.

Moving beyond empathy, a helping relationship involves providing support to the other individual enabling him to be effective in action. Finally, helping involves some sacrifice on the part of the helper, giving some of his time and energy to the other person. The helper is prepared to suffer some inconvenience in order to be useful to the other person.

A healthy helping relationship is a two-way process. While a role occupant is ready to empathize, support, and sacrifice his time, he is also prepared to seek help from the other role occupant. Such mutuality should exist in all relationship, including the one between a boss and the employees. The boss can (and should) also take the subordinates' help in various matters as much as he helps the employees.

Superordination

The concept of super ordination is derived from the concept of super ordinate goals. As super ordinate goal is one, which is valuable to two or more persons, or the groups involved; which is shareable; and which cannot be achieved by a single person or group working alone. The term super ordination is used to indicate the relevance of a person or a role to a much larger entity. Superordination may take several form, some of which are suggested below.

Superordination may be reflected in the perception of common goals, which are desirable and the achievement of which would require collaboration with the other role occupants. Superordination of a role also increases if the role occupants realize that they are part of a prestigious organization, which is working for larger causes.

A role occupant has sense of super ordination when he realizes that the role is useful (and is seen as such) for the organization. A sense of higher linkage is developed.

Superordination is higher when a role occupant perceives that what he does in the role contributes to a higher cause.

Superordination is also higher when the role occupants see their role as providing opportunity to serve others.

And finally, super ordination emerges from linkages of a role with a larger group outside the organization, for example, professional groups such as engineers, doctors, cost accountants, etc. The occupants to increase the super ordination of their roles can generate several action suggestions. Similarly an organization can also take steps to raise the level of super ordination for the various roles.

The objective /purpose of the RES is to determine how much role efficacy a person has. It helps to assess Role Effectiveness.

Operational Definitions

Centrally: If a person occupying a particular role in an organization feels that the role he occupies is central in the organization, his role efficacy is likely to be high.

Integration

When the qualities and the background of a person match with the functions of the role (expectations by the significant persons, and those of the role occupant), the role efficacy will be high.

Proactivity

Proactivity involves unusual behaviour. In this sense, proactivity means freeing oneself from, and taking action beyond the immediate concern. Proactivity gives initiative to the person to start a new process or set a new pattern of behaviour.

Creativity

There are several aspects of creativity in an organization. It is reflected in new suggestions generated by employees, attempts at improving upon previous ways of working, trying out a new idea to which one has been exposed, innovating new methods, and thinking about a problem while ignoring the so called 'constraints'.

Inter-Role Linkage

Interlinkages may be built when two or more role occupants work for a common goal. Most of the interdepartmental linkages are built around common goals.

Helping

A helping relationship goes beyond work-related linkages. Helping can be personal or role-related. In either case at least three processes are involved in helping: empathy, support and sacrifice.

Superordination

The term Superordination is used to indicate the relevance of a person or a role to a much larger entity. Superordination may be reflected in the perception of common goals which are desirable and the achievement of which would require collaboration with the other role occupants. Superordination of a role also increases if the role occupants realize that they are part of a prestigious organization, which is working for larger causes.

Influence

Power or influence is the scope a person has of making impact on the other individuals, matters, things or groups. The impact can vary from a complete control to a kind of indirect impact, which can sometimes be far more extensive and deeper than the former.

Growth

Self-development or personal growth is an important motivating force contributing to role efficacy. A role occupant has a need to grow to make his role more effective. There is also strong need to grow into the next higher role (advancement or promotion). Any employee is interested in his development in general. Thus there are three dimensions of growth; current role, transition to the next role, and general development. Attention should be paid to all these aspects.

Confrontation

The terms confrontation is being used with some reservation and means 'putting a front' contrasted with "putting the back" (escaping) the problem. A better term would be confrontation-exploration (CE).

Let us use the term confrontation in this sense of confrontation-exploration, i.e. facing a problem and working jointly with others to find a solution to the problem.

Controls

1. Noise and distractions are kept at the bare minimum.
2. Instructions are given properly.
3. Made sure that the employees have understood the instructions properly.

Methodology

Sample:- S^1 - Mr. Anand Nair (Sr. Project Manager)

S^2 - Ms. Disha Parab (Executive, HR Manager)

Materials Used

Role efficacy scale has been developed by Udai Pareek and has high reliability. The Role Efficacy Scale is a structured instrument consisting 20 triads of statements. A respondent marks one statement in each triad, which describes his role most accurately. These three alternatives are pre-weighted. There are two statements for each dimension of Role Efficacy and the same pattern is followed (+2, +1, or –1). The regular scale is to be completed by a role occupant for his own role.

Instructions

"In each of the following sets of three statements, check the one (a, b, or c) that most accurately describes your own experience in your organizational role. You must choose only one statement in each set."

Discussion

The role efficiency scale measures how efficient or rather potential efficiency of a role is in an organization. Role efficiency is an important dimension, which is linked to many other important dimensions. Thus it is a very useful tool.

The first S who was given this test was Disha Parab, who is an Executive HR Manager working for Rediffusion Ad Agency.

The S has a high score of 4 on creativity helping relationship and confrontation. This implies her present role, gives here the opportunity to try new and unconventional ways. She also feels and even gives other people help. The firm also gives her the chance to confront problems and find relevant solutions for them.

On integration and growth she has the next score of 3. She does feel the job allows her to grow and develop but she thinks it would be better. The role she plays gives here the opportunity to use here special skills but once in a while it becomes monotonous.

On centrality, super-ordination and influence she has a moderate score. She does not feel what is doing is really important for the society and her influence in the organization is again related to the fact that she is an executive manager in the organization.

Her inter-role linkage score is very low; she cannot link her role with the others in the organization. Also as a trainee she is not expected to take initiative in any thing so her score on proactivity is 0. Personally also the S does not like to take initiative.

But overall her efficiency is quite high, it is 71% that is she is infact overqualified to do this work. Thus a redesigning effort will definitely help to increase her motivation and performance level.

The 2nd S Mr. Anand Nair, Sr. Project Manager, Vishan Projects Pvt. Ltd. had almost the same scores and therefore the above discussion holds true for him also.

8. Team Building

What is teamwork?

The idea of teamwork is not always an easy one to grasp. Most organizations organize their work force into groups of people who work together but each have their own jobs to do; and these are often referred to as teams. But simply having an arrangement whereby people work together isn't the same as having on organization, which has converted to teamwork. Essentially, the message of teamwork is delegation and empowerment. Team working is all about passing responsibility over to working team, so that they can get on with what they have to do without continually having to refer to higher levels in their organization. That means that the teams need to be given enough authority to make day-to-day decisions about their work and enough power to make sure that things are done properly.

Team working, then, is very different from the old-fashioned, high-control, authoritarian management that is still, unfortunately, so common. But it is also much more effective. Organizational psychologists have known for a long time that when people are given responsibility, they act in a much more responsible way. Strict, authoritarian systems produce resentful and passive employees and interfere with communication into the bargain. But team working gives people a sense of being valued and we all work better when we feel that our efforts are appreciated. Team working also encourages people to be more professional in their approach and to take their responsibilities seriously. All of which is a tremendous benefit to any organization.

Types of Teams

Production or Service Teams–The type of team which most commonly comes to mind when we th..ık about teams in organizations are those teams which are actively involved in manufacturing, production, or service. They include teams of stewardesses or stewards on aircraft, production-line assembly teams involved in direct manufacturing, mining or drilling teams, computing or data processing teams and maintenance teams such as those involved in municipal gardening or building maintenance.

Teams of this type usually consist of full-time workers, who may sometimes have worked together over many years. These teams are largely self-managing in terms of the rest of their organization, in that they organize their own work and get on with it. How far individual team members have a say in what they do, though, is usually up to the team manager, who is also the link between the team and the rest of the organization.

Action / Negotiation Teams

Another type of team consists of highly skilled individuals who come together to engage in special activities where each person's role is clearly defined. These teams include surgical teams, musical groups, and sports teams, tend to be entirely task-focused, with each team member having tend to be entirely task – focused, with the team has to perform which effectively defines how the team members operate.

Since the tasks, which these teams perform, are complex and sometimes unpredictable, it is vital that each team member is able to draw from their own expertise to contribute to the whole. That way, it is possible to improvise in unusual situations. The role of management in these is really about establishing the task or mission, which the team has to perform. Once that has been done, the team takes over. Within the team itself, leadership is not about directing individual activities. Instead, it is mainly concerned with co-ordination and timing.

Project and Development Teams

Product development team, research teams and project teams from a third type of team. These teams tend to operate across a much longer time span: they can sometimes take years to complete a particular development project, such as the design of a new type of car or computer. Sometimes, these teams have come together for a single project and the team members go on to different work once their task is completed. Sometimes, through, they are ongoing, permanent teams with a general research role in the organization. Whichever type of lifespan they have, these teams tend to consist of highly skilled technical or professional people, with a mixture of different specialisms. They tend to organize their work internally and will often have a reasonably high level of autonomy, in respect to the rest of the organization.

Advice and Involvement Teams

The fourth type of team is concerned with providing organizational advice and decision-making. High-level management teams are the classic example, of course, but this category also includes specialist advisory teams such as personnel or financial planning teams. Not all of these teams are at high levels in an organization, though; this category can also include quality control circles and employee involvement groups, whose role is to generate ideas, advice and to pass on suggestions.

Most advice and involvement teams have a fairly restricted scope, and don't take up a great deal of working time – their members have other roles within the organization. At the lower levels in the organization, such teams often don't have all that much autonomy, although that depends to a very large degree on the organization's commitment to teamwork.

What Makes a Good Team?

There is some consensus in the management and organizational literature about the characteristics of a good team. A good team has a clear sense of itself as a special group, but its members are also able to interact positively with other people in the organization. The team as a whole cultivates and negotiates positive assumptions and beliefs among its members, which help them to operate effectively with their organization. They communicate clearly with one another and effectively with the rest of the organization. And working together, the team is more effective than those same people would be if they were working as individuals.

Some team managers appear to know how to foster these mechanisms instinctively to encourage positive team qualities, and to head off destructive or counter-productive events. Other, equally good, team managers have had to learn how to manage their teams effectively. Part of learning how to do it involves understanding some of the mechanisms which are important in making teams work.

Psychological Dimensions of Team Work

Whatever type of team it is, a team consists of a number of individual people working together to achieve a common goal. Simply because they are human beings, this means that teamwork involves psychology - and quite a lot of it. Effective communication, for instance, draws on body language as well as choice of words and metaphors.

But there are some over-arching psychological mechanisms, which permeate the whole process of working in teams. These are absolutely central to why human beings work well in team at all and if we really want to understand what is going on, we need psychological mechanisms.

The two psychological mechanisms, which are particularly helpful when we are trying to understand the psychology of teamwork, are known as social identification and social representations. Put in its simplest form, social identification is our human tendency to see the world in terms of 'them-and-us' – to see us as located in various social groups, which are different from 'the others'. Social representations are the shared beliefs or assumptions, which we pick, up from others and adjust until they fit into out own personal beliefs and opinions.

Team Roles

As research interest shifted into the idea of the team, interest in-group roles made a transition to that of team roles. Belbin, in 1981, proposed a set of eight significant roles, which, according to Belbin, were also essential in other kinds of teamwork in organizational life. These roles are listed in Table. A recent revision (Belbin 1993) changed the name of 'chairperson' to 'co-ordinator' and 'company worker' to 'implementer', although the role descriptions themselves remained essentially similar.

Belbin arrived at these roles through a series of simulation exercises, in which managers attending management development courses were asked to work in-groups to analyze the implications of particular case studies. By combining individuals with different attributes, Belbin showed that successful team consisted of a mixture of different individuals. Moreover, Belbin argued that successful teams would always, of necessity, involve people playing different roles in a team, in which nobody acted as 'plant'.

Although Belbin did accept that some people might be able to play more than one role, he also argued that effective management would need to ensure that all of these roles were covered in a given team – if necessary. 'Importing' someone to play a part if it wasn't already being played. That suggestion reveals quite a change of emphasis: rather than being a temporary stance which reflects the demands and issues of the moment, the concept of role had become transformed into the idea of a consistent pattern, relevant for all working groups, and tied to particular individuals. Unfortunately, this shift of emphasis severely weakened team role theory as it developed since it then became unable to cope well with individual flexibility.

Team roles (adapted from Belbin 1981)

Role	*Activities*	*Characteristics*
Chairperson	Clarifies goal and objects; helps allocate roles, responsibilities and duties; articulates group conclusions	Calm, average intellect trusting, impartial, self-disciplined, positive thinker, self-confident.
Shaper	Seeks patterns in group discussions; pushes group towards agreement and decision-making	High-achiever, highly-strung, impatient, outgoing, argumentative and provocative, dynamic.
Plant	Advance proposals and offers new ideas; gives new insights on courses of action.	Individualistic, serious-minded and knowledgeable, unorthodox, intellectual.
Monitor / evaluator	Analyses problems and complex issues; assesses the contributions of others.	Sober, clever, discreet, detached, unemotional, not easily aroused.
Company worker	Transforms talk and ideas into practical activities.	Tough-minded, practical, tolerant, conscientious.
Team worker	Gives personal support and help to others.	Gregarious, sensitive, team-oriented, indecisive
Resource investigator	Introduces external information; negotiates with outsiders.	Curious, versatile, sociable, innovative, communicative.
Completer	Emphasizes the need for meeting schedules and targets and completing task.	Perfectionist, perseverance, conscientious, attention to detail, anxious

While it is clear that a successful team does involve different contributions from the participants and while it is equally clear that different roles may be crucial to the overall success or otherwise of the team, tying the role to the individual much more contentious. Much of the experimental evidence supporting the idea of team roles has derived from a relatively narrow range of research situations: for example, Belbin provided each group with case studies and asked them to use the information to solve a particular problem. Although the content of the case study and of the problem varied, the task itself was essentially pretty consistent. So it may not be surprising that the managers concerned acted in reasonably consistent ways.

The problem, though, is that a very different situation may bring an entirely different facet of personality to the fore. People act in different ways in different situations. One person may take the role of 'shaper' with respect to one type of task, while adopting an evaluative role in another and a 'plant' rolc in a third. It depends on expertise and knowledge, as well as on people are working positively and efficiently together, the role which they play at any one time will depend as much on the nature of the immediate task, and the skills which it requires, as it does on the other members of the team. Of course, people are likely to adopt consistent areas of responsibility but the whole point of a strong team is that it is able to bring out other abilities and resources in its members.

The Team Management Wheel

Belbin's typology is undoubtedly valuable in showing how people can make different contributions to a team's work, and how positive team action often requires a mixture of different types of activity. However, it is better to think of team roles as just that – types of activity–and it may not be all that helpful to think of individual people as automatically representing the appropriate roles.

Four Different Approaches

When we look at the various approaches to team building, which are described in the organization literature, it is possible to distinguish four general approaches.

The first approach–the interpersonal approach–focuses on developing very high levels of social and personal awareness between team members, for example, by helping team members to learn how to listen to one another, or to become aware of the past experiences of the other members of the team. The idea is that a better understanding of one another's personalities, and a better ability to communicate with one another, will help people to work together more easily. It will encourage people to see the other team members as 'us', rather than simply as a collection of people that they have to work with.

A second approach to team building focuses; on the role and norms, which exist within the team.

For some management consultant, this way of understanding teams became the framework, which defined how a team could be built, and so team-building emphasized role expectations, the norms of the group as a whole and the shared responsibilities of the different group members. This would mean that the team would become aware of itself as a working unit. It would be able to operate effectively and efficiently because each member had a clear understanding of his or her place, role and responsibility.

A third approach to team to team building also focuses on developing a shared understanding between team members. This time, though, the emphasis is on the overall stance, which team members take towards what they are doing, and the value, which they adopt, rather than the characters of the individuals making up the team, or the roles, which they are playing.

By ensuring that everyone in the team holds common values and the working aims of the team actually reflect those values, it is felt that the team members will be able to work together effectively, and will be able to perceive how their own personal activity contributes to the team's shared aims and reflects its shared values.

A fourth approach to team building emphasizes the team's task and the unique way that each team member can contribute to the achievement of that task. In this approach, the emphasis is not so much on what people are like, as on what skills they have and how those skills can contribute to the whole. This approach, therefore, places a heavy emphasis on the interchange of information between the various team members. It also emphasizes the realistic analysis of the team's task in terms of the resources, skills and practical steps, which it will require to carry, is cut out. This approach is manifest in many current discussions of high-performance team working (e.g. Katzenbach and Smith).

Most, if not all, methods of team building derive from one of these four approaches. Their effectiveness depends on three factors: the context in which the team is being built; the nature of the people involved; and the types of organizational task which the team is expected to carry out.

The Belbin Team Roles Self-Protection Inventory

Belbin (1981) had developed a model of eight team roles, derived from observations of genera' managers on training courses. The managers concerned would undertake a particular simulation exercise, the executive Management exercise, as part of their course. They had taken the 16PF personality test and the Watson Glaser Critical Thinking Appraisal before hand, and their behaviour during the exercise was observed, using a system based on Bales' interaction analysis. Belbin derived the set of team roles from the information provided by these measures, and also produced a self-report questionnaire, known as the Belbin Team Role Self-Perception Inventory (BTRSPI).

The BTRSPI rapidly became a very popular method of evaluating team roles and was widely adopted by a number of commercial organizations and management consultancies, and used for training courses as well as team building and development. However, in 1993, Furnham et al. published a detailed psychometric evaluation of the BTRSPI and found a number of weaknesses (Furnham, Steele and Pendleton 1993). One of the problems was that the questions were vague and inconsistent. For example, respondents were asked to specify their typical behaviour in situations such as 'when I am involved in a project with other people. Since this type of questioning is so general, it can lead to misunderstandings and is likely to produce very inconsistent results – and the more experience people have of working in diverse teams, the more unreliable those results are likely to be.

Another problem, which they identified, was that the BTRSPI was an Ipsative test, which was being used as if it was a normative one. Ipsative tests are ones, which assess a person's stronger and weaker traits – or in this case, the roles people may be more or less likely to adopt. The problem is that Ipsative tests give results which only relate to the particular individual who has taken the test and can't really be used to compare one person with another (Johnson, Wood and Blinkhorn 1988). This is because of the way that Ipsative tests work.

In an Ipsative test, scores are distributed between the items in the test in such a way that they always make up the same total. Stronger characteristics get more points from the pool, so this automatically means that weaker characteristics are allocated less.

Furnham et. al. also argued that the BTRSPI had not been properly evaluated as a psychometric test. There was no published evidence of its reliability (whether the test gave consistent answers when it was administered to the same people at different times), of its validity (whether it really measured what it claimed to measure), or of its dimensionality (how the different roles and role-measurements related to one another). Each of these is a fundamental requirement for a valid psychometric test and yet a search of the published literature had produced virtually nothing of this kind.

Belbin (1993) responded to this criticism by arguing that the Belbin Team Role Self-Perception Inventory had never been marketed as a psychometric test. It had been included in the Appendix to a book about team management, as a quick and easy way of indicating own key roles to managers who had read the book. The formally marketed test was what Belbin described as a more robust way of assessing the potential team role contribution of individuals, known as Interplace (Belbin Associates 1988). This was based on the same model, but used additional sources of data. However; Furnham et. al. (1993) pointed out that since the BTRSPI was actually used as the basis for organizational decision-making, it was important that it was actually valid for its purpose. Moreover, they argued, their criticisms also appeared to apply to the Interplace model, which was marketed as a psychometric tool.

Furnham, Steele and Pendleton (1993) conducted three studies designed to investigate the reliability and dimensionality of the Belbin Team Role Self-Perception Inventory. Their results indicated that there was a considerable degree of unreliability in the test items, and also that there seemed to be little connection between the dimensionality of the test items which was revealed by factor analysis, and the descriptions of their relationship which had been suggested in BellBin's own writing. In other words, Bellbin had suggested that some of the team roles linked together, but the empirical analysis didn't give much evidence for those connectionsî

These studies, however, were rather more controversial than the critical analysis, which the researchers had made, partly because of the way that Furnham et. al. used the BTRSPI itself. As other researchers have shown (Johnson, Wood and Blinkhorn 1998), it is inappropriate to use factor analysis on an Ipsative test, because it doesn't have independent measuring scales – the size of the scores on one item will have been affected by the size of the scores on the others. To take account of that, two of Furnham, Steele and Pendleton's three studies had used a 'de-ipsativized' version of the test. This gave results, which were quite different from the third study, which had used the original test. Furnham et. al. suggested that this was evidence that the BTRSPI was unreliable, but Belbin (1993) argued that the test had been changed so much by rendering it non-ipsative that it was hardly a fair evaluation. Although Furnham et. al. challenged this point too, their case here was weaker. And since they themselves had observed that it was inappropriate to use factor analysis on ipsative test data, their third study was not really a valid assessment even on their own terms.

Summary of Belbin's Team Roles

Implementer

- Stable and controlled–a practical organizer
- Turns ideas into manageable tasks
- Sorts out what is feasible and actionable
- Strength of character and disciplined approach
- Sincere, has integrity and trust; not easily deflated or discouraged
- May be thrown by sudden change of plan
- Needs stable structures and tries to create them
- Does not like 'airy-fairy' ideas
- Can be over-competitive for status
- But usually near the balance of the team; go to him or her to find out what is happening

Coordinator

- Clarifies group's objectives and sets agenda
- Stable, dominant, extrovert
- Presides over and co-ordinates; not necessarily brilliant and rarely originates many of the good ideas

- Self-discipline and 'character'
- Is dominant but in a relaxed, non-aggressive way
- Trusts people unless has reasons not to
- Not jealous
- Focuses people on what they can do best
- Good communicator
- Sets criteria but does not domineer
- Social leader.

Shaper

- Anxious, dominant, extrovert
- Task leader
- Lot of nervous energy
- Often has considerable charm
- Impulsive, impatient – easily frustrated
- Quick to challenge and quick to respond to challenges
- Does not harbor grudges
- Most prone to paranoid
- Principal function to give shape to the application of the team's efforts.
- Tries to unite ideas and produce patterns
- Exudes self-confidence which often belies self-doubts
- Sees team as an extension of own ego
- Intolerant of wolliness and vagueness – can make team uncomfortable but make things happen.

Creator

- Dominant, very high IQ
- Scatters seeds which other nourish
- Ideas-person – originality and radical thinking
- Imaginative as well as intelligent
- Most likely to start searching for original approaches
- More concerned with fundamentals – large issues rather than details – and can make careless mistakes.

- Can be prickly, especially when criticized.
- Danger that spends too much time on own ideas rather than on what group is there for
- May be bad at taking criticism of own ideas and may be offended and sulk.

Resource Investigator

- Stable, dominant, extrovert
- Most immediately likeable–relaxed and sociable
- Tends to be positive and enthusiastic but puts things down as quickly as picks them up.
- Masses of outside contacts
- A salesman, diplomat and liaison officer.
- Can be mistaken for the 'ideas-person' but lack the personal originality that distinguishes the plant
- Needs pressure
- Preserves the team from stagnation and from losing touch with the outside world.

Monitor–Evaluator

- High IQ; stable introvert in a balanced team; it is only plant and evaluator who need a high IQ serious
- Serious, not exciting; measured, dispassionate analysis
- No original ideas but most likely to stop team from committing itself to a misguided project
- Least personally motivated – ego involvement does not cloud judgement.
- Best skills are assimilating, interpreting and evaluating large volumes of complex written material.
- Can lower group's morale by being a damper at the wrong time
- Can be competitive with those who overlap with him or her, i.e. chairman or the plant
- Lacks warmth and imagination
- But judgement rarely wrong.

Team Worker

- Stable, extrovert, low in dominance
- Most sensitive of the team; most aware of individual needs and worries.
- Knows about private lives and families
- Likeable, popular smoother – cement of the team
- Loyal to team and build on ideas
- Good listener, communicates freely and encourages others
- Counterbalances friction of shaper and plant
- Does not like confrontation
- Particularly valued when team is in difficulty
- Certainly missed not there.

Finisher

- Anxious, introvert
- Only at ease when has personally checked every detail
- Maintains permanent sense of urgency
- Self-control; impatient and intolerant of more casual members of the team
- Compulsive about order
- Can be bogged down in detail and might worry the group.

Specialist

- High degree of expertise in own field
- Introvert
- Narrowly focused on own knowledge and/or skill base; not interested in people or in broader team issues
- Can be a bit a 'law unto him-or herself'
- Adds significantly to the capability of the team.

What can team Managers Do?

It is essential to provide the team with the resources that it will need–including dedicated time for team-building and other activities. It is important to establish communication mechanisms, not just within the team but also between the team and the rest of the organization. It is necessary to make sure that the team is able to obtain the expertise, which it needs: either through training or through establishing effective liaison with the appropriate specialists.

What is particularly important for a team manager, though, is to make sure that all necessary conditions for positive social identification within the team are in place. The best way to think of this is in terms of the three features of social identifications: boundaries, cohesion and a clear sense of their boundaries and this should not be left to evolve by itself, in case the boundaries appear in the wrong place and the team becomes hampered by factionalism and in-fighting. It is up to the team manager to establish conditions whereby each team has a clear definition of itself and a clear sense of the part that it plays in the wider organization.

The team manager also needs to make sure that the communication mechanisms, which will promote effective tea cohesion, are in place. That communication can (indeed, should) be both formal and informal; it can be about the organization as a whole or the department as well as about the team and it should ensure that team members understand each others' roles and specialiality as well as the task demands and organizational contexts within which they are working. It also needs to work in all direction: one-way communication mechanisms simply won't serve the purpose.

In particular, the team manager needs to foster a sense of pride in belonging to the team and in working for the organization. That can happen in many ways: through emphasizing achievements, through building high professional standards, through encouraging positive customer care, or all three and some others besides. But it is an important part of the team manager's job to ensure that people are able to feel proud of belonging to their team. In this way, the manager will be able to harness the psychological processes of social identification, to aid and amplify team working.

What can Direction Do?

The hands-on aspects of team management don't really apply to high-level management, which is more likely to be involved at the level of policy and strategic decision-making. But, without support at the higher levels of the organization, team working is unlikely to become particularly successful. High-level management needs to provide the vision, the strategy and the resources to make team-working work.

High-level management needs to spend some time working out the organizational support team working will need, if is to achieve the productive synergy which can so transform an organization.

Directions and high-level management, too, can benefit from keeping social identity processes in mind. It is they who can provide the content of communications, which will help employees to feel proud of the organization's achievements. It is they who can establish the resources for building professionalism and customer care into daily work. And it is they who can ensure that the organization has a definite, positive direction, with clearly delineated values, which are understood and shared by all of its members.

It is possible, of course, for teams to operate with departmental support alone. Team managers can achieve a great deal to promote co-operative and mutually productive working. But teams working in that way are unlikely to achieve the powerful synergy and dynamism of their potential. They need active consideration and help from high-level management, as well as from their own lineïlX managers.

The high-level management of an organization is generally referred to as a team, but too often we find that it really works as a collection of individuals, each with a separate agenda and little shared vision. Spending time working on the characteristics of the team, and in participative safety, is always time well spent.

The objective of the team-building test was to determine if the respondent shows task related behavior or maintenance related behavior.

Operational Definition

Task related behavior: Here the focus is on the targets and on completing the tasks at hand. It is Achievement Oriented.

Maintenance related behavior: They are focused on what is already been done, and continuing to concentrate on its maintenance. They maintain the status quo.

Controls

1. Noise and distractions are kept at the bare minimum level.
2. Instructions are given properly.

3. Made sure that the employee has understood the instructions well.

Methodology

Sample: - S^1 - Ms. Disha Parab

Exec. HR Manager, Rediffusion Ad Agency

S^2 - Mr. Anand Nair

Sr. Project Manager, Vishan Projects Pvt. Ltd.

Materials Used

Team questionnaire. It consists of 16 statements that have to be rated. The scoring would help you identify a respondent's scores on task related and maintenance related behavior.

Instructions

"Below is a list of statements describing possible contributions to effective teams. Score each statement according to the following scale.

1 = Not very often true of me

2 = Sometime true of me

3 = Very often true of me".

Discussion

The first respondent was Disha Parab who was the HR Executive and the second respondent was Anand Nair who was the Sr. Project Manager.

Disha has got a higher score of 20 on maintenance related behavior as compared to task related behavior, where he has got a score of 18. This indicates that she has a higher orientation for maintenance related behavior than task related behavior, as she is a senior employee, she plays the role of a maintainer than meeting targets etc. She works more of a support system than concentrating on completion of tasks.

Anand on the other hand has maintained an equal score of 23 on both, task and maintenance related behavior which indicate that he is equally good at meeting and reaching targets, deadlines, at the same time maintaining systems and the status quo required. According to him one must be a blend of both. Being good at task and not at maintenance could be a drawback, even its vice versa is not recommended. One has to adopt a more task related behavior when targets are not being met, or when people are unable to reach goals, once the targets have been met then its important to maintain the same, in this case then, one must adopt a more of maintenance related behavior.

One has to always strike a balance of various styles. As one style might not work in one situation, he has to understand the importance and the various perspectives of each style.

9. Conflict Management

Organizations by definition require people to work together and communicate with one another-often in pairs. Ideally, these interpersonal relationships should be productive, cooperative and satisfying. In reality, managers find that they are not always that way,

Almost every working relationship will produce some degree of conflict across time. Whether the conflicts will be destructive or constructive depends on the attitudes and skills of the participants as well as time pressures and resource shortages.

Interpersonal behaviour in complex organizations inevitably produces power differences.

Nature of Conflict

Conflict is any situation in which two or more parties feel themselves in opposition, conflict is an interpersonal process that arises from disagreements over the goals to attain or the methods to be used to accomplish those goals. In organizations everywhere, conflict among different interests is inevitable, and sometimes the amount of conflict is substantial.

One survey reported that managers spend an estimated 20% of their time dealing with the conflict. They may be either direct participants or mediators trying to resolve conflict between two or more of their employees. In either case, knowledge and understanding of conflict and the methods for resolving it are important.

Levels of Conflict

Conflict can occur within an employee, between individuals or groups, and across organizations as they compete.

Intrapersonal Conflict

Although most role conflicts occur when an employee's supervisor or peers send conflicting expectations to him or her, it is possible for Intrapersonal role conflict to emerge from within an individual, as a result of competing roles taken.

Interpersonal Conflict

Interpersonal conflicts are a problem to many people because they deeply affect a person's emotions. There is a need to protect one's self-image and self esteem from damage by others. When self-concept is threatened, serious upset occurs and relationships deteriorate. Sometimes the temperaments of two persons are incompatible and their personalities clash. In other instances, conflicts develop from failures of communication or differences in perception.

Intergroup Conflict

Intergroup conflicts, e.g., between different departments, also cause problems. Conflicts arise from such causes as different viewpoints, group loyalties, and competition for resources. Resources are limited in any organization struggle to be competitive. Since most groups feel that they need more than they can secure, the seeds of intergroup conflict exist wherever there are limited resource.

Some conflicts can be constructive, and this is certainly true at the intergroup level. Here, conflict may provide a clue that a critical problem between two departments needs to be resolved rather than allowed to smolder. Unless issues are brought into the open, they cannot be fully understood or explored. Once intergroup conflict emerges, it creates a motivating force encouraging the two groups to resolve the conflict so as to move the relationship to a new equilibrium. Intergroup conflict is sometimes escalated – intentionally stimulated in organizations because of its constructive consequences. On other occasions it may be desirable to de-escalate it – intentionally decrease it because of its potentially destructive consequences. The managerial challenge is to keep conflict at a moderate level (where it is most likely to stimulate creative thought but not interfere with performance) conflict should not become so intense that individual parties either hide it or escalate it to destructive levels.

Sources of Conflict

Interpersonal conflict arises from a variety of sources. Organizational change: people hold differing views over the direction to go, the routes to take and their likely success, the resources to be used, and the probable outcomes. With the pace of technological, political, and social change increasing and the marketplace hurtling toward a global economy, organizational changes will be ever present.

Personality Clashes

The concept of individual differences is fundamental to organizational behaviour. Not everyone thinks, feel, look, or acts like the other. Some people simply "rub us the wrong way", and we cannot necessarily explain why. Although personality differences can cause conflict, they are also a rich resource for creative problem solving. Employees need to accept respect, and learn how to use these differences when they arise.

Different Sets of Values

People hold different beliefs and adhere to different value systems. Their philosophies may diverge, or their ethical values may lead them in different directions. The resulting disputes can be difficult to resolve, since they are less objective than disagreements over alternative products inventory levels, or the social rank of person in a group, is very important to many individuals. When one's status is threatened, face saving becomes a powerful, driving force as a person struggles to maintain a desired image. Conflict may arise between the defensive person and whoever created a threat to status.

Contrasting Perceptions

People perceive things differently as a result of their prior experiences and expectations. Since their perceptions are very real to them (and they feel that theses perceptions must be equally apparent to others), they sometimes fail to realize that others may hold contrasting perceptions of the same object or event. Conflict may arise unless employees learn to see things as others see them and help others do the same.

Lack of Trust

Every continuing relationship requires some degree of trust – the capacity to depend on each other's word and actions. Trust opens up boundaries, provides opportunities in which to act and enriches the entire social fabric of an organization. It takes time to build, but it can be destroyed in an instant. When someone has a real or perceived reason not to trust another, the potential for conflict arises.

Effects of Conflict

Conflict is not all bad, but rather may result in either productive or non-productive outcomes. A more positive view, then, is to see that conflict is nearly inevitable and to search for ways in which it can result in constructive outcomes.

Advantages

One of the benefits produced by conflict is that people are stimulated to search for improved approaches that lead to better results. It energizes them to be more creative and to experiment with new ideas.

Another benefit is that once –hidden problems are brought to the surface, where they may be confronted and solved. And once the conflict is resolved, the individuals may be more committed to the outcome through their involvement in solving it.

Disadvantages

If the conflict lasts a long time, becomes too intense, or is allowed to focus on personal issues. At the interpersonal level, cooperation and teamwork may deteriorate. Distrust may grow among people who need to coordinate their efforts. At the individual level some of others will decline and personal stress levels will rise. Predictably, the motivation level of some employees will be reduced. It is important, then, for managers to be aware of the potential for interpersonal and intergroup conflicts, to anticipate their likely outcomes, and to use appropriate conflict resolution strategies.

Model of Conflict

Conflict arises from many sources and directions. It also varies in the speed of its emergence and in the degree of its predictability. Sometimes it smolders for a long time and then springs to life when the hot coal is fanned. Other times it simply seems to explode without warning, like the sudden eruption of a volcano. And just like the flame that can warm us in need or scar us with its heat, conflict can be constructive or destructive. Managers, therefore, must know when to stimulate conflict and when to resolve it. If conflict will be harmful, managers need to apply a conflict resolution strategy to prevent, diminish or remove it. Then the outcomes of conflict (winning or losing) must be evaluated from the perspectives of both parties.

Conflict Outcomes

Conflict may produce four distinct outcomes depending on the approaches taken by the people involved. The first quadrant, termed ("lose-lose"), depicts a situation in which a conflict deteriorates to the point that both parties are worse off than they were before.

An extreme example is the case of an executive who fires the only person who knows the secret formula for the organization's most successful product. The second quadrant is ("lose-win"), a situation in which one person (individual A) is defeated while the other one (individual B) is victorious.

In quadrant three ("win-lose") the situation is reversed with B losing A. The fourth quadrant is the ("win-win") outcome of the conflict, in which both parties perceive that they are in a better position than they mere before the conflict began. This is the preferred outcome to try and achieve in ongoing relationships, such as with suppliers, customers, and employees. Although it may be an unrealistic ideal in some situations, it is a fundamental organizational behaviour perspective toward which all parties should aim.

Conflict Resolution

Different people use different strategies for managing conflicts. These strategies are learned, usually in childhood, and they seem to function automatically. Usually we are not aware of how we act in conflicting situations. We just do whatever seems to come naturally. But we do have a personal strategy, and because it was learned, we can always change it by learning new and more effective ways of managing conflicts. When you become engaged in a conflict, there are two major concerns you have to take into account:

Achieving your personal goals-you are in conflict because you have a goal those conflicts with another person's goal. Your goal may be highly important to you, or it may be of little importance.

Keeping a good relationship with the other person- you may need to be able to interact effectively with the other person in the future. The relationship may be very important to you, or it may be of little importance. How important your personal goals are to you and how important the relationship is to you affects how you act in a conflict.

Intentions help participants select their strategies. Once they have been chosen, the strategies implemented will have a substantial impact on the outcomes reached given these two concerns, five styles of managing conflicts can be identified. Each style is associated to an animal.

Avoiding: The Turtle

Turtles withdraw into their shells to avoid conflicts. They give up their personal goals and relationships. They stay away from the issues over which the conflict is taking place and from the people they are in conflict with. Turtles believe it is hopeless to try to resolve conflicts. They feel helpless. They believe it is easier to withdraw (physically and psychologically) from a conflict than to face it. For e.g.

If, in a conflicting situation, party A is concerned neither about himself nor the other, A is likely to avoid facing or handling the conflict. When the situation is thus ignored or neglected, then B might just get the better of A by taking advantage of A's avoidance behaviour.

Competing: The Shark

Sharks try to overpower opponents by forcing them to accept their solution to the conflict. Their goals are highly important to them, and the relationship is of minor importance. They seek to achieve their goals at all costs. They are not concerned with the needs of other people. They do not care if other people like or accept them. Sharks assume that one-person winning and one-person losing settle conflicts. They want to be winner. Winning gives sharks a sense of pride and achievement. Losing gives them a sense of weakness, inadequacy and failure. They try to win by attacking, over-powering, overwhelming and intimidating other people.

If on the other hand, A has very high concern for himself and very low concern for the other, then A will take a highly competitive stance and would approach the conflict situation from a "I win-you lose" stance. This, competitive mode of handling the conflict will then resolve who wins and who loses in the situation.

Confrontation: The Owl (collaboration)

Owls highly value their own goals and relationships. They view conflicts as problems to be solved and seek a solution that achieves both their own goals and the goals of the other person in the conflict.

Owls see conflicts as improving relationships by reducing tension between two people. They try to begin a discussion that identifies the conflict as a problem. By seeking solutions that satisfy both themselves and the other person, owls maintain the relationship. Owls are not satisfied until a solution is found that achieves their own goals and the other person's goals. And they are not satisfied until the tensions and negative feeling have been fully resolved. The higher the total score for each conflict strategy, the more frequently you tend to use that strategy. The lower the total score for each conflict strategy, the less frequently you tend to use that strategy.

If A has high concern for both, the self and other, then A would approach the conflict situation in a collaborative mode with a desire to solve whatever problem exists in a way that would benefit both parties. A "win-win" stance will be taken in such a case and the resolution of the conflict will result in satisfying experiences for both the parties.

Accommodation: The Teddy Bear

To Teddy Bear, the relationship is of great importance, while their goals are of little importance. Teddy Bears want to be accepted and liked by other people. They think that conflict should be avoided in favor of harmony and believe that conflicts cannot be discussed without damaging relationships. They are afraid that if conflict continues, someone will get hurt and that would ruin.

If A is highly concerned about the other and not so much about himself, that is, A, is cooperative but very unassertive about satisfying his own concerns, then, he will be eager to give in to B and please B. To ensure that B's concerns are satisfied, A would be very accommodating and thus try to resolve conflicts through a policy of appeasement.

Compromise: The Fox

Foxes are moderately concerned with their own goals and about their relationships with other people. Foxes seek a compromise. They give up part of their goals and persuade the other person in a conflict to give up part of his goals. They seek a solution to conflicts where both sides gain something- the middle ground between two extreme positions. They are willing to sacrifice part of their goals and relationships in order to find agreement for the common good.

If A has medium level of concern for both himself and the other, then, he would take a compromising stance with an attitude of "give and take" and be willing to share the resources so that neither totally wins nor totally loses.

Materials Used

A conflict management questionnaire, that consists of several pairs of statements that describe possible behavioral responses to situations. For each pair consisting A and B (2 statements). There is a set of 30 statements.

A scoring sheet, that consists of five styles/ ways to deal with a conflict. The scoring sheet helps the analyzer to find out the dominant style of conflict management that is used to by the person.

Operational Definitions

Conflict

Any tension as psychologically defined that is experienced when one perceives that her needs or desircs are likely to be thwarted.

Avoidance

Is the physical and/or mental withdrawal from conflicts. This approach reflects a low concern for either party's outcomes and often results in a lose-lose situation.

Competing

Using power tactics to achieve a mix. This strategy relies on aggressiveness and dominance to achieve personal goals at the expense of the concern for the other party. The likely result is a win-lose situation.

Collaborating

Is facing the conflict directly and working it through to a mutually satisfactory resolution. Also known as problem solving or integrating, this tactic seeks to maximize achievement of both party's goals, resulting in a win-win outcome.

Accommodating

Accommodating the other party's interests. This approach places greatest emphasis on concern for others, usually to one's own detriment, resulting in a lose-win outcome.

Compromising

Searching for middle ground or being willing to give up something in exchange for gaining something else. This strategy reflects a moderate degree of concern for self and others, with no clear-cut outcome.

Methodology

Sample: - S^1 - Ms. Mamta Jha

Exec. HR Manager, Rediffusion Ad Agency

S^2 - Mr. Anand Nair

Sr. Project Manager, Vishan Projects Pvt. Ltd.

Instructions

"This is a very simple questionnaire that you have to solve. Imagine that you are in situations where you do not agree with another person and try to respond to the following with that orientation. In that questionnaire you will find several pairs of statements describing possible behavioral responses to situations. For each pair, circle the 'A' or the 'B' statement, which is the most characteristic of your own behaviour. In some cases neither the 'A' nor the 'B' statement would be representative of your behaviour, even so, try to select that which comes closest to what you may be likely to do. The responses which you circle will offer you a good understanding of your conflict – handling style."

Discussion

As seen above there are five different styles of conflict management and none of them is good in every situation. In fact one should be cautious of using any of the styles consistently across all situations. This questionnaire developed by Thomas and Kilmann (1974) identifies the frequency of the conflict style most preferred by the individual.

The 1st S was Mamta Jha, Executive HR Manager, Rediffusion Ad Agency. Her scores for the styles of conflict management are:

Competing 3

Collaborating 9

Compromising 6

Avoiding 5

Accommodating 7

Thus, the scores for collaborating style is highest. The S has a high concern for self as well as for others. She would tend to solve problems in a way, which would benefit both parties. She would take a win-win stand. She may get to try to get solutions by joint efforts of both the parties.

Collaborations are both time and energy consuming. Not all situations need collaborating solutions. The Ss score for just this style is high; on the rest of the styles it is quite average. Thus, this seems to be her dominant style of conflict management.

Compromising and accommodating styles that are low on the concern for self are going to be used by the individual if she really feels collaboration cannot be used.

The least preferred styles are those of avoiding and competing, thus for this individual conflict management styles that are low on the concern for others are the last preference.

The 2nd subject was Mr. Anand Nair, Sr. Project Manager, Vishan Projects Pvt. Ltd.

His Score are follows: -

Competing 5

Collaborating 8

Compromising 8

Avoiding 5

Accommodating 4

The S's score is highest on collaborating and compromising. This shows that he tries to find some expedient, mutually acceptable solution, which partially satisfies both sides though neither is fully satisfied. A compromising, stance addresses the issue without avoiding it, but does not explore the alternatives in a way that would be completely satisfying.

Sometimes compromising just gives a temporary solution to settle complex issues in the short run till a more thorough and permanent solution to the problem can be found. People who score high on this style should be aware of the fact that this mode of operation on a constant or consistent basis can create a climate of "gamesmanship" in the work environment, which might then lead to distrust among members.

The next style, which is preferred, is the avoidance style thus the employee will not face the conflict situation itself and avoid resolving the conflict. This style again is non-effective unless the conflict is very trivial or if it needs to be resolved urgently. The next two preferred styles are competing and accommodating. At first the individual shows high concern for self but then focuses that attention and concern on others.

10. Counseling Style Inventory

Counseling is an interactive process characterized by a unique relationship between counselor and client that leads to change in the client in one or more of the following areas:

Behavior (overt changes in the ways clients act, their coping skills, decision making skills, and/or relationship skills).

Beliefs (ways of thinking about oneself, others, and the world) or emotional concerns relating to these perceptions.

Levels of emotional distress (uncomfortable feelings or reactivity to environmental stress).

The desire for change can stem from identified problems, such as loneliness, uncontrollable anxiety, or poor social skills, or from a desire for a fuller life, even in the even in the absence of clear problems in functioning. Counseling may also enhance and individual's ability to cope with life situations. Certain environmental conditions are adverse and difficult to change, but learning how to manage one's life in the face of adversity creates room for accomplishment and enjoyment in spite of such conditions. It may also contribute to a client's ability to make important life decisions.

Counseling is discussion with an employee of a problem that usually has emotional content in order to help the employee cope with it better. Counseling seeks to improve employee mental health, good mental health means that people feel comfortable about themselves right about other people, and able to meet the demands of life.

Since it helps employees cope with problems, it should improve organizational performance, because the employee becomes more cooperative, worries less about personal problems, or improves in other ways. Counseling also helps the organization become more human and considerate of people's problems. Counseling may be performed by both professionals and nonprofessionals both a human resource specialist in counseling and a supervisor who is not trained in counseling may counsel employees. Company physicians also counsel employees, and even an employee's friends may provide counseling.

Counseling usually is confidential so that employees will feel free to talk openly about their problems. It also involves both job and personal problems, since both types of problems may affect an employee's performance on the job. For example, one employee may be experiencing the stress of new job expectations, while another may be distraught with grief following the death of a family member. Both employees are potential candidates for receiving the benefits of counseling at work.

Although a few companies had employee counseling programs at an earlier date, the recognized-beginning of employee counseling was in 1936 at Western Electric Company in Chicago. It is believed that this was the first time company that used the term "personnel counseling" for employee counseling services. Employee job satisfaction definitely improved as a result of the counseling.

Elements of Counseling:

- Listening.
- Recognizing the "Presenting Problem"
- Finding the core problem.
- Recognizing and admitting feelings.
- Criticism.
- The problem solving process.
- Influencing the directions.

Need for Counseling

The need for counseling arises from a variety of employee problems, including stress. When these problems exist, employees benefit from the understanding and guidance that counseling can provide. For example, one employee feels insecure about retirement. Another employee is hesitant to take the risk required by a promotion and thus ceases growing on the job. A third employee may become unstable in the job. In all cases, counseling is a necessity.

What Counseling Can Do?

The general objective of counseling is to help employees develop better mental health so that they will grow in self-confidence, understanding, self-control, and ability to work effectively. This objective is consistent with the supportive and collegial models of organizational behavior, which encourage employee growth and self-direction. It is also consistent with Maslow's higher-order needs and Alderfer's growth needs, such as self-esteem and self-actualization.

Reassurance	Giving a person courage and confidence to face a problem
Communication	Providing information and understanding
Release of emotional tension	Helping a person feel more free of tensions
Clarified thinking	Encouraging more coherent, rational thought
Reorientation	Encouraging an internal change in goals and values

Functions of Counseling

	Nondirective Counseling	*Directive Counseling*
Counseling method	The employee primarily controls the direction of the conversation and does most of the talking.	The counselor primarily controls the direction of the conversation and does most of the talking.
Status of participants	The employee and the counselor are on an equal level.	The counselor is at least implicitly superior to the employee.
Role of participants	The employee is psychologically independent as a person, choosing a solution and growing in ability to make choices in the future.	The employee is psychologically dependent on the counselor, whose role as a problem –solver tends to limit the employee's personal growth.
Emphasis placed	Psychological adjustment is paramount, with deep feeling and emotional problems accented.	Solution of current problems is emphasized with feelings and emotions often ignored.

Use by professionals: Professional counselors usually practice some form of nondirective counseling and often accomplish four counseling functions. Communication occurs both upward and downward through the counselor. Emotional release takes place even more effectively than with directive counseling, and clarified thinking tends to follow. The unique advantage of nondirective counseling is its ability to cause the employee's reorientation. It emphasizes changing the person instead of dealing only with the immediate problem, in the usual manner of directive counseling.

Professional counselors treat each counselee as a social and organizational equal. They primarily listen in a caring and supportive fashion and try to help the counselee discover and follow improved courses of action. They constantly encourage the counselee to open up and reveal deeper feelings that may help solve the employee's Problem.

Who is the Needy Person?

The human being has always been and will always remain a needy person. Also perhaps he has always looked up to certain external forces as well as some internal powers for meeting his needs. Whenever he has not succeeded in attaining his objective through the use of resources at his own command, he has tried to seek, the assistance of someone who, in his view, happened to know better. Thus seeking counsel in some form or other must have always existed. The world of today, however, has become much more complicated than what it was a few centuries ago. His needs are also expanding. Discussion of this phenomenon is in no way suggestive of the necessity of all expanding needs of man to be fulfilled. The Psychological truth to be underscored in this situation is that any need tends to create tension which is painful, and often an individual when unable to cope with the need requires assistance from an expert to deal with the situation. So, it may be said that while in the broadest possible sense, every individual is a needy person; an individual who is troubled by a situation, which he is unable to cope with, may be more specifically called a needy person who should seek special assistance.

The Expert

This brings us to the second important dimension of the counseling behaviour viz. The Expert. Literally the term Expert connotes a combination of extraordinary proficiency and adeptness in an individual with regard to a specific field of work. Proficiency implies competency above the average, and adeptness indicates an added presence of aptitude for the job in the concerned person. Thus a person who can be deemed, as an Expert in a particular field needs to firstly, have certain basic attitudes involved in successful performance at a job. These basic characteristics have to be developed towards maturity through a well-planned professional training program. Experiences given during such a program would result in developing the needed competencies, skills, information, knowledge, etc. in the prospective Expert. And last of all, but not the least important, will be the experience of the person in the actual job that can elevate him to the status of an expert.

Personal Qualities of a Counselor as an Expert

In continuation to the general discussion related to all personnel involved in human centered jobs, it may be logical to first stress some desirable personal qualities of a counselor and then proceed to an examination of other necessary professional variables, relevant to the counselor's job.

- **A Good Listener:** To become a Counselor needs to be basically interested in listening to others rather than having others to listen to him. He has to-in the interest of his job – give up the natural fondness of ''love for one's own voice."
- **Empathy:** An expert counselor is able to put himself m the situation of another individual without getting unduly involved in if. The expert should succeed in understanding the feelings of the needy person as he (the needy person) views them.
- **Patience:** Wooing with such a complex psychological construct, as the human personality, requires a lot of patience. "Take time to solve problems and make decisions."
- **Integrity:** Basically the quality of integrity implies a moral soundness and uprightness in the character of an individual. Literally, it connotes such a rectitude that makes the individual incapable of being a fake to a trust or pledge. A non-verbal pledge binds the Expert counselor and a needy counselee in the counseling situation, and it is one of the greatest responsibilities of the expert to uphold that pledge. This responsibility makes the basic theme in the code of conduct of a counselor.
- **Emotional Maturity:** One of the prime objectives of counseling is to assist the needy individual in moving from immaturity

towards a state of maturity. It is but natural that an expert who is supposed to lead a human being along this path should be himself a mature person. Again the expert's maturity and the needy person's conviction about this maturity alone can lay the foundations of the expert-needy relationship in a counseling situation.

(i) **The Counseling Situation**–In trying to discuss the counseling situation, we are in fact bringing together and adding to the previous two dynamic dimensions involved in the counseling behaviour. It is in the counseling situation that the two separately dynamic dimensions interact with each other, and also react towards the counseling environment. It is, therefore, very difficult to fully view and specifically -pinpoint the variety of dynamic forces at work with an unusually subtle complexity during the counseling situation.

(a) **A Unique Relationship:** The individuals come together in one of the most unique relationships in human life, when they meet in the interpersonal situation of counseling. The counseling expert, as we have seen, is expected to have an unusual grasp in the field of interpersonal relations.

- **Expert-Needy Person Relationship:** First and foremost, it is an Expert-needy person relationship, This aspect of interpersonal relation, as we saw, is also the central feature of human relationships existing in some other human centered jobs like that of the teacher or the doctor. There is however a basic difference between the interpersonal relationship of an Expert-Client nature in the above-mentioned jobs and that of a Counselor. No doubt in all these jobs, the client, who is a needy person looks up to the expert with confidence that his specific need will be understood, and his particular problem will be adequately dealt with. But while in jobs other than that of a Counselor, the Expert generally directs, orders, or instructs the needy person regarding his behavioral patterns, a counseling expert merely guides the counselee about the course of action. He really assists him in taking his own decisions with a sense of responsibility. The crucial challenge of the counseling expert lies in leading the counselee towards an expertise in understanding himself in the context of his environment, in viewing his needs and problems in a correct perspective based on scientific data, and then making realistic choices and wise decisions in an independent manner.

Voluntary Nature

The notable feature of the unique relationship between the counselor and the counselee is the willing cooperation of both the participants involved in the counseling situation. The ideal state of affairs however in a counselor-counselee relationship is that the counselee should really come to the expert counselor as a needy person who has a full cognizance of and respect for his needs. While a professional counselor is generally expected to carry on his duties in a willing manner, it is specifically his client, the counselee, who needs to enter this unique relationship in a voluntary manner.

It cannot be overstressed that the counseling profession essentially involves job tasks of a very personal nature and the work is not easy; in fact, it is highly delicate, and demands the strictest degree of ethical code. The professional counselor needs to be constantly alert that his voluntary attitudes towards his work may not, in the slightest, degenerate into -an undue curiosity about the details of another person's life. Whatever he is looking for or whatever he succeeds in obtaining in the counseling situation should be strictly looked upon as data, which is scientifically collected, objectively analysed, and judiciously/impersonally used.

There is one more caution to which the counselor needs to remain alert. Compared to some other jobs, the counselor's job does not require physical exertion; but it demands a very high degree of mental alertness, and a keen level of constant concentration. Even the preparations before the counseling interviews are ions exercises in mental-intellectual work. During the counseling situation, an unusual promptness of response to various dynamic clues becomes the most difficult challenge in the job. Particularly while dealing with serious problems of competent persons, the counselor may discover that grasping the nuances of what may 1e reserved, distorted or even unknown by the counselee, may be very relevant to his work in hand; and it is not easy to grasp them

The slightest unwillingness or indifference towards his client's needs is bound to bring up obstacles in an initial structuring of the needed rapport between these two individuals who are or should be—bound together in a unique relationship.

(b) The Nature of Communication: Meaningful communication is the essence of any interpersonal relationship. Any communication can be meaningful only if the media of communication carry the same meaning for the parties involved in the communication process.

Counseling Process

Counseling is helping people help themselves.

Processes	*Counselor Uses*	*Helps the Client*
Relationship building skills	Respect Genuineness Empathy	To feel valued, understood and prepared to trust the counselor.
Exploring and clarifying goals.	Contracting Open questions Summarizing Focussing Reflecting Immediacy Clarifying Concreteness Confronting	To talk and explore. To understand more about how he feels and why to consider options and examine alternatives to choose an alternative.
Outcome.	Objective setting Action planning Problem solving	To develop clear objectives To form specific action plans To do, with support, what needs to be done.

The Manager's Counseling Role

Much of a manager's time with his subordinates is spent in listening to them. The ideal manager is a helper who provides personal support for his staff. Leonard Sayles calls this function 'responsiveness' and notes that it a manager is accessible to his staff they will often come just to have him listen. Listening is a key managerial skill and one of the aspects, which subordinates value most.

In the hectic environment of the work world, there is also the need for action. A manager achieves results through other people working well and some of his most important actions concern the motivation of subordinates. This is rarely a simple 'carrot and stick' exercise, but a complex process requiring a detailed knowledge of the individual needs of subordinates, and considerable helping skills.

Managers usually can perform the counseling functions successfully. They will at times perform all counseling functions. On other occasions, if professional counseling services are available, they will refer employees to the professional counselors. The point is that when counseling services are established, managers must not conclude that all their counseling responsibilities have been transferred to the counseling staff, Managers are important counselors because they are the ones in day-to-day interaction with employees. If managers close their eyes to the emotional problems of employees and refuse to discuss them, it appears that managers are saying to employees, "I don't care about you, just your work." Managers cannot, when an emotional upset arises, say, 'This is not part of my job. Go see a counselor." Emotions are part of the whole employee and must be considered a part of the total employment situation for which a manager is responsible. For this reason all managers, from the lowest to the highest levels, need training to help them understand problems of employees and counsel them effectively.

Since almost all problems brought to a manager have a combination of factual and emotional content, a manager should not spend all day looking for emotional content when a rational answer will solve the problem.

Misconceptions about Counseling:

- Advising
- A burden on the management.
- Is only a professional's job.
- Time Overload.
- Leads to spoiling relationships.

The objective of conducting the Counselling style inventory was to identify the Counselling Styles of Managers.

Operational Definitions

Evaluative style: the person always tries to evaluate matters, events, situations and relationship between the same. They are judgmental people. Not a recommended style of counselling.

Interpretative style: the person tries to interpret various events and relations, tries to read between lines.

Support style: the person acts as a good support system. How one uses this style is important. It's good to be of this style.

Probing: the person tries to get more information about the client, asks questions, and clarifies things, issues. Tries to learn about the client by asking open-ended questions.

Understanding: this is the best style of counselling, as the counselor is non-judgmental, non-evaluative, non-interpretative. Trying to understand the clients view point.

Controls

1. Noise and Distractions are kept at the bare minimum level.
2. Instructions are given properly.
3. Made sure that the employees have understood instructions properly.

Methodology

Sample:

S^1 - Ms. Disha Parab

Exec. HR Manager, Rediffusion Ad Agency

S^2 - Mr. Anand Nair

Sr. Project Manager, Vishan Projects Pvt. Ltd.

Materials Used

A counselling questionnaire, which contains 5 situations. Each situation has 5 alternative counselling styles that a person could adopt. The 5 styles are Evaluative, Interpretative, Supportive, Probing and understanding. After the scoring is done one would be able to identify his/her counselling style.

Discussion

The first respondent was Anand Nair Sr. Project Manager Vishan Projects Pvt. Ltd., and the second respondent, Disha Parab who was the Assistant HR Manager in Rediffusion DY&R. Both the respondents have been considered for this test as they actually play the role of a counselor all the time with their subordinates, whenever they need assistance or help, Disha and Anand have always been of good support system to them and helped them solve their problems.

The scores obtained by Anand and Disha on the five counselling styles, which are Evaluative, Interpretative, Supportive, Probing and Understanding.

Anand has scored a 0 on Evaluative and Interpretative, 8 on Supportive, 9 on Probing, and 1 on Understanding. This indicates that he has scored the least on Evaluative and Interpretative. These styles are not recommended anyway, so its good that he has scored 0 on these two styles, his dominant counseling style is of Probing and Supportive. He is able to be a good support system; he is always there to help the needy people. His style is also of asking a lot of questions and probing, trying to find out more about the client.

Disha has also scored a 0 on Evaluative and interpretative style. She has a higher score of 9 on Understanding, 6 on Supportive and 1 on Probing style. The recommended style is a proper mix of Understanding and Supportive style. One should never be judgmental, evaluative or interpretative. So Disha fits in perfect as a counselor, while Anand still needs to be more understanding and less of probing.

11. Behaviorally Anchored Rating Scale

To try to rectify some of the problems, with the other rating systems, Smith and Kendall developed Behaviorally Anchored Rating Scales, better known as BARS. The BARS format deals with measurable behaviors, not personality, provides raters and ratees with clear statements of performance goals, and is based on a specific, thorough job analysis.

Using BARS, raters focus on specific ratee behaviors. These behaviors are compared to specific examples (job dimensions and anchors developed from the job analysis) that provide concrete benchmarks for making appraisal judgments.

Behaviorally Anchored Rating Scales (BARS)

BARS, a behaviorally based performance appraisal tool, designed to objectively measure employee behaviors. BARS require observers (raters) select from a prescribed set of behaviors that best fit behaviors exhibited by the person being evaluated. An integral part of BARS is that both those working in the job(s), along with the supervisor, determine which job dimensions should be evaluated and which behaviors are least and most desirable.

The job dimension indicates that an employee is being evaluated on his/her behavior in managing clients. The behaviors, known as anchors, are placed on a nominal scale ranging from (1) being the least favorable behavior to (5) being the most favorable. These behaviors could be given on a survey to persons who are best positioned to observe the employee's behavior. Mentioned later in the findings under the subtitle 360-degree feedback are examples possible raters for the training coordinator, including self.

Developing BARS for the training coordinator position can provide the director with information regarding what area an employee need to development to effectively carryout the various dimensions of the job. "BAR can facilitate effective training programs as the behavioral deficiencies noted in performance reviews sessions can serve as objective around which training program content is built." Schneier & Beatty, (1982). Adding Behaviorally Anchored Rating Scales with Management by Objectives as part of an appraisal system should not only help the director and employees attain departmental goals, but ensure the desirable behaviors are being carried out. A BARS is often mentioned as one way to improve rating scales. It does this by providing a description of behavior along the scale, or continuum. A BARS is based on critical incidents of job performance. Normally, BARS consists of a series of five to ten vertical scales, one for each important dimension of job performance. The assessor marks along a scale, which lists examples of definite, observable and measurable job behaviour. Effective behaviors are related higher than ineffective, and all behaviour is job specific rather than general. Problems lie in the development of BARS for each job, though this can be turned to advantage by asking employees to make out the scales.

BARS are developed in 5 steps.

1. A list of critical incidents is generated.
2. A group of people (usually supervisors) clusters the incidents into a smaller set of performance dimensions (usually 5-10) that they typically represent. The result is given a number of performance dimensions, each containing several illustrative critical incidents.
3. Another group of knowledgeable people is instructed to perform the following task. The critical incidents are "scrambled" so that they are no longer listed under the dimensions described in step 2. The incidents might be written, on separate note cards and presented to the people in random order. The rater's task is to assign again or retranslate all the critical incidents back to the original performance dimensions. The goal is to have critical incidents that clearly represent the performance dimensions under consideration. Incidents that are not retranslated successfully are discarded.
4. The people who translated the items are asked to rate each "surviving" critical incident on a scale (typically 7 or 9 points) of just how effectively or ineffectively it represents performance on the appropriate dimension. The ratings given to each incident are then averaged, and the standard deviation for each item is computed. Low standard deviations indicate low rater agreement. A standard deviation criterion is then set for deciding which incidents will be retained for inclusion in the final form.
5. The final form of the instrument consists of critical incidents that survived both the retranslation and standard deviation criteria. The incidents serve as behavioral anchors for the performance dimension scales. The final BARS instrument is a series of scales listed vertically and anchored by the retained incidents. Each incident is located along the scale according to its established rating.

References and Further Reading

1. Aronson, E., Wilson, T.D. and Akert, R.M. (2003). Social Psychology, Upper Saddle River, NJ: Prentice Hall.
2. Aswathappa K. (2002). Human Resource and Personnel Management New Delhi: Tata McGraw-Hill Publishing Company Limited, 32-33.

3. Davis K; Newstrom, J.W.(1998). Organizational Behavior. Human Behavior at Work (10th ed). New Delhi: Tata McGraw-Hill Edition,101-103,430-434, 442.
4. Jones, E. E., D. E. Kannouse, H. H. Kelley, R E. Nisbett, S. Valins, and B. Weiner, Eds. (1972). Attribution: Perceiving the Causes of Behavior. Morristown, NJ: General Learning Press.
5. Luthans F.(2002). Organizational Behavior (9th ed). NewDelhi: Mc Graw-Hill International Edition, 122-124,397-399,411-414.
6. Mamoria C.B; Gankar S.V. (2001). Personnel Management. Mumbai: Himalaya Publishing House, 316-347.
7. Pareek, Udai (1997). Training instruments for HRD. New Delhi: Tata McGraw Hill Publication. 123-129.
8. Robbins S.P. (2003). Organisational Behavior. New Delhi: Prentice Hall Inc.,524-525, 582-586.
9. Schuler, H. / Thornton, G.C. / Frintrup, A. / Mueller-Hanson, R,,Test manuals,2002,US.
10. Weiner, B. (1986). An attributional theory of motivation and emotion. New York: Sprinper-Verlag.

26

Performance Appraisal Format

Introduction

There have been two prevalent approaches to performance appraisal. The first approach has been the traditional approach. This approach has also been known as the organizational or overall approach. The traditional approach has been primarily concerned with the overall organization and has been involved with past performance. The second approach to performance appraisal has been the developmental approach. This approach viewed the employees as individuals and has been forward looking through the use of goal setting.

Performance: It refers to the results achieved vis-a-vis the organization's expectations.

Organization expectations are the standards of performance. These standards of performance are used for measurement of employee's performance. The goals/objectives set for the employee are organizational expectations.

Appraisal: Is the process of measurement, assessment and comparison of performance.

Therefore Performance Appraisal means measurement, assessment, and comparison of performance of employees of an organization. It is usually for and during a specific period of time mostly a year.

Why is Performance Appraisal Important?

It unifies the appraisal procedure by using same methods and approach so that ratings of different employees are comparable.

It provides useful and thorough information for taking important decisions about selection, training promotions, pay increase, transfers, lay-offs, discharges, and salary adjustment.

All the information collected about rating is recorded, so that it can be used to produce evidence, if decisions of rating are challenged in court of law.

Appraisal programs provide information on the weakness of employees and enable them to gauge their own value and accomplishments and to know what they are doing. If used properly such periodical appraisal will establish an atmosphere in which criticism can be taken without resentment and can be used constructively for self-improvement.

Each employee according to his skills and capacity can be placed in the right place.

It enhances better employer and employee relationship.

Objectives of Performance Appraisal

Objectives, which an appraisal system is likely to accomplish, can be classified into three parts and those are.

Organizational Goals:

- Generate manpower information.
- Human resource development.
- Efficiency and effectiveness.
- Developing harmonious employee relationship.
- Control over all working system.
- Device national basis of employee compensation.

Individual Goals

- Personal development.
- Effort linked rewards.
- Feedback about performance.
- Career involvement.

Mutual Goal

- Growth, development and harmony of organizations.

- Effectiveness and profitability of both individual and organization.

Performance Appraisal is Also Applied/Useful In Various Functions of HRD Like

1. Organizational development.
2. Staffing.
3. Training and development.
4. Salary and wage administration.
5. Motivation.
6. Employee relations.
7. Employee services.
8. Employee welfare.
9. Employee records.
10. Job analysis and job evaluation.
11. Career planning and succession planning.
12. Productivity.
13. QWL.
14. Personnel research.
15. Health and safety.

Who Can Do Performance Appraisal?

1. Self.
2. Self and immediate superior.
3. Self and immediate superior and second superior.
4. Immediate superior immediate superior and second superior.
5. Performance appraisal committee.
6. Head of the department.
7. Personnel manager and HRM.
8. 360-degree feedback.

When To Do Performance Appraisal?

It has two aspects:

- It should be done continuously.

- Recording of performance appraisal may be periodical.

Performance appraisal may be done.

1. Daily.
2. Weekly.
3. Monthly.
4. Quarterly.
5. Half yearly.
6. Annual.
7. Bi-annual basis.

How To Do Performance Appraisal?

It is done by:

1. Observation.
2. Examination or test.
3. Interviews.
4. Diary method.
5. Logbook method.
6. Critical incidents method.
7. Descriptive method/essay method.
8. Behaviorally anchored rating scales.
9. Ranking.
10. Rating.
11. Paired comparison.

Why Appraisal Techniques Proved to be Failure?

1. Bias.
2. Time consuming.
3. Limited stress on self-improvement.
4. Absence of uniform standards.
5. Absence of effective participation of employees.
6. Resistançe of employees to appraisal.
7. Considerable time gap between two appraisals.

8. Prejudices.
9. Faulty perceptions.
10. Favoritism.
11. Central tendency.
12. Halo Effect.
13. Recent incidents.
14. Spill over effect.
15. Extreme tendencies.
16. Non-performance related considerations.

How Appraisals May be Made Successful?

1. Comprehensive and transparent performance appraisal system.
2. Raters must be trained for performance appraisal.
3. Forum for redressal of grievances.
4. HR auditors should audit performance appraisal.
5. Should cultivate atmosphere of trust and confidence between superior and subordinate.
6. Stress should be on performance rather than on personality traits
7. The process should less time consuming.

Strengths and weaknesses of the employees should be identified and the later should be conveyed to him as soon as possible

Purposes of Traditional Performance Appraisals

Performance appraisal for evaluation using the traditional approach has served the following purposes: Promotion, separation and transfer decisions and Feedback to the employee regarding how the organization viewed the employee's performance

Purposes of Developmental Performance Appraisals

The developmental approach to performance appraisal has been related to employees as individuals. This approach has been concerned with the use of performance appraisal as a contributor to employee motivation, development, and human resources planning. The development approach contained all of the traditional overall organizational performance appraisal purposes and the following additional purposes: 1. Provided employees the opportunity to formally indicate the direction and level of the employee's ambition 2. Show organizational interest in employee development, which was cited to help the enterprise retain ambitious, capable employees instead of losing the employees to competitors 3. Provided a structure for communications between employees and management to help clarify expectations of the employee by management and the employee 4. Provide satisfaction and encouragement to the employee who has been trying to perform well.

The Performance Appraisal Process

The performance appraisal process typically consists of four inter-related steps as follows:

1. Establish a common understanding between the manager (evaluator) and employee (evaluate) regarding work expectations; mainly, the work to be accomplished and how that work is to be evaluated.
2. Ongoing assessment of performance and the progress against work expectation. Provisions should be made for the regular feedback of information to clarify and modify the goals and expectations, to correct unacceptable performance before it was too late, and to reward superior performance with proper praise and recognition.
3. Formal documentation of performance through the completion of a performance and development appraisal form appropriate to the job family.
4. The formal performance and development appraisal discussion, based on the completed appraisal form and ending in the construction of a Developmental Plan.

Basic Purposes

Effective performance appraisal systems contain two basic systems operating in conjunction: an EVALUATION system and the FEEDBACK system. The main aim of the Evaluation system is to identify the performance gap (if any). This gap is the shortfall that occurs when performance does not meet the standard set by the organization as acceptable. The main aim of the Feedback system is to inform the employee about the quality of his/her performance. (However, the information flow is not exclusively one way. The appraiser also receives feedback from the employees about the job problems etc.). One of the best ways to appreciate the purposes of performance appraisals is to look at it from the different viewpoints of the main stakeholders: The employee and the organization.

Employee viewpoint: From the employee viewpoint, the purpose of performance appraisal is four-fold.1. Tell me what you want me to do? 2. Tell me how well I have done it. 3. Help me improve my performance. 4. Reward me for doing well.

Organizational viewpoint: From the organization's viewpoint, one of the most important reasons for having a system of performance appraisal is to establish and uphold the principle of the accountability. For decades it has been known to researchers that one of the chief causes of organizational failure is "non – alignment of responsibility and accountability. "Non-alignment occurs where employees are given responsibilities and duties, but are not held accountable for the way in which those responsibilities and performed. In this event, Organizational failure is the only; possible outcome. In cases where the non-alignment is not so severe, the organization may continue to function, albeit inefficiently. The objective is to align responsibility and accountability at every organizational level.

Benefits of Appraisal

Appraisal offers a valuable opportunity to focus on work activities and goals, to identify and correct existing problems, and to encourage better future performance. Thus the performance of the whole organization is enhanced.

Performance appraisal form an example format

Employee name:
Employee code: head quarter:
Designation:
Date of joining:
Reporting manager:
Review quarter: first/second/third/fourth (final)
Review period:

Signature:...

(Reviewer) (Reviewed)

Date:

Goal setting

Priorities	*Key result areas*	*Measurement criteria*	*Achieve-ments*	*Reason for variance*
Quantitative goals				
A				
B				
C				
D				
E				
F				
Qualitative goals				
A				
B				
C				
D				
E				
F				
total score obtained (a)				

Section—I

Sales Performance details for the specified quarter:

Quarter	*Month*	*Target Sales*	*Actual Sales*	*% Achieved*
Scores per month				Total Score

Average score for 3 months (B): ____________

Section—II

Field working details for the specified quarter:

Averages

Month July

Month August

Month September

Exp.

Ach

%

Exp

Ach.

%

Exp.

Ach.

%

Total Score: __________ Average Score for 3 months (C)______

Section–III

Join Working details for the specified quarter: Quarter: I/II/III/IV

Month	*Accng. Manager*	*Days of Field work*	*Training*	*Counseling*
			Areas Covered	

Section—IV

Rating on Functional and personality Traits:

Functional Traits	*Poor*	*Average*	*Good*	*Excellent*	*Specific Comments*

Personality Traits	***Poor***	***Average***	***Good***	***Excellent***	***Specific Comments***

	Grand Total
Poor	0
Average	2
Good	4
Excellent	5

	Total Score
Below 20	0
20 – 50	5
51 - 70	10
71 – 90	15
91 - 105	25

Section—V

Employee Development Details:

Has the assessee:

Attended the induction training programme organized by the company?

YES ...... NO......

Attended any other training programme

In previous employment: YES..... NO......

If YES, Please specify:______________________________

In current employment YES..... NO......

If YES, Please specify:______________________________

Identification of Developmental Areas:

Functional Areas: (Refer to the Functional Traits)

Behavioral Areas: (Refer to the Personality Traits)

Needs to take more initiative. Requires to plan in a better way in order to optimize on time and opportunity.

Section—VI

Comments/review actions to be filled by the statelead

Comments/review actions: (to be filled by the dgm/gm – sales)

Date of review: ______________

Signature of the Reviewing Manager: ________________________

Signature of the State Head: ________________________

Signature of DGM/GM – Sales: ________________________

27

Six Sigma

Introduction

In the olden times there was the concept of "Zero Defect" but it was considered more as a hypothetical term rather than having a more practical aspect because though the companies propagated that their processes or services were of Zero Defect but very few customers relied on them because defects were always there. A "Defect" can be defined as any product or service that does not conform to the set standards or satisfaction of the customer. Now, Six Sigma is a concept that tries to achieve a near zero defect in a million events.

Six Sigma stands for Six Standard Deviations (Sigma is the Greek letter used to represent standard deviation in statistics) from mean. Six Sigma methodology provides the techniques and tools to improve the capability and reduce the defects in any process. It was started in Motorola in 1980, in its manufacturing division, where millions of parts are made using the same process repeatedly. Eventually Six Sigma evolved and applied to other non-manufacturing processes. Today you can apply Six Sigma to many fields such as Services, Medical and Insurance Procedures, Call Centers.

History

While Six Sigma was invented at Motorola in the late 1980s, Six Sigma has had antecedents over the past 100 years. As far back as 1776, in The Wealth of Nations, Adam Smith identified the economies of scale made possible with specialization in manufacturing. During the early years of the twentieth century, systems were developed for disaggregating manufacturing work processes into subsystems and components in the effort to increase efficiency. Modern organizations are still based on the specialization of labor and the fragmentation of processes into simpler tasks. These principles are generally thought of as starting with Frederick W. Taylor and the scientific theory of management.

Six Sigma: Natural Progression of Quality, or Totally New Event and a New Thrust

1900 to 1920s: Scientific Management and Statistics

Taylor and Scientific Management

Frederick W. Taylor's techniques, which became known as scientific management, made work tangible and measurable through analyzing manufacturing processes and turning them into a set of tasks that could be standardized and made repetitive. With work fragmented into a multitude of tasks, a managerial system was then required to control work. The concept of the separation of planning and execution was central to Taylor's system.

Taylor's system dealt a blow to the concept of craftsmanship in managing work or quality as a single end-to-end process. In 1911, The Principles of Scientific Management, a collection of his writings, was published. By the 1920s, Taylor's methods were widely adopted and Taylor's ideas had influence across the globe.

Ford Assembly Line

Henry Ford adopted four principles in his goal to efficiently produce an automobile at an affordable price: interchangeable parts, continuous flow, division of labor, and a reduction of wasted effort. Influenced by Taylor's ideas and Ford's own observations of improved work flow in other industries, the assembly of the Model T, first produced in 1908, was broken down into 84 distinct steps, with each worker trained to do just one. Ford had Taylor do time-and-motion studies to determine the exact speed at which the work should proceed and the exact motions workers should use to accomplish their tasks. In 1913, Ford's experiments and innovations came together in the first moving assembly line used for large-scale manufacturing. Ford's early methods are a foundation of Just-in-Time and Lean manufacturing.

Walter A. Shewhart and Statistical Process Control (SPC)

Quality engineering can trace its origins to the applications of statistical methods for control of quality in manufacturing. Much of the early work was done at Bell Telephone Lab-oratories, where both Walter Shewhart and Dr. Joseph M. Juran worked in the 1920s. In 1924, Shewhart first sketched out the control chart. What has survived of that early work is the Shewhart control chart and what has become known as Statistical Process Control. Shewhart's work laid the foundation not only for the use of engineering methods to specify work processes, but also for the use of statistical methods that quantify the quality and variability of processes.

1950s: Deming, Juran, and Feigenbaum and the Japanese Quality Emergency

Japanese upper management—presidents and general managers—assumed the leadership of the quality function in response to the quality emergency of the 1950s. Shoddy quality had made Japanese goods uncompetitive. The postwar rebuilding of Japanese industry was seen by industry leaders as a unique opportunity to radically deal with this problem. Dr. W. Edwards Deming, Dr. Armand Feigenbaum, and Dr. Joseph M. Juran are widely credited with helping the Japanese revolutionize their quality and competitiveness after World War II, and they served as consultants to the Japanese in the ensuing decades. The three became prominent in the United States after the Japanese quality revolution struck fear into American business. Although their contributions are many and complex, what we want to do here is simply point out contributions that are important to our understanding of the origins of Six Sigma.

Dr. W. Edwards Deming

Known for introducing statistical quality control to Japan, Deming also placed great importance on the responsibility of management, believing it to be responsible for 94 percent of quality problems. Deming is also associated with the "plan-do-check-act" (PDCA) cycle as a universal improvement cycle (also known as the Shewhart cycle, as Shewhart first advocated its use).

Dr. Joseph M. Juran

Juran developed the quality trilogy—quality planning, quality control, and quality improvement. Juran associated quality with customer satisfaction and dissatisfaction, emphasized ongoing quality improvement through a succession of improvement projects, and believed upper management leadership of the quality function was critical. Juran also emphasized reducing the cost of poor quality as a key to competitiveness.

Dr. Armand Feigenbaum

Known as the originator of "total quality control" or "total quality," Feigenbaum defined total quality as an effective system to ensure production and service at the most economical levels that allow customer satisfaction.

1960s to 1980s: Japanese Quality Revolution

Japanese companies chose to train almost all managers in the science of quality. Unlike in the West, quality responsibility and training were not confined to members of specialized quality functions. From the 1950s onward, Japanese companies undertook a massive training program in quality for employees and instituted annual programs of quality improvement. They also instituted a project concept of quality improvements. Improvement breakthroughs were made project by project under the guidance of managers who selected the improvement projects and mobilized and guided project teams.

The Toyota Production System (TPS)

TPS is perhaps the premier example known in the West of these Japanese methodologies. Its practices—quality circles, for example—have been widely studied and used in the West, often without achieving the same results. In the 1970s, TPS was equated with Just-in-Time production methods. Stephen Spear and H. Kent Bowen believe the reason that U.S. companies have rarely achieved the kind of results that Toyota has is that they confuse the tools with the system itself.

In Toyota, expert knowledge requires the addition of the knowledge of the people doing the work to improve the process; the people doing the work need the guidance and help of leader-teachers to apply the scientific method in a controlled project to achieve improvement. In the Toyota Production System and in Japanese concepts of quality in general, processes, people, and behaviors are seen as inextricably linked in a culture of continuous improvement.

1980s to 1990s: The American Quality Movement

Loss of market share, especially dramatic in the automotive and electronic industries, ultimately led to a reinvention of manufacturing in North America, beginning with the rediscovery of Statistical Process control (SPC) and the introduction of quality circles, through Just-in-Time (JIT) and Total Quality Management (TQM) to Lean Manufacturing and Six Sigma.

Just-in-Time and Lean Manufacturing

Lean Manufacturing represents a rebirth in the United States of the powerful methods and concepts of the Toyota Production System. JIT, like its predecessor, failed in many cases because its implementation focused on the tools and characteristics rather than on the underlying principles of TPS. Lean and Six Sigma are used side by side in some organizations known as Lean Six Sigma.

Total Quality Management (TQM)

In application, TQM generally focused on organizational results rather than on business results. Although the mantra of customer focus was chanted, the tools for integrating what the customer required were not rigorous. Also, even while having a mind-set toward improving processes, entrenched Taylorism, along with the tendency of companies to enhance these improvement efforts as engineering and quality disciplines, have led to overall disappointment with TQM. TQM evolved during the mid-1980s into the first generation of Six Sigma at Motorola.

First Generation Six Sigma

In the mid-1980s, Motorola, under the leadership of Robert W. Galvin, was the initial developer of Six Sigma. Most credit the late Bill Smith for inventing Six Sigma; Smith, a senior engineer and scientist within Motorola's Communications Division, had noted that its final product tests had not predicted the high level of system failure rates Motorola was experiencing. He suggested that the increasing level of complexity of the system and the resulting high number of opportunities for failure could be possible causes for this. He came to the conclusion that Motorola needed to require a higher level of internal quality, and he brought this idea to then-CEO Bob Galvin's attention, persuading him that Six Sigma should be set as a quality goal. This high goal for quality was new, as was Smith's way of viewing reliability of a whole process (as measured by mean time to failure) and quality (as measured by process variability and defect rates).

Motorola decided to take quality seriously. Motorola's CEO at the time, Bob Galvin, started the company on the quality path known as Six Sigma and became a business icon largely as a result of what he accomplished in quality at Motorola. Today, Motorola is known worldwide as a quality leader and a profit leader. After Motorola won the Malcolm Baldrige National Quality Award in 1988 the secret of their success became public knowledge and the Six Sigma revolution was on. Today it's hotter than ever.

For Motorola, the originator of Six Sigma, the answer to the question "Why Six Sigma?" was simple: survival. Motorola came to Six Sigma because it was being consistently beaten in the competitive marketplace by foreign firms that were able to produce higher quality products at a lower cost. When a Japanese firm took over a Motorola factory that manufactured Quasar television sets in the United States in the 1970s, they promptly set about making drastic changes in the way the factory operated. Under Japanese management, the factory was soon producing TV sets with 1/20th the number of defects they had produced under Motorola management. They did this using the same workforce, technology, and designs, making it clear that the problem was Motorola's management.

Second Generation of Six Sigma

To put Six Sigma in perspective, we started by discussing the beginnings of Six Sigma in the 1980s and then its antecedents from the early twentieth century to the recent history of TQM, JIT, and Lean. The Six Sigma of the late 1980s and early 1990s—the first generation—was part of continuous improvement or total quality efforts at companies that were led for the most part by quality professionals. These efforts often became islands of isolated change that died when unsupported by the business leadership. What can be called the second generation of Six Sigma can be fairly said to have first emerged at AlliedSignal in 1994, where it was led by CEO Larry Bossidy. Hallmarks of the second generation are that Six Sigma is part of the corporate business plan and is key to achieving business objectives, with top leadership support and often-intimate involvement. Another key difference from the first generation is that the second generation of Six Sigma starts with the Voice of the Customer. In its first generation, Six Sigma process improvement methodology included four logically linked phases: measure-analyze-improve-control.

In the second generation, during the GE Capital deployment in 1995, a new first phase, define, was added, becoming the DMAIC methodology now used in most Six Sigma implementations. In the define phase, data is used to verify customer needs and requirements and to identify the Critical-to-Quality characteristics for customer satisfaction. The define phase guarantees that the Voice of the Customer is central to every Six Sigma project by adding rigor to the front end of the create processes with maximum efficiency and effectiveness. And by integrating process improvement (DMAIC), process, product and service design (i.e., Design for Six Sigma, or DFSS), and process management into a comprehensive approach to implementing business strategy, Six Sigma finally evolved into a program that could be used to drive the business instead of narrowly focusing on quality. According to Jack Welch CEO of GE, "Six Sigma is the most challenging and potentially rewarding strategy that GE has ever undertaken". Indian organizations such as Wipro, Tata Motors, Hero Motors, Godrej-GE have also adopted Six Sigma strategies to improve their businesses (Business Today, Sept 22, 1999).

Definitions of Six Sigma

Six Sigma (6) is a business-driven, multi-faceted approach to process improvement, reduced costs, and increased profits. With a fundamental principle to improve customer satisfaction by reducing defects, its ultimate performance target is virtually defect-free processes and products [3.4 or fewer defective parts per million (ppm).]

Six Sigma is a methodology used to improve any business process by constantly reviewing, updating and retuning the existing process. Six Sigma provides the tools to improve the capability of any business process. Six Sigma professionals evaluate a business process and determine ways to improve upon the existing process. Six Sigma incorporates the same principles and techniques used in Business, Statistics, and Engineering.

Six Sigma improves the process performance, decreases variation and maintains consistent quality of the process output. This leads to defect reduction and improvement in profits, employee morale, product quality and finally customer satisfaction.

Six Sigma Strives for perfection. It allows for only 3.4 defects per million opportunities for each product or service transaction. It relies heavily on statistical techniques to reduce defects and measure quality.

Six Sigma is a rigorous and disciplined methodology that uses data and statistical analysis to measure and improve a company's operational performance by identifying and eliminating "defects" in manufacturing and service-related processes.

The Six Sigma methodology, consisting of the steps "Define - Measure-Analyze-Improve-Control," is the roadmap to achieving this goal. Within this improvement framework, it is the responsibility of the improvement team to identify the process, the definition of defect, and the corresponding measurements. This degree of flexibility enables the Six Sigma method, along with its toolkit, to easily integrate with existing models of software process implementation.

It would be a mistake to think that Six Sigma is about quality in the traditional sense. Quality, defined traditionally as conformance to internal requirements, has little to do with Six Sigma. Six Sigma is about helping the organization make more money. To link this objective of Six Sigma with quality requires a new definition of quality. For Six Sigma quality can be defined as the value added by a productive endeavor. Quality comes in two flavors: potential quality and actual quality. Potential quality is the known maximum possible value added per unit of input. Actual quality is the current value added per unit of input. The difference between potential and actual quality is waste. Six Sigma focuses on improving quality (i.e., reducing waste) by helping organizations produce products and services better, faster and cheaper. In more traditional terms, Six Sigma focuses on defect prevention, cycle time reduction, and cost savings. Unlike mindless cost-cutting programs which reduce value and quality, Six Sigma identifies and eliminates costs which provide no value to customers: waste costs.

For non-Six Sigma companies, these costs are often extremely high. Companies operating at three or four sigma typically spend between 25 and 40 percent of their revenues fixing problems. This is known as the cost of quality, or more accurately the cost of poor quality. Companies operating at Six Sigma typically spend less than 5 percent of their revenues fixing problems. The dollar cost of this gap can be huge. General Electric estimates that the gap between three or four sigma and Six Sigma was costing them between $8 billion and $12 billion per year.

How Companies Define Six Sigma

It is enlightening to compare how various companies—including leading proponents of Six Sigma—define it for their employees and their customers.

General Electric: Six Sigma is the Road Map to Customer Impact

"First, what it is not. It is not a secret society, a slogan, or a cliché. Six Sigma is a highly disciplined process that helps us focus on developing and delivering near-perfect products and services. Why 'Sigma'? The word is a statistical term that measures how far a given process deviates from perfection.

The central idea behind Six Sigma is that if you can measure how many 'defects' you have in a process, you can systematically figure out how to eliminate them and get as close to 'zero defects' as possible. Six Sigma has changed the DNA at GE—it is now the way we work—in everything we do and in every product we design."

TRW: What Is Six Sigma?

"Six Sigma is a structured and disciplined, data-driven process for improving business. TRW is committed to the implementation of Six Sigma focusing on how we can dramatically improve our competitiveness by increasing customer focus, enhancing employee involvement, instilling positive change into our culture and ultimately creating bottom and top line growth. At the highest level, Six Sigma is all about satisfying customer needs profitably. It is a highly disciplined methodology that helps develop and effectively deliver near-perfect products and services. It will help TRW in all of our operations, engineering, manufacturing and staff areas."

Honeywell: Six Sigma Plus

"Six Sigma is one of the most potent strategies ever developed to accelerate improvements in processes, products, and services, and to radically reduce manufacturing and/or administrative costs and improve quality. It achieves this by relentlessly focusing on eliminating waste and reducing defects and variations.

"Leading-edge companies are applying this bottom-line enhancing strategy to every function in their organizations—from design and engineering to manufacturing to sales and marketing to supply management— for dramatic savings. "Now, Honeywell has developed a new generation of Six Sigma...Six Sigma Plus is Morris Township, NJ–headquartered Honeywell's principal engine for driving growth and productivity across all its businesses, including aerospace, performance polymers, chemicals, automation and control, transportation, and power systems, among others. In addition to manufacturing, Honeywell applies Six Sigma Plus to all of its administrative functions."

At the end of the day, Six Sigma is much less of a technical program, although it has a lot of technical tools, than it is a leadership and cultural change program.

—Interview with Dave Cote, President and CEO, Honeywell International

Six Sigma is a management framework that, in the past 15 years, has evolved from a focus on process improvement using statistical tools to a comprehensive framework for managing a business. The results that world-class companies such as General Electric, Johnson & Johnson, Honeywell, Motorola, and many others have accomplished speak for themselves. Six Sigma has become a synonym for improving quality, reducing cost, improving customer loyalty, and achieving bottom-line results.

Distinction Between Six Sigma and TQM

According to Mikel Harry Six Sigma is now squarely focused on quality of business, where TQM is concerned with the business of quality. That is, when you adopt TQM, you become involved in the business of doing quality, and when you adopt Six Sigma, you're concerned about the quality of business. In a nutshell, TQM is a defect-focused quality improvement initiative, whereas Six Sigma is an economics-based strategic business management system.

Six Sigma came as a vector change, looking across the history of quality from the era of craftsmanship; it's fairly continuous; each step is a logical continuance of the preceding step, built off the same fundamental core beliefs and principles, whereas Six Sigma represents a radical departure from that continuum. It's actually a reassessment of quality from a whole new perspective and frame of reference. It's been the evolution of a business management revolution.

While Six Sigma was originally created as a continuous quality improvement technique, today it is significantly different than the TQM approach of the 1980's. Here are the key differences between Six Sigma and TQM.

SIX SIGMA	*TQM*
Executive ownership	Self directed work teams
Business strategy executive system	Quality initiative
Truly cross functional	Largely within a single function
Focus training with verifiable returns	No mass training in statistics and quality
Business results oriented	Return on investment quality oriented

Six Sigma Levels and Process

The Greek letter for Sigma,, represents one standard deviation from the normal or average. The higher the sigma level the better the quality level.

Normal Distribution and Sigma Levels

Normal Distribution

In practice generally we come across data which is of variable type and is measured on continuous scale. If there are no extraneous factors it follows a systematic pattern known as "Normal Distribution".

Most Commonly Used Intervals

In normal distribution, the most common intervals are:

1. Process mean - SD and process mean + SD i.e 1 Sigma

2. Process mean - 2 SD and process mean + 2 SD i.e 2 Sigma
3. Process mean - 3 SD and process mean + 3 SD i.e 3 Sigma

Levels of Sigma

% population between Mean –SD and Mean +SD (1 Sigma)

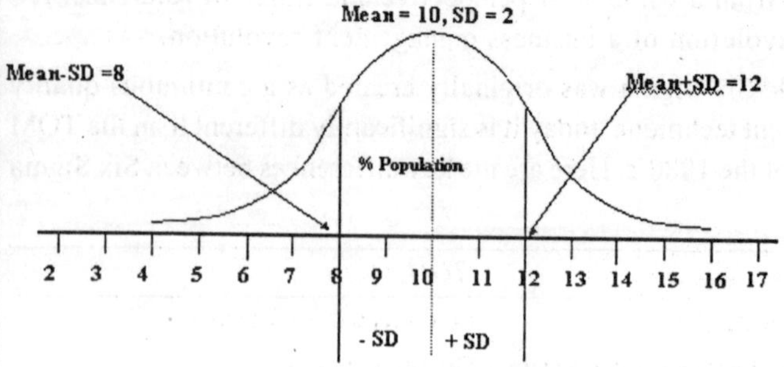

% population between Mean –SD and Mean +SD or 1 Sigma = 68.3,
This implies that 68.3% population lies between dimensions of 8 and 12

% population between Mean –2 SD and Mean + 2 SD (2 Sigma)

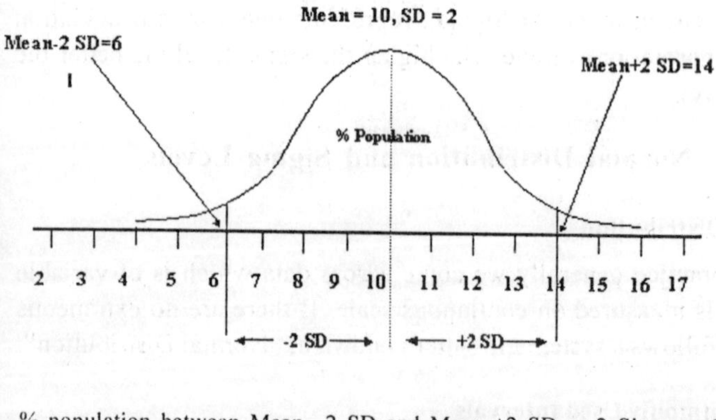

% population between Mean –2 SD and Mean +2 SD or 2 Sigma = 95.5.
This implies that 95.5% population lies between dimensions of 6 and 14.

% Population between Mean –3SD and Mean –3SD (3 Sigma)

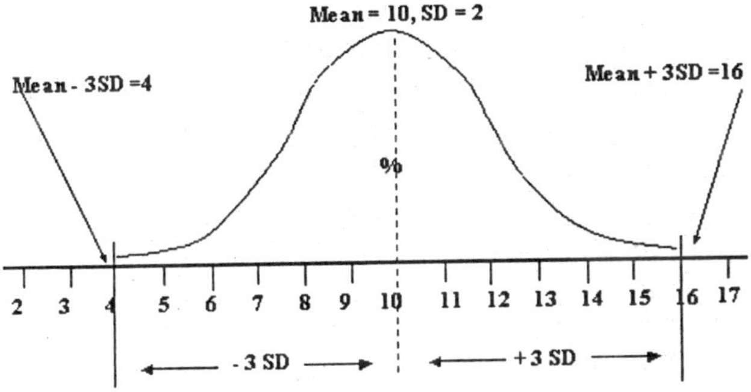

% population between Mean –3SD and Mean +3SD or 3 Sigma = 99.73, This implies that 99.73% population lies between dimensions of 4 and 16

Range of Observations for Nearly 100% Population

Range of observations for nearly 100% population (to be precise 99.73%) depends upon, mean of the process and standard deviation of the process. If it follows normal distribution the population lies between –

Mean - 3 SD & Mean + 3 SD i.e (3Sigma)

Sigma Process

From a sigma process we come to know that at what distance, in terms of the standard deviation, the specification limits are placed from the target value.

Move beyond 3 sigma

Until a few years back all statistical process controls were designed on the basis of 3 sigma limits. It is only in the recent years that this concept has been challenged and the organizations have started looking for quality levels beyond 3 Sigma.

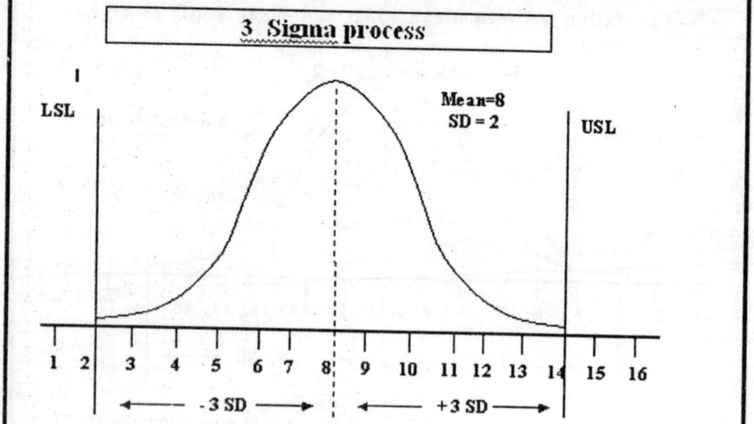

Note: LSL is Lower specification limit and USL is Upper specification limit.

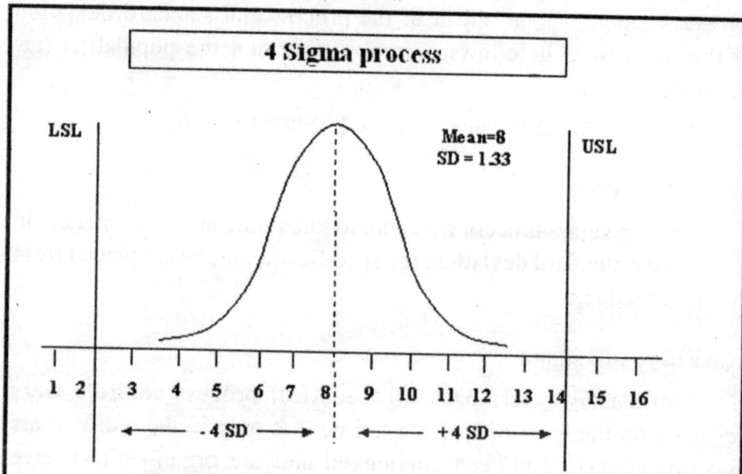

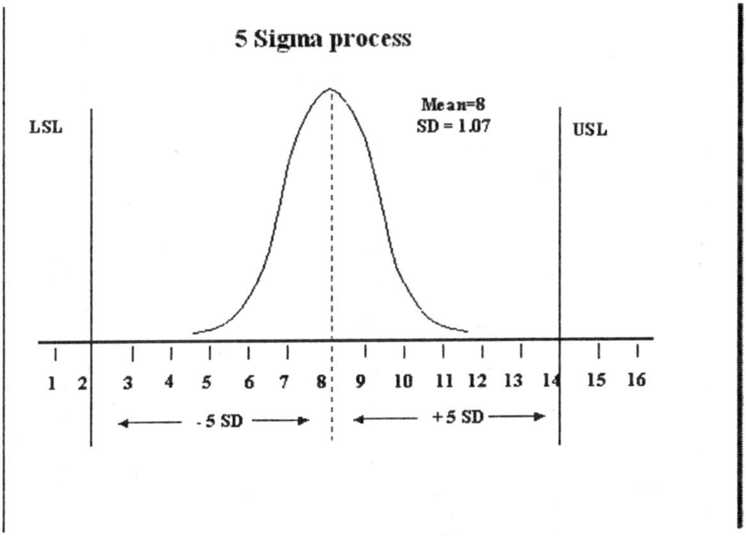
5 Sigma process
LSL
Mean=8
SD = 1.07
USL
1 2 3 4 5 6 7 8 9 10 11 12 13 14 15 16
- 5 SD
+ 5 SD

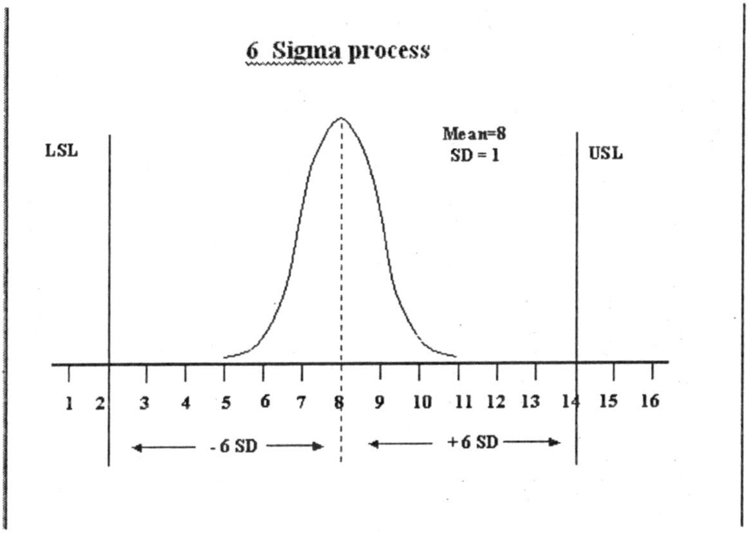
6 Sigma process
LSL
Mean=8
SD = 1
USL
1 2 3 4 5 6 7 8 9 10 11 12 13 14 15 16
- 6 SD
+ 6 SD

Precision

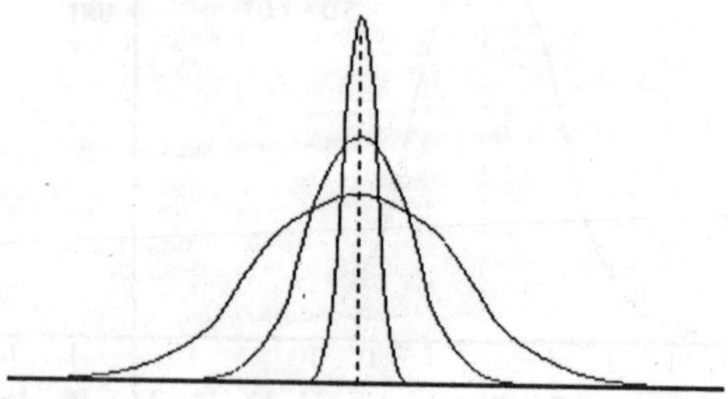

Lesser the standard deviation of the process, more precise or consistents is the process

3 Sigma Vs 6 Sigma

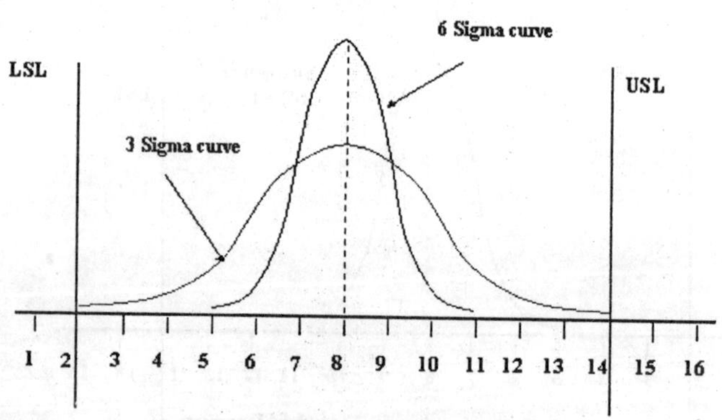

In a 3 sigma process the values are widely spread along the centre line, showing the higher variation of the process. Whereas in a 6 sigma process, the values are closer to the centre line showing less variation in the process.

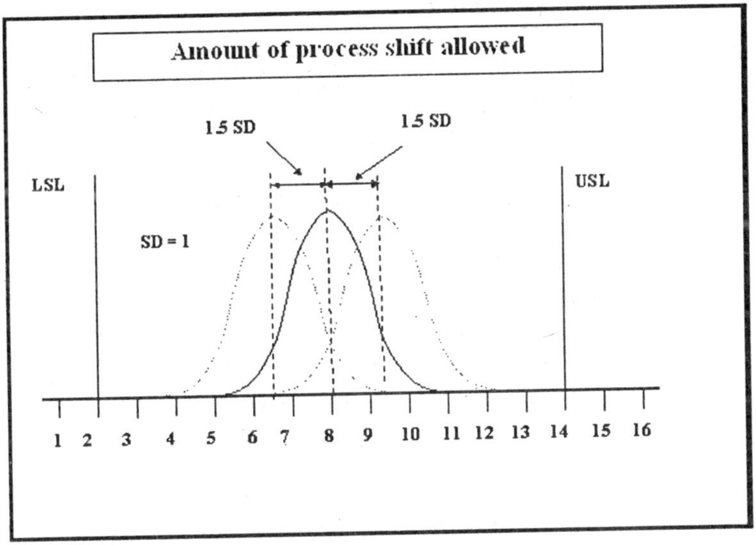

Six Sigma Process

Motorola developed a

five phase approach to the Six Sigma Process called DMAIC which is a continuous process as the diagram shows until the highest level in the Six Sigma is achieved, i.e., 3.4 defects per million.

DMAIC

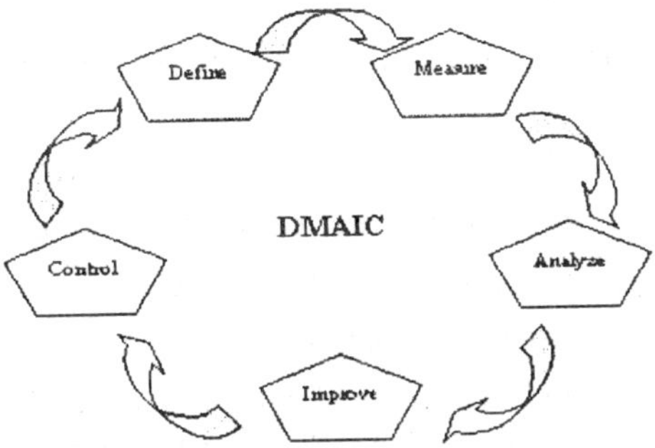

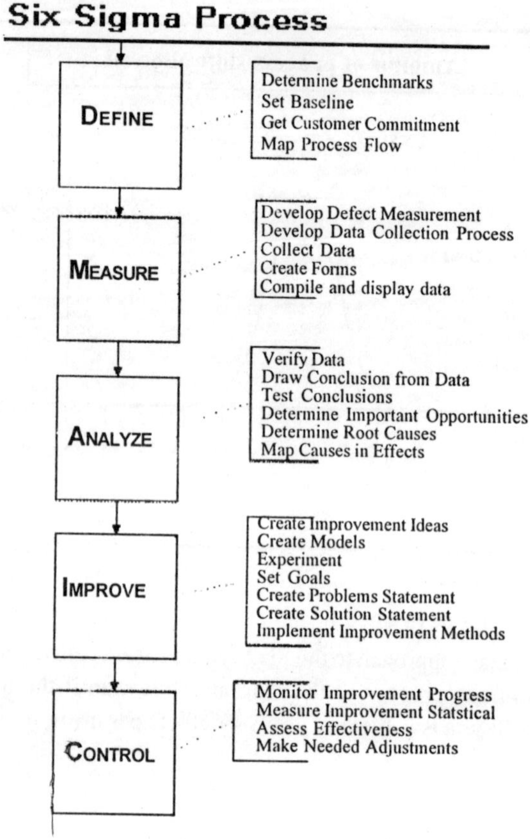

The DMAIC methodology breaks down as follows:

Define the project goals and customer (internal and external) requirements.

Measure the process to determine current performance.

Analyze and determine the root cause(s) of the defects.

Improve the process by eliminating defect root causes.

Control future process performance

When most people refer to Six Sigma, they are in fact referring to the DMAIC methodology. The DMAIC methodology should be used when a product or process is in existence at your company but is not meeting customer specification or is not performing adequately.

The DMAIC methodology is almost universally recognized and defined as comprising of the following five phases: Define, Measure, Analyze, Improve and Control. In some businesses, only four phases (Measure, Analyze, Improve and Control) are used; in this case the Define deliverables are then considered pre-work for the project or are included within the Measure phase. Some companies also use DMAIIC, where the first I stands for Improve and the second I stands for Implement.

DFSS

DFSS is the acronym for Design for Six Sigma. Unlike the DMAIC methodology, the phases or steps of DFSS are not universally recognized or defined—almost every company or training organization will define DFSS differently. Many times a company will implement DFSS to suit their business, industry and culture; other times they will implement the version of DFSS used by the consulting company assisting in the deployment. Because of this, DFSS is more of an approach than a defined methodology.

DFSS is used to design or re-design a product or service from the ground up. The expected process Sigma level for a DFSS product or service is at least 4.5 (no more than approximately 1 defect per thousand opportunities), but can be 6 Sigma or higher depending the product. Producing such a low defect level from product or service launch means that customer expectations and needs (CTQs) must be completely understood before a design can be completed and implemented.

One popular Design for Six Sigma methodology is called DAMADV, and retains the same number of letters, number of phases, and general feel as the DMAIC acronym. The five phases of DMADV are defined as: Define Measure, Analyze, Design and Verify.

Define the project goals and customer (internal and external) requirements.

Measure and determine customer needs and specifications; benchmark competitors and industry.

Analyze the process options to meet the customer needs.

Design (detailed) the process to meet the customer needs.

Verify the design performance and ability to meet customer needs.

A slight modification on the DMADV methodology is DMADOV: Define, Measure, Analyze, Design, Optimize and Verify. There are a few other "flavors" of DFSS that you might be interested to know about: DCCDI, IDOV and DMEDI.

DCCDI is being popularized by Geoff Tennant and is defined as Define, Customer Concept, Design and Implement. You can see that there are many similarities between these phases and the DMADV phases.

Define the project goals.

Customer analysis is completed.

Concept ideas are developed, reviewed and selected.

Design is performed to meet the customer and business specifications.

Implementation is completed to develop and commercialize the product/service.

IDOV is a well known design methodology, especially in the manufacturing world. The IDOV acronym is defined as Identify, Design, Optimize and Validate.

Identify the customer and specifications (CTQs).

Design translates the customer CTQs into functional requirements and into solution alternatives. A selection process whittles down the list of solutions to the "best" solution.

Optimize uses advanced statistical tools and modeling to predict and optimize the design and performance.

Validate makes sure that the design you've developed will meet the customer CTQs.

DMEDI is being taught by Price water house Coopers and stands for Define, Measure, Explore, Develop and Implement. I'm sure you won't have much trouble identifying the main objectives in each of these phases based on the title of each phase.

The DFSS approach can utilize any of the many possible methodologies. The fact is that all of these DFSS methodologies use the same advanced design tools (Quality Function Deployment, Failure Modes and Effects Analysis, benchmarking, Design of Experiments, simulation, statistical optimization, error proofing, Robust Design, etc.).

Each methodology primarily differs in the name of each phase and the number of phases (and, of course, the acronym).

Six Sigma Organizational Architecture

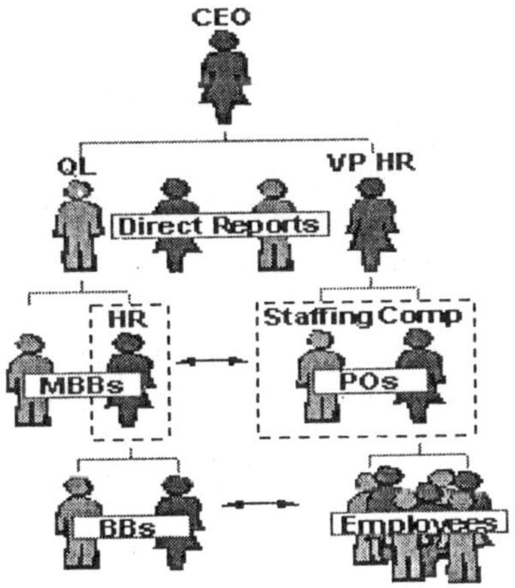

Six Sigma can produce significant benefit to businesses and organizations. The roles and responsibilities in a Six Sigma organization are as give below:

Roles and Responsibilities

Quality Leader/Manager (QL/QM)

The quality leader's responsibility is to represent the needs of the customer and to improve the operational effectiveness of the organization. The Quality function is typically separated from the manufacturing or transactional processing functions in order to maintain impartiality. The quality manager sits on the CEO/President's staff, and has equal authority to all other direct reports.

Master Black Belt (MBB)

Master Black Belts are typically assigned to a specific area or function of a business or organization. It may be a functional area such as human resources or legal, or process specific area such as billing or tube rolling. MBBs work with the owners of the process to ensure that quality objectives and targets are set, plans are determined, progress is tracked, and education is provided. In the best Six Sigma organizations, process owners and MBBs work very closely and share information daily.

Process Owner (PO)

Process owners are exactly as the name sounds – they are the responsible individuals for a specific process. For instance, in the legal department there is usually one person in charge — maybe the VP of Legal—that's the process owner. There may be a chief marketing officer for your business—that's the process owner for marketing. Depending on the size of your business and core activities, you may have process owners at lower levels of your organizational structure. If you are a credit card company with processes around billing, accounts receivable, audit, billing fraud, etc., you wouldn't just have the process owner be the chief financial officer, you would want to go much deeper into the organization where the work is being accomplished and you can make a big difference.

Black Belt (BB)

Black Belts are the heart and soul of the Six Sigma quality initiative. Their main purpose is to lead quality projects and work full time until they are complete. Black Belts can typically complete four to six projects per year with savings of approximately $230,000 per project. Black Belts also coach Green Belts on their projects, and while coaching may seem innocuous, it can require a significant amount of time and energy.

Green Belt (GB)

Green Belts are employees trained in Six Sigma who spend a portion of their time completing projects, but maintain their regular work role and responsibilities. Depending on their workload, they can spend anywhere from 10% to 50% of their time on their project(s). As your Six Sigma quality program evolves, employees will begin to include the Six Sigma methodology in their daily activities and it will no longer become a percentage of their time — it will be the way their work is accomplished 100% of the time.

A specific strategy for Six Sigma manufacturing and non-manufacturing processes would look similar to what is shown below:

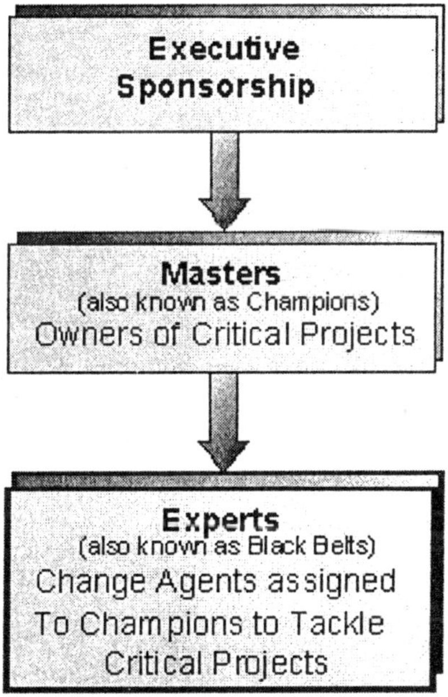

The executives must have a total commitment to the implementation of Six Sigma and accomplish the following:

- Establish a Six Sigma Leadership Team.
- Identify key business issues.
- Assign Masters to each key business issue.
- Assist the Masters and Leadership Team in identifying critical projects that are tied to the key business issues.
- Assist the Masters and Leadership Team in selecting Expert candidates.
- Allocate time for change agents (Experts) to make breakthrough improvements.
- Set aggressive Six Sigma goals.
- Incorporate Six Sigma performance into the reward system.
- Direct finance to validate all Six Sigma ROI.

- Evaluate the corporate culture to determine if intellectual capital is being infused into the company.
- Continuously evaluate the Six Sigma implementation and deployment process and make changes if necessary.

The roles of the Leadership Team, Masters, and Experts are defined next.

	Expert	Master	Leadership team
Profile	Technically oriented respected by peers and management. Master of basic and advanced tools	Senior manager respected leader and mentor of business issues. Strong proponent of Six Sigma who asks the right questions	Highly visible in company trained in Six Sigma. Respected leaders and mentors for Experts
Role	Leads strategic, high impact process improvement projects. Change agent trains and coaches on tools and analysis teaches and mentors cross-functional team members full-time project leader converts gains into $	Selects projects and Experts provides resources and strong leadership for projects inspires a shared vision establishes plan and creates infrastructure develops metrics converts gains into $	Develop a training Master Plan to implement Six Sigma. Schedule training select projects and Experts determine certification requirements and certify Experts. develop an Expert network to enhance communication review and improve the Six Sigma process
Training	three to four 1-week sessions with three to six weeks between sessions to apply to project project review in every session	4 days of Masters training Six Sigma development and implementation plan	one day of Basics of Six Sigma training or four days of Masters training
Numbers	1 per 50 employees (2 %)	1 per business group or major working site	4 - 6 member team

The overall approach to obtaining the right kind of knowledge is focused on finding the answers to the 14 questions shown next. These questions, which are partitioned into a 4-phase strategy of Prioritize, Characterize, Optimize, and Realize, form the Six Sigma Project Master Strategy.

Six Sigma Project Master Strategy

Prioritize	*Characterize*	
1. What processes are you responsible for? Who is the owner of these processes? Who are the team members? How well does the team work together? 2. Which processes have the highest priority for improvement? How did you come to this conclusion? Where is the data that supports this conclusion?	3. How is the process performed? 4. What are the process performance measures? Why? How accurate and precise is the measurement system? 5. What are the customers driven specifications for all of the performance measures? How good or bad is the current performance? Show me the data. What are the improvement goals for the process? 6. What are all the sources of variability in the process? Show me what they are. 7. Which sources of variability do you control? How do you control them and how is it documented? 8. Are any sources of variability supplier-dependent? If so, what are they, who's the supplier and what's being done about it?	9. What are the key variables that affect the average and variation of the measures of performance? How do you know this? Show me the data. 10. What are the relationships between the measures of performance and the key variables? Do any key variables interact? How do you know for sure? Show me the data.

Optimize	*Realize*
11. What setting for the key variables will optimize the measures of performance? How do you know this? Show me the data.	13. How much improvement has the process shown in the last 6 months? How do you know this? Show me the data.
12. For the optimal setting of the key variables, what kind of variability exists in the performance measures? How do you know? Show me the data.	14. How much time and/or money have your efforts saved or generated for the company? How did you document all of your efforts? Show me the data.

The Six Sigma tools and methodology must be taught to Masters, Experts and other managers at a level they can grasp and feel confident to apply. A proven instructional approach developed by Air Academy Associates is shown next:

A Keep-It-Simple-Statistically (KISS) approach is used, with the intention to avoid statistical complexity. Statistics is not presented as an "end", but rather the means to gaining knowledge for making good decisions, which are critical for success. There are a variety of Six Sigma tools and techniques, and we will use the "Present / Practice / Apply / Review" instructional strategy. That is, we will present a tool or method, give you a chance to practice that tool in class, then have you apply that tool to your project, and finally have you review the results of the application to your project. A final report will be written to document your success story and its impact to the company's bottom line.

Six Sigma Deployment and Implementation

All Six Sigma proponents agree to the fact that the key to Six Sigma improvement success is the building up of an effective infrastructure. An effective infrastructure lays the foundation for the success of the organization in its implementation of Six Sigma. It is a known fact today that the success of Six Sigma lays on the projects selected and their link to the strategy of their organization.

When we discuss the building up of an implementation structure what we are embarking on is a project in itself, which follows the DMAIC (Define, Measure, Analyze, Improve and Control) methodology:

D: Define the Strategic Direction of the organization

M: Set Measures for the strategic objectives of the organization

A: On a continual basis collect data on the measures set and analyze using Six Sigma tools and techniques.

I: Identify the opportunities for improvement and convert them to Six Sigma projects for improvement.

C: Set up a management control action of continuous reviews on the improvements made on the Six Sigma Projects.

The objectives of the Define and Measure phase of this project are defined as below:

Building up a set of metrics for the organization that give definition to the organizations Vision.

M	**Measure**
E	**Everything**
T	**That**
R	**Results**
I	**In**
C	**Customer**
S	**Satisfaction**

- Metrics that are Integrated with the Strategic direction and objectives of the organization Metrics that align people and work with their strategic objectives.
- Metrics that serve as effective means of communication for the organization both horizontally and vertically.
- Metrics that provide insight needed for making decisions, setting direction and correcting course.
- Metrics which will serve as a continuous source for identifying gaps in the organization and plugging them with Six Sigma Projects.

The problem most organizations face in the phases of Define and Measure is how to build such an organizational dashboard, which will help achieve the objectives cited above.

First Step

The first step an organization needs to embark on is conducting a self-assessment based on proven assessment models like the Malcom

Baldridge which will help the organization in understanding its "as is" state more clearly and help identify the various opportunities for improvement. The organizations could use the checklist type of approach in conjunction with interviews for identifying the gaps in Approach-Deployment-Results. Once the assessment of the organization is completed the findings need to be shared with the top management and the employees. This step is extremely crucial as this is what binds the organization together and helps create the cultural change needed aspect within the organization combined with the need for Six Sigma.

Second Step

Once the first step is conducted the organization is now clear about its current strategies for growth and customer satisfaction. Based on the assessment conducted the organization can re-evaluate all its strategies and strategic objectives. New strategic objectives can now be identified.

Third Step

Most organizations after having articulated and identified their various objectives are unable to communicate the strategies of the organization. One of the most effective methods for communicating the strategy of the organization is building a strategy map encompassing the now widely adopted Kaplan and Norton's Balanced score card spanning the four perspectives. Answering the questions related to the perspectives helps understand the strategy better and also build a good strategy map. The strategy map helps provide the vital cause and effect linkages in an organization and helps link the Business processes to the strategic destination of the organization. Before attempting to build the map it is essential for the organization to identify all its core processes and support processes as they help in completing the strategy map.

Six Sigma Implementation

Implementation of Six Sigma begins with education and training within an organization. The beauty of this Quality Management Concept is that it has various levels of Six Sigma training which are: -

Six Sigma Champion: Champions undergo five days of training and are taught how to manage projects and act as advisors to various project teams.

Green Belts: They undergo two weeks of training that includes project-oriented tasks. They act as team members to the Six Sigma project team. Their cooperation and involvement is necessary for projects success.

Black Belts: They receive four weeks of trainings and are directly involved in the implementation of Six Sigma Projects. They are the project leaders and go through in-depth training on Six Sigma approach and tools and work full time on the project.

Master Black Belts: These are the people who conduct Six Sigma Training and also have on the job training and experience.

The Six Sigma implementation can be done by following the steps in the given model: -

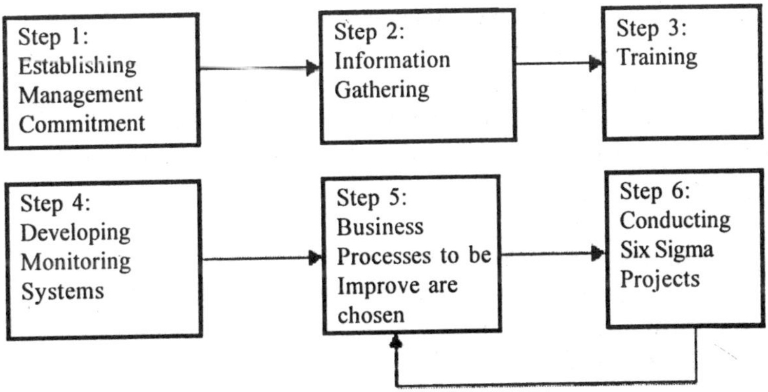

Step 1

In order for Six Sigma to be successful, top level management and everyone below them must fundamentally believe in the strength of it. Managers need to support all individuals and teams involved in improving the quality of the product or service or process.

Step 2

In this step information gathering through intensive communication with customers, suppliers, and employees takes place. Information about the conditions of the processes, products and services that can be improved, are found and analyzed.

Step 3

Training this is the most important step and the organizations should strive to have all of its employees trained on Six Sigma on various levels. An organization should have a mix of Black Belts and Green Belts for effectively implementing a Six Sigma project. Black Belts are the all day problem solvers who also operate as team leaders in Six Sigma projects. Green Belts are the team members in Six Sigma projects.

Step 4

In this step we develop a monitoring system that can be both internal and external. Internal like the amount of wastages and external like the customer satisfaction.

Step 5

In this step the business processes that are to be improved are chosen the problems that were identified are removed and valueless activities and sub processes are terminated. Here the Six Sigma project is at a critical stage. Before improvements it is necessary that a plan is made and the changes are communicated throughout the organization. Documentation of the improvements is very necessary so that these improvements can be replicated everywhere in the organization.

Step 6

In this step the Six Sigma project is at its mature stage and the changes and improvements are made and analyzed by simulations and statistical methods and if any discrepancies are found then again the cycle is repeated.

Another critical piece to a successful Six Sigma experience is the reward structure. Recall that many companies struggled to engage the entire organization in implementing TQM. To overcome this problem, Jack Welch has made the following statements:

- To get promoted you must be Six Sigma trained.
- Forty percent of top management bonuses are tied to Six Sigma goals.
- Stock options are tied to Six Sigma performance.
- As you can imagine, General Electric has very few problems engaging the entire organization in its Six Sigma initiative.

Thus, the modern day Six Sigma movement has fully embraced a Knowledge Based Management approach. Numerous companies, such as General Electric and Sony, are demonstrating that this approach has a high return on investment. This new and improved Six Sigma business strategy is much more powerful than the original Six Sigma developed at Motorola.

Costs and Limitations

Institutionalizing Six Sigma into the fabric of a corporate culture can require significant investment in training and infrastructure. There are typically three different levels of expertise cited by companies: Green Belt, Black Belt Practitioner, Master Black Belt. Each level has increasingly greater mastery of the skill set. Roles and responsibilities also grow from each level to the next, with Black Belt Practitioners often in team/project leadership roles and Master Black Belts often in mentoring/teaching roles. The infrastructure needed to support the Six Sigma environment varies. Some companies organize their trained Green/ Black Belts into a central support organization. Others deploy Green/ Black Belts into organizations based on project needs and rely on communities of practice to maintain cohesion.

Critical Success Factors For Six Sigma

Customer Centricity

The Six Sigma culture is customer centric; its goal is to delight customers. The quality of a product or service is measured from the customer's perspective by its contribution to their success. This customer focus comes through the Six Sigma drives:

- **Voice of the Customer:** What the customers say they want.
- **Requirements:** Voice of the customer input that is translated into specific, measurable elements.
- **Critical to Quality (CTQ):** Requirements those are most important to customers.
- **Defect:** Failing to deliver to a customer's CTQ.
- **Design for Six Sigma:** designing products and processes based on customer requirements.

The gaps between what customer desire and what you can currently deliver are the areas where significant value can be created for both supplier and customer.

Six Sigma provides the discipline to help companies go beyond and anecdotal understanding of customer wants and needs to specific requirements driven process matrix. This changes behavior from fire fighting to disciplined improvement based on customer satisfaction. Every defect in a process reduces quality but creates a time delay, generates an additional cost and produces an associated loss of operating profit. The actual cost of defects depends on the process.

Financial Results

At the heart of Six Sigma is a focus on financial results that reflects lessons learned the hard way. Total quality management, the principle quality initiative that immediately preceded Six Sigma, often positioned the need to solve quality problem as a moral imperative. TQM as often lead by people who had a modest understanding of the drivers of shareholder values and tended to invent their own metrics. All that changed with Six Sigma, where financial performance is paramount.

Six Sigma speaks the language of CEO that's why Six Sigma is quite explicit about financial benefit expected from each and every effort. Black belts and champions are expected to contribute between $250,000 and $1,000,000 of incremental operating profit each year. Theses expectations tie Six Sigma to the financial goals of the company as no other improvement process has before it. These some upfront costs; a lot of time and money is invested in the training and start-up phase. But a well-designed élan Six Sigma process more than pays its costs during the first year of implementation.

Management Engagement

The CEO, executives, and managers are engaged in Six Sigma. They have responsibilities for overseeing and guiding Six Sigma projects to make sure those projects stay focused on organizational priorities

Six Sigma has changed all this with its emphasis on financial results that make it clear what executives will gain and have gained through their continued involvement. As with TQM, however, the results are self-evident the biggest gains have been made in companies where executives are an integral part of Six Sigma deployment.

Resource Commitment

Typical fulltime commitment of personnel to Six Sigma effort is roughly 1 per cent of the company's population, though there have been situations where it is reached 3 per cent because there were sufficient opportunities for achieving significant gains. Black belts and champions must be fulltime to achieve sustainable results. Six Sigma requires that champions and black belts be selected based on their potential for becoming the future leaders of the corporation. One needs to make sure that the projects selected are of highest priority to the organization and its customers. Ultimately, the champion will present the opportunities to his P&L manager for approval.

One of the benefits of selecting the future leaders as black belts and champions is that they will receive an exemplary experience in every facet of business management and effective use of resources. Further, the potential foe fast track advancement based on a few years of success as a black belt works to retain this intellectual capital of the corporation.

Execution Infrastructure

Six Sigma possess an infra structure that effectively translates the CEO"S agenda into a customer centric set of projects chosen to maximize share holder value and provides effective management and monitoring of his results versus plan.

Starting at the top

- The corporate champions are armed with CEO and P&L managers agenda for financial performance and shareholder values increase.
- These strategic goals are translated to an operational agenda by the business unit champions who report to the P&L managers. Theses unit champions are trained in the methods of identifying key value streams and prioritizing projects based on net present value.
- The customer critical to quality issues and the time traps within the key values stream are developed into projects and the prioritized. These projccts are then executed by black belts who have been trained in the tools and team leadership skills of lean Six Sigma.

- Project sponsors own the process that is to be improved by the specific project. They have the specific authority to implement improvements and have ultimate long term accountability for ensuring that the improvements and financial benefits stick.
- Implementation is accomplished by a mix of team members including green belts, black belts and master black belts. whereas the black belts and champions are assigned full time to improvement activities, the green belts whose support black belt projects are generally part time and have received less training.

Starting form the front line, the black belts and others can propose project ideas to their champions and business unit managers. These ideas are transmitted to the business unit champions who reports to the business unit GM. the business unit GM and controller review the projects with the champion and provide required financial data and verifies savings potential. These projects are then ready to be prioritized against other known projects to ensure that those with the highest returns are executed next.

Conclusion

The culture of Six Sigma is the reason for its success. It has been wisely stated that "culture eats strategy for breakfast". Six Sigma provides the cultural framework to convert good strategy into good execution.

References and Further Reading

1. Breyfogle III, Forrest W. (1999) Implementing Six Sigma: Smarter Solutions using Statistical Methods. New York: Wiley
2. George, M.L. (2002) Lean Six Sigma: Combining Six Sigma Quality with Lean Speed. New Delhi: Tata McGraw Hill Edition.
3. www.sixsigmatutorial.com
4. www.encyclopedia.thefreedictionary.com/Dabbawalas
5. www.isixsigma.com
6. www.qaiindia.com/Training/blackbelt.htm
7. www.qualityamerica.com/knowledgecente/articles.htm

Index

F

K

L

N

O

P

S